THE DISENTANGLERS

ANDREW LANG

1ST WORLD
LIBRARY
Literary Society

The Disentanglers

Andrew Lang

© 1st World Library, 2007
PO Box 2211
Fairfield, IA 52556
www.1stworldlibrary.com
First Edition

LCCN: 2007934221

Softcover ISBN: 978-1-4218-9692-2
Hardcover ISBN: 978-1-4218-9792-9
eBook ISBN: 978-1-4218-9592-5

Purchase *"The Disentanglers"*
as a traditional bound book at:
www.1stWorldLibrary.com/purchase.asp?ISBN=978-1-4218-9692-2

1st World Library is a literary, educational organization
dedicated to:

- Creating a free internet library of downloadable ebooks

- Hosting writing competitions and offering book publishing
scholarships.

1st World Library Literary Society

Giving Back to the World

"If you want to work on the core problem, it's early school literacy."

- James Barksdale, former CEO of Netscape

"No skill is more crucial to the future of a child, or to a democratic and prosperous society, than literacy."

- Los Angeles Times

"Literacy... means far more than learning how to read and write... The aim is to transmit... knowledge and promote social participation."

- UNESCO

"Literacy is not a luxury, it is a right and a responsibility. If our world is to meet the challenges of the twenty-first century we must harness the energy and creativity of all our citizens."

- President Bill Clinton

"Parents should be encouraged to read to their children, and teachers should be equipped with all available techniques for teaching literacy, so the varying needs and capacities of individual kids can be taken into account."

- Hugh Mackay

TO HERBERT HILLS, ESQ.

These Studies OF LIFE AND CHARACTER *ARE DEDICATED*

PREFACE

It has been suggested to the Author that the incident of the Berbalangs, in The Adventure of the Fair American, is rather improbable. He can only refer the sceptical to the perfectly genuine authorities cited in his footnotes.

I

THE GREAT IDEA

The scene was a dusky shabby little room in Ryder Street. To such caves many repair whose days are passed, and whose food is consumed, in the clubs of the adjacent thoroughfare of cooperative palaces, Pall Mall. The furniture was battered and dingy; the sofa on which Logan sprawled had a certain historic interest: it was covered with cloth of horsehair, now seldom found by the amateur. A bookcase with glass doors held a crowd of books to which the amateur would at once have flown. They were in 'boards' of faded blue, and the paper labels bore alluring names: they were all First Editions of the most desirable kind. The bottles in the liqueur case were antique; a coat of arms, not undistinguished, was in relief on the silver stoppers. But the liquors in the flasks were humble and conventional. Merton, the tenant of the rooms, was in a Zingari cricketing coat; he occupied the arm-chair, while Logan, in evening dress, maintained a difficult equilibrium on the slippery sofa. Both men were of an age between twenty-five and twenty-nine, both were pleasant to the eye. Merton was, if anything, under the middle height: fair, slim, and active. As a freshman he had coxed his College Eight, later he rowed Bow in that vessel. He had won the Hurdles, but been beaten by his Cambridge opponent; he had taken a fair second in Greats, was believed to have been 'runner up' for the Newdigate prize poem, and might have won other laurels, but that he was found to do the female parts very fairly in the dramatic performances of the University, a thing irreconcilable with study. His father was a rural dean. Merton's most obvious vice was a thirst for general information. 'I know it is awfully bad form to know anything,' he had been heard to say, 'but everyone has his failings, and mine is occasionally useful.'

Logan was tall, dark, athletic and indolent. He was, in a way, the last of an historic Scottish family, and rather fond of discoursing on the ancestral traditions. But any satisfaction that he derived from them was, so far, all that his birth had won for him. His little patrimony had taken to itself wings. Merton was in no better case. Both, as they sat together, were gloomily discussing their prospects.

In the penumbra of smoke, and the malignant light of an ill trimmed lamp, the Great Idea was to be evolved. What consequences hung on the Great Idea! The peace of families insured, at a trifling premium. Innocence rescued. The defeat of the subtlest criminal designers: undreamed of benefits to natural science! But I anticipate. We return to the conversation in the Ryder Street den.

'It is a case of emigration or the workhouse,' said Logan.

'Emigration! What can you or I do in the Colonies? They provide even their own ushers. My only available assets, a little Greek and less Latin, are drugs in the Melbourne market,' answered Merton; 'they breed their own dominies. Protection!'

'In America they might pay for lessons in the English accent . . . ' said Logan.

'But not,' said Merton, 'in the Scotch, which is yours; oh distant cousin of a marquis! Consequently by rich American lady pupils "you are not one to be desired."'

'Tommy, you are impertinent,' said Logan. 'Oh, hang it, where is there an opening, a demand, for the broken, the stoney broke? A man cannot live by casual paragraphs alone."'

'And these generally reckoned "too high-toned for our readers,"' said Merton.

'If I could get the secretaryship of a golf club!' Logan sighed.

'If you could get the Chancellorship of the Exchequer! I reckon that there are two million applicants for secretaryships of golf clubs.'

'Or a land agency,' Logan murmured.

'Oh, be practical!' cried Merton. 'Be inventive! Be modern! Be up to date! Think of something *new*! Think of a felt want, as the Covenanting divine calls it: a real public need, hitherto but dimly present, and quite a demand without a supply.'

'But that means thousands in advertisements,' said Logan, 'even if we ran a hair-restorer. The ground bait is too expensive. I say, I once knew a fellow who ground-baited for salmon with potted shrimps.'

'Make a paragraph on him then,' said Merton.

'But results proved that there was no felt want of potted shrimps—or not of a fly to follow.'

'Your collaboration in the search, the hunt for money, the

quest, consists merely in irrelevancies and objections,' growled Merton, lighting a cigarette.

'Lucky devil, Peter Nevison. Meets an heiress on a Channel boat, with 4,000*l.* a year; and there he is.' Logan basked in the reflected sunshine.

'Cut by her people, though—and other people. I could not have faced the row with her people,' said Merton musingly.

'I don't wonder they moved heaven and earth, and her uncle, the bishop, to stop it. Not eligible, Peter was not, however you took him,' Logan reflected. 'Took too much of this,' he pointed to the heraldic flask.

'Well, *she* took him. It is not much that parents, still less guardians, can do now, when a girl's mind is made up.'

'The emancipation of woman is the opportunity of the indigent male struggler. Women have their way,' Logan reflected.

'And the youth of the modern aged is the opportunity of our sisters, the girls "on the make,"' said Merton. 'What a lot of old men of title are marrying young women as hard up as we are!'

'And then,' said Logan, 'the offspring of the deceased marchionesses make a fuss. In fact marriage is always the signal for a family row.'

'It is the infernal family row that I never could face. I had a chance—'

Merton seemed likely to drop into autobiography.

Andrew Lang

'I know,' said Logan admonishingly.

'Well, hanged if I could take it, and she—she could not stand it either, and both of us—'

'Do not be elegiac,' interrupted Logan. 'I know. Still, I am rather sorry for people's people. The unruly affections simply poison the lives of parents and guardians, aye, and of the children too. The aged are now so hasty and imprudent. What would not Tala have given to prevent his Grace from marrying Mrs. Tankerville?'

Merton leapt to his feet and smote his brow.

'Wait, don't speak to me—a great thought flushes all my brain. Hush! I have it,' and he sat down again, pouring seltzer water into a half empty glass.

'Have what?' asked Logan.

'The Felt Want. But the accomplices?'

'But the advertisements!' suggested Logan.

'A few pounds will cover *them*. I can sell my books,' Merton sighed.

'A lot of advertising your first editions will pay for. Why, even to launch a hair-restorer takes—'

'Oh, but,' Merton broke in, '*this* want is so widely felt, acutely felt too: hair is not in it. But where are the accomplices?'

'If it is gentleman burglars I am not concerned. No Raffles for me! If it is venal physicians to kill off rich relations, the lives of the Logans are sacred to me.'

'Bosh!' said Merton, 'I want "lady friends," as Tennyson says: nice girls, well born, well bred, trying to support themselves.'

'What do you want *them* for? To support them?'

'I want them as accomplices,' said Merton. 'As collaborators.'

'Blackmail?' asked Logan. 'Has it come to this? I draw the line at blackmail. Besides, they would starve first, good girls would; or marry Lord Methusalem, or a beastly South African *richard.*'

'Robert Logan of Restalrig, that should be'—Merton spoke impressively—'you know me to be incapable of practices, however lucrative, which involve taint of crime. I do not prey upon the society which I propose to benefit. But where are the girls?'

'Where are they not?' Logan asked. 'Dawdling, as jesters, from country house to country house. In the British Museum, verifying references for literary gents, if they can get references to verify. Asking leave to describe their friends' parties in *The Leidy's News*. Trying for places as golfing governesses, or bridge governesses, or gymnastic mistresses at girls' schools, or lady laundresses, or typewriters, or lady teachers of cookery, or pegs to hang costumes on at dressmakers'. The most beautiful girl I ever saw was doing that once; I met her when I was shopping with my aunt who left her money to the Armenians.'

'You kept up her acquaintance? The girl's, I mean,' Merton asked.

'We have occasionally met. In fact—'

'Yes, I know, as you said lately,' Merton remarked. 'That's one, anyhow, and there is Mary Willoughby, who got a second in history when I was up. *She* would do. Better business for her than the British Museum. I know three or four.'

'I know five or six. But what for?' Logan insisted.

'To help us in supplying the widely felt want, which is my discovery,' said Merton.

'And that is?'

'Disentanglers—of both sexes. A large and varied staff, calculated to meet every requirement and cope with every circumstance.' Merton quoted an unwritten prospectus.

'I don't follow. What the deuce is your felt want?'

'What we were talking about.'

'Ground bait for salmon?' Logan reverted to his idea.

'No. Family rows about marriages. Nasty letters. Refusals to recognise the choice of a son, a daughter, or a widowed but youthful old parent, among the upper classes. Harsh words. Refusals to allow meetings or correspondence. Broken hearts. Improvident marriages. Preaching down a daughter's heart, or an aged parent's heart, or a nephew's, or a niece's, or a ward's, or anybody's heart. Peace restored to the household. Intended marriage off, and nobody a penny the worse, unless—'

'Unless what?' said Logan.

'Practical difficulties,' said Merton, 'will occur in every

enterprise. But they won't be to our disadvantage, the reverse—if they don't happen too often. And we can guard against *that* by a scientific process.'

'Now will you explain,' Logan asked, 'or shall I pour this whisky and water down the back of your neck?'

He rose to his feet, menace in his eye.

'Bear fighting barred! We are no longer boys. We are men—broken men. Sit down, don't play the bear,' said Merton.

'Well, explain, or I fire!'

'Don't you see? The problem for the family, for hundreds of families, is to get the undesirable marriage off without the usual row. Very few people really like a row. Daughter becomes anaemic; foreign cures are expensive and no good. Son goes to the Devil or the Cape. Aged and opulent, but amorous, parent leaves everything he can scrape together to disapproved of new wife. Relations cut each other all round. Not many people really enjoy that kind of thing. They want a pacific solution—marriage off, no remonstrances.'

'And how are you going to do it?'

'Why,' said Merton, 'by a scientific and thoroughly organised system of disengaging or disentangling. We enlist a lot of girls and fellows like ourselves, beautiful, attractive, young, or not so young, well connected, intellectual, athletic, and of all sorts of types, but all *broke*, all without visible means of subsistence. They are people welcome in country houses, but travelling third class, and devilishly perplexed about how to tip the servants, how to pay if they lose at bridge, and so forth. We enlist them, we send them out on demand, carefully selecting our agents to meet the circumstances in

Andrew Lang

each case. They go down and disentangle the amorous by—well, by entangling them. The lovers are off with the old love, the love which causes all the worry, without being on with the new love—our agent. The thing quietly fizzles out.'

'Quietly!' Logan snorted. 'I like "quietly." They would be on with the new love. Don't you see, you born gomeral, that the person, man or woman, who deserts the inconvenient A.—I put an A. B. case—falls in love with your agent B., and your B. is, by the nature of the thing, more ineligible than A.—too poor. A babe could see that. You disappoint me, Merton.'

'You state,' said Merton, 'one of the practical difficulties which I foresaw. Not that it does not suit *us* very well. Our comrade and friend, man or woman, gets a chance of a good marriage, and, Logan, there is no better thing. But parents and guardians would not stand much of that: of people marrying our agents.'

'Of course they wouldn't. Your idea is crazy.'

'Wait a moment,' said Merton. 'The resources of science are not yet exhausted. You have heard of the epoch-making discovery of Jenner, and its beneficent results in checking the ravages of smallpox, that scourge of the human race?'

'Oh don't talk like a printed book,' Logan remonstrated. 'Everybody has heard of vaccination.'

'And you are aware that similar prophylactic measures have been adopted, with more or less of success, in the case of other diseases?'

'I am aware,' said Logan, 'that you are in danger of personal suffering at my hands, as I already warned you.'

'What is love but a disease?' Merton asked dreamily. 'A French *savant*, Monsieur Janet, says that nobody ever falls in love except when he is a little bit off colour: I forget the French equivalent.'

'I am coming for you,' Logan arose in wrath.

'Sit down. Well, your objection (which it did not need the eyes of an Argus to discover) is that the patients, the lovers young, whose loves are disapproved of by the family, will fall in love with our agents, insist on marrying *them*, and so the last state of these afflicted parents—or children—will be worse than the first. Is that your objection?'

'Of course it is; and crushing at that,' Logan replied.

'Then science suggests prophylactic measures: something akin to vaccination,' Merton explained. 'The agents must be warranted "immune." Nice new word!'

'How?'

'The object,' Merton answered, 'is to make it impossible, or highly improbable, that our agents, after disentangling the affections of the patients, curing them of one attack, will accept their addresses, offered in a second fit of the fever. In brief, the agents must not marry the patients, or not often.'

'But how can you prevent them if they want to do it?'

'By a process akin, in the emotional region of our strangely blended nature, to inoculation.'

'Hanged if I understand you. You keep on repeating yourself. You dodder!'

Andrew Lang

'Our agents must have got the disease already, the pretty fever; and be safe against infection. There must be on the side of the agent a prior attachment. Now, don't interrupt, there always *is* a prior attachment. You are in love, I am in love, he, she, and they, all of the broken brigade, are in love; all the more because they have not a chance. "Cursed be the social wants that sin against the strength of youth." So, you see, our agents will be quite safe not to crown the flame of the patients, not to accept them, if they do propose, or expect a proposal. "Every security from infection guaranteed." There is the felt want. Here is the remedy; not warranted absolutely painless, but salutary, and tending to the amelioration of the species. So we have only to enlist the agents, and send a few advertisements to the papers. My first editions must go. Farewell Shelley, Tennyson, Keats, uncut Waverleys, Byron, *The Waltz*, early Kiplings (at a vast reduction on account of the overflooded state of the market). Farewell Kilmarnock edition of Burns, and Colonel Lovelace, his *Lucasta*, and *Tamerlane* by Mr. Poe, and the rest. The money must be raised.' Merton looked resigned.

'I have nothing to sell,' said Logan, 'but an entire set of clubs by Philp. Guaranteed unique, and in exquisite condition.'

'You must part with them,' said Merton. 'We are like Palissy the potter, feeding his furnace with the drawing-room furniture.'

'But how about the recruiting?' Logan asked. 'It's like one of these novels where you begin by collecting desperados from all quarters, and then the shooting commences.'

'Well, we need not ransack the Colonies,' Merton replied. 'Patronise British industries. We know some fellows already and some young women.'

'I say,' Logan interrupted, 'what a dab at disentangling Lumley would have been if he had not got that Professorship of Toxicology at Edinburgh, and been able to marry Miss Wingan at last!'

'Yes, and Miss Wingan would have been useful. What a lively girl, ready for everything,' Merton replied.

'But these we can still get at,' Logan asked: 'how are you to be sure that they are—vaccinated?'

'The inquiry is delicate,' Merton admitted, 'but the fact may be almost taken for granted. We must give a dinner (a preliminary expense) to promising collaborators, and champagne is a great promoter of success in delicate inquiries. *In vino veritas*.'

'I don't know if there is money in it, but there is a kind of larkiness,' Logan admitted.

'Yes, I think there will be larks.'

'About the dinner? We are not to have Johnnies disguised as hansom cabbies driving about, and picking up men and women that look the right sort, in the streets, and compelling them to come in?'

'Oh no, *that* expense we can cut. It would not do with the women, obviously: heavens, what queer fishes that net would catch! The flag of the Disentanglers shall never be stained by—anything. You know some likely agents: I know some likely agents. They will suggest others, as our field of usefulness widens. Of course there is the oath of secrecy: we shall administer that after dinner to each guest apart.'

'Jolly difficult for those that are mixed up with the press to keep an oath of secrecy!' Logan spoke as a press man.

'We shall only have to do with gentlemen and ladies. The oath is not going to sanction itself with religious terrors. Good form—we shall appeal to a "sense of form"—now so widely diffused by University Extension Lectures on the Beautiful, the Fitting, the—'

'Oh shut up!' cried Logan. 'You always haver after midnight. For, look here, here is an objection; this precious plan of yours, parents and others could work it for themselves. I dare say they do. When they see the affections of a son, or a daughter, or a bereaved father beginning to stray towards A., they probably invite B. to come and stay and act as a lightning conductor. They don't need us.'

'Oh, don't they? They seldom have an eligible and satisfactory lightning conductor at hand, somebody to whom they can trust their dear one. Or, if they have, the dear one has already been bored with the intended lightning conductor (who is old, or plain, or stupid, or familiar, at best), and they won't look at him or her. Now our Disentanglers are not going to be plain, or dull, or old, or stale, or commonplace— we'll take care of that. My dear fellow, don't you know how dismal the *parti* selected for a man or girl invariably is? Now *we* provide a different and superior article, a *fresh* article too, not a familiar bore or a neighbour.'

'Well, there is a good deal in that, as you say,' Logan admitted. 'But decent people will think the whole speculation shady. How are you to get round that? There is something you have forgotten.'

'What?' Merton asked.

'Why it stares you in the face. References. Unexceptionable

references; people will expect them all round.'

'Please don't say "unexceptionable"; say "references beyond the reach of cavil."' Merton was a purist. 'It costs more in advertisements, but my phrase at once enlists the sympathy of every liberal and elegant mind. But as to references (and I am glad that you have some common sense, Logan), there is, let me see, there is the Dowager.'

'The divine Althaea—Marchioness of Bowton?'

'The same,' said Merton. 'The oldest woman, and the most recklessly up- to-date in London. She has seen *bien d'autres*, and wants to see more.'

'She will do; and my aunt,' Logan said.

'Not, oh, of course not, the one who left her money to the Armenians?' Merton asked.

'No, another. And there's old Lochmaben's young wife, my cousin, widely removed, by marriage. She is American, you know, and perhaps you know her book, *Social Experiments*?'

'Yes, it is not half bad,' Merton conceded, 'and her heart will be in what I fear she will call "the new departure." And she is pretty, and highly respected in the parish.'

'And there's my aunt I spoke of, or great aunt, Miss Nicky Maxwell. The best old thing: a beautiful monument of old gentility, and she would give her left hand to help any one of the clan.'

'She will do. And there's Mrs. Brown-Smith, Lord Yarrow's daughter, who married the patent soap man. *Elle est capable de tout*. A real good woman, but full of her fun.'

'That will do for the lady patronesses. We must secure them at once.'

'But won't the clients blab?' Logan suggested.

'They can't,' Merton said. 'They would be laughed at consumedly. It will be their interest to hold their tongues.'

'Well, let us hope that they will see it in that light.' Logan was not too sanguine.

Merton had a better opinion of his enterprise.

'People, if they come to us at all for assistance in these very delicate and intimate affairs, will have too much to lose by talking about them. They may not come, we can only try, but if they come they will be silent as the grave usually is.'

'Well, it is late, and the whisky is low,' said Logan in mournful tones. 'May the morrow's reflections justify the inspiration of—the whisky. Good night!'

'Good night,' said Merton absently.

He sat down when Logan had gone, and wrote a few notes on large sheets of paper. He was elaborating the scheme. 'If collaboration consists in making objections, as the French novelist said, Logan is a rare collaborator,' Merton muttered as he turned out the pallid lamp and went to bed.

Next morning, before dressing, he revolved the scheme. It bore the change of light and survived the inspiration of alcohol. Logan looked in after breakfast. He had no new objections. They proceeded to action.

II

FROM THE HIGHWAYS AND HEDGES

The first step towards Merton's scheme was taken at once. The lady patronesses were approached. The divine Althaea instantly came in. She had enjoyed few things more since the Duchess of Richmond's ball on the eve of Waterloo. Miss Nicky Maxwell at first professed a desire to open her coffers, 'only anticipating,' she said, 'an event'—which Logan declined in any sense to anticipate. Lady Lochmaben said that they would have a lovely time as experimental students of society. Mrs. Brown-Smith instantly offered her own services as a Disentangler, her lord being then absent in America studying the negro market for detergents.

'I think,' she said, 'he expects Brown-Smith's brand to make an Ethiopian change his skin, and then means to exhibit him as an advertisement.'

'And settle the negro question by making them all white men,' said Logan, as he gracefully declined the generous but compromising proposal of the lady. 'Yet, after all,' thought he, 'is she not right? The prophylactic precautions would certainly be increased, morally speaking, if the Disentanglers were married.' But while he pigeon-holed this idea for future reference, at the moment he could not see his way to accepting

Mrs. Brown-Smith's spirited idea. She reluctantly acquiesced in his view of the case, but, like the other dames, promised to guarantee, if applied to, the absolute respectability of the enterprise. The usual vows of secrecy were made, and (what borders on the supernatural) they were kept.

Merton's first editions went to Sotheby's, 'Property of a gentleman who is changing his objects of collection.' A Russian archduke bought Logan's unique set of golf clubs by Philp. Funds accrued from other sources. Logan had a friend, dearer friend had no man, one Trevor, a pleasant bachelor whose sister kept house for him. His purse, or rather his cheque book, gaped with desire to be at Logan's service, but had gaped in vain. Finding Logan grinning one day over the advertisement columns of a paper at the club, his prophetic soul discerned a good thing, and he wormed it out 'in dern privacy.' He slapped his manly thigh and insisted on being in it—as a capitalist. The other stoutly resisted, but was overcome.

'You need an office, you need retaining fees, you need outfits for the accomplices, and it is a legitimate investment. I'll take interest and risks,' said Trevor.

So the money was found.

The inaugural dinner, for the engaging of accomplices, was given in a private room of a restaurant in Pall Mall.

The dinner was gay, but a little pathetic. Neatness, rather than the gloss of novelty (though other gloss there was), characterised the garments of the men. The toilettes of the women were modest; that amount of praise (and it is a good deal) they deserved. A young lady, Miss Maskelyne, an amber-hued beauty, who practically lived as a female jester at the houses of the great, shone resplendent, indeed, but magnificence of apparel was demanded by her profession.

'I am *so* tired of it,' she said to Merton. 'Fancy being more and more anxious for country house invitations. Fancy an artist's feelings, when she knows she has not been a success. And then when the woman of the house detests you! She often does. And when they ask you to give your imitation of So-and-so, and forget that his niece is in the room! Do you know what they would have called people like me a hundred years ago? Toad-eaters! There is one of us in an old novel I read a bit of once. She goes about, an old maid, to houses. Once she arrived in a snow storm and a hearse. Am I to come to that? I keep learning new drawing-room tricks. And when you fall ill, as I did at Eckford, and you can't leave, and you think they are tired to death of you! Oh, it is I who am tired, and time passes, and one grows old. I am a hag!'

Merton said 'what he ought to have said,' and what, indeed, was true. He was afraid she would tell him what she owed her dress-makers. Therefore he steered the talk round to sport, then to the Highlands, then to Knoydart, then to Alastair Macdonald of Craigiecorrichan, and then Merton knew, by a tone in the voice, a drop of the eyelashes, that Miss Maskelyne was—vaccinated. Prophylactic measures had been taken: this agent ran no risk of infection. There was Alastair.

Merton turned to Miss Willoughby, on his left. She was tall, dark, handsome, but a little faded, and not plump: few of the faces round the table were plump and well liking. Miss Willoughby, in fact, dwelt in one room, in Bloomsbury, and dined on cocoa and bread and butter. These were for her the rewards of the Higher Education. She lived by copying crabbed manuscripts.

'Do you ever go up to Oxford now?' said Merton.

'Not often. Sometimes a St. Ursula girl gets a room in the town for me. I have coached two or three of them at little reading parties. It gets one out of town in autumn: Bloomsbury in August is not very fresh. And at Oxford one can "tout," or "cadge," for a little work. But there are so many of us.'

'What are you busy with just now?'

'Vatican transcripts at the Record Office.'

'Any exciting secrets?'

'Oh no, only how much the priests here paid to Rome for their promotions. Secrets then perhaps: not thrilling now.'

'No schemes to poison people?'

'Not yet: no plots for novels, and oh, such long-winded pontifical Latin, and such awful crabbed hands.'

'It does not seem to lead to much?'

'To nothing, in no way. But one is glad to get anything.'

'Jephson, of Lincoln, whom I used to know, is doing a book on the Knights of St. John in their Relations to the Empire,' said Merton.

'Is he?' said Miss Willoughby, after a scarcely distinguishable but embarrassed pause, and she turned from Merton to exhibit an interest in the very original scheme of mural decoration behind her.

'It is quite a new subject to most people,' said Merton, and he mentally ticked off Miss Willoughby as safe, for Jephson, whom he had heard that she liked, was a very poor man, living on his fellowship and coaching. He was sorry: he had never liked or trusted Jephson.

'It is a subject sure to create a sensation, isn't it?' asked Miss Willoughby, a little paler than before.

'It might get a man a professorship,' said Merton.

'There are so many of us, of them, I mean,' said Miss Willoughby, and Merton gave a small sigh. 'Not much larkiness here,' he thought, and asked a transient waiter for champagne.

Miss Willoughby drank a little of the wine: the colour came into her face.

'By Jove, she's awfully handsome,' thought Merton.

'It was very kind of you to ask me to this festival,' said the girl. 'Why have you asked us, me at least?'

'Perhaps for many besides the obvious reason,' said Merton. 'You may be told later.'

'Then there is a reason in addition to that which most people don't find obvious? Have you come into a fortune?'

'No, but I am coming. My ship is on the sea and my boat is on the shore.'

'I see faces that I know. There is that tall handsome girl, Miss Markham, with real gold hair, next Mr. Logan. We used to call her the Venus of Milo, or Milo for short, at St. Ursula's. She has mantles and things tried on her at Madame Claudine's, and stumpy purchasers argue from the effect (neglecting the cause) that the things will suit *them*. Her people were ruined by Australian gold mines. And there is Miss Martin, who does stories for the penny story papers at a shilling the thousand words. The fathers have backed horses, and the children's teeth are set on edge. Is it a Neo-Christian dinner? We are all so poor. You have sought us in the highways and hedges.'

'Where the wild roses grow,' said Merton.

'I don't know many of the men, though I see faces that one used to see in the High. There is Mr. Yorker, the athletic man. What is he doing now?'

'He is sub-vice-secretary of a cricket club. His income depends on his bat and his curl from leg. But he has a rich aunt.'

'Cricket does not lead to much, any more than my ability to read the worst handwritings of the darkest ages. Who is the man that the beautiful lady opposite is making laugh so?' asked Miss Willoughby, without moving her lips.

Merton wrote 'Bulstrode of Trinity' on the back of the menu.

'What does *he* do?'

'Nothing,' said Merton in a low voice. 'Been alligator farming, or ostrich farming, or ranching, and come back shorn; they all come back. He wants to be an ecclesiastical "chucker out," and cope with Mr. Kensitt and Co. New profession.'

'He ought not to be here. He can ride and shoot.'

'He is the only son of his mother and she is a widow.'

'He ought to go out. My only brother is out. I wish I were a man. I hate dawdlers.' She looked at him: her eyes were large and grey under black lashes, they were dark and louring.

'Have you, by any chance, a spark of the devil in you?' asked Merton, taking a social header.

'I have been told so, and sometimes thought so,' said Miss Willoughby. 'Perhaps this one will go out by fasting if not by prayer. Yes, I *have* a spark of the Accuser of the Brethren.'

'*Tant mieux*,' thought Merton.

All the people were talking and laughing now. Miss Maskelyne told a story to the table. She did a trick with a wine glass, forks, and a cork. Logan interviewed Miss Martin, who wrote tales for the penny fiction people, on her methods. Had she a moral aim, a purpose? Did she create her characters first, and let them evolve their fortunes, or did she invent a plot, and make her characters fit in?

Miss Martin said she began with a situation: 'I wish I could get one somewhere as secretary to a man of letters.'

'They can't afford secretaries,' said Logan. 'Besides they are family men, married men, and so—'

'And so what?'

'Go look in any glass, and say,' said Logan, laughing. 'But how do you begin with a situation?'

'Oh, anyhow. A lot of men in a darkened room. Pitch dark.'

'A seance?'

'No, a conspiracy. They are in the dark that when arrested they may swear they never saw each other.'

'They could swear that anyhow.'

'Conspirators have consciences. Then there comes a red light shining between the door and the floor. Then the door breaks down under a hammer, the light floods the room. There is a man in it whom the others never saw enter.'

'How did he get in?'

'He was there before they came. Then the fighting begins. At the end of it where is the man?'

'Well, where is he? What was he up to?'

'I don't know yet,' said Miss Martin, 'it just comes as I go on. It has just got to come. It is a fourteen hours a day business. All writing. I crib things from the French. Not whole stories. I take the opening situation; say the two men in a boat on the river who hook up a sack. I don't read the rest of the Frenchman, I work on from the sack, and guess what was in it.'

'What was in the sack?'

'*In the Sack*! A name for a story! Anything, from the corpse of a freak (good idea, corpse of a freak with no arms and legs, or with too many) to a model of a submarine ship, or political papers. But I am tired of corpses. They pervade my works. They give "a *bouquet*, a fragrance," as Mr. Talbot Twysden said about his cheap claret.'

'You read the old Masters?'

'The obsolete Thackeray? Yes, I know him pretty well.'

'What are you publishing just now?'

'This to an author? Don't you know?'

'I blush,' said Logan.

'Unseen,' said Miss Martin, scrutinising him closely.

'Well, you do not read the serials to which I contribute,' she went on. 'I have two or three things running. There is *The Judge's Secret.*'

'What was that?'

'He did it himself.'

'Did what?'

'Killed the bishop. He is not a very plausible judge in English: in French he would be all right, a *juge d'instruction*, the man who cross- examines the prisoners in private, you know.'

'Judges don't do that in England,' said Logan.

'No, but this case is an exception. The judge was such a very old friend, a college friend, of the murdered bishop. So he takes advantage of his official position, and steals into the cell of the accused. My public does not know any better, and, of course, I have no reviewers. I never come out in a book.'

'And why did the judge assassinate the prelate?'

'The prelate knew too much about the judge, who sat in the Court of Probate and Divorce.'

'Satan reproving sin?' asked Logan.

'Yes, exactly; and the bishop being interested in the case—'

'No scandal about Mrs. Proudie?'

'No, not that exactly, still, you see the motive?'

'I do,' said Logan. 'And the conclusion?'

'The bishop was not really dead at all. It takes some time to explain. The *corpus delicti*—you see I know my subject—was somebody else. And the bishop was alive, and secretly watching the judge, disguised as Mr. Sherlock Holmes. Oh, I know it is too much in Dickens's manner. But my public has not read Dickens.'

'You interest me keenly' said Logan.

'I am glad to hear it. And the penny public take freely. Our circulation goes up. I asked for a rise of three pence on the thousand words.'

'Now this *is* what I call literary conversation,' said Logan. 'It is like reading *The British Weekly Bookman*. Did you get the threepence? if the inquiry is not indelicate.'

'I got twopence. But, you see, there are so many of us.'

'Tell me more. Are you serialising anything else?'

'Serialising is the right word. I see you know a great deal about literature. Yes, I am serialising a featured tale.'

'A featured tale?'

'You don't know what that is? You do not know everything yet! It is called *Myself.*'

'Why *Myself?*'

'Oh, because the narrator did it—the murder. A stranger is found in a wood, hung to a tree. Nobody knows who he is. But he and the narrator had met in Paraguay. He, the murdered man, came home, visited the narrator, and fell in love with the beautiful being to whom the narrator was engaged. So the narrator lassoed him in a wood.'

'Why?'

'Oh, the old stock reason. He knew too much.'

'What did he know?'

'Why, that the narrator was living on a treasure originally robbed from a church in South America.'

'But, if it *was* a treasure, who would care?'

'The girl was a Catholic. And the murdered man knew more.'

'How much more?'

'This: to find out about the treasure, the narrator had taken priest's orders, and, of course, could not marry. And the other man, being in love with the girl, threatened to tell, and so the lasso came in handy. It is a Protestant story and instructive.'

'Jolly instructive! But, Miss Martin, you are the Guy Boothby of your sex!'

At this supreme tribute the girl blushed like dawn upon

the hills.

'My word, she is pretty!' thought Logan; but what he said was, 'You know Mr. Tierney, your neighbour? Out of a job as a composition master. Almost reduced to University Extension Lectures on the didactic Drama.'

Tierney was talking eagerly to his neighbour, a fascinating lady laundress, *la belle blanchisseuse*, about starch.

Further off a lady instructress in cookery, Miss Frere, was conversing with a tutor of bridge.

'Tierney,' said Logan, in a pause, 'may I present you to Miss Martin?' Then he turned to Miss Markham, formerly known at St. Ursula's as Milo. She had been a teacher of golf, hockey, cricket, fencing, and gymnastics, at a very large school for girls, in a very small town. Here she became society to such an alarming extent (no party being complete without her, while the colonels and majors never left her in peace), that her connection with education was abruptly terminated. At present raiment was draped on her magnificent shoulders at Madame Claudine's. Logan, as he had told Merton, 'occasionally met her,' and Logan had the strongest reasons for personal conviction that she was absolutely proof against infection, in the trying circumstances to which a Disentangler is professionally exposed. Indeed she alone of the women present knew from Logan the purpose of the gathering.

Cigarettes had replaced the desire of eating and drinking. Merton had engaged a withdrawing room, where he meant to be closeted with his guests, one by one, administer the oath, and prosecute delicate inquiries on the important question of immunity from infection. But, after a private word or two with Logan, he deemed these conspicuous formalities needless. 'We have material enough to begin with,' said Logan. 'We knew beforehand that some of the men were safe, and certain of the women.'

There was a balcony. The providence of nature had provided a full moon, and a night of balm. The imaginative maintained that the scent of hay was breathed, among other odours, over Pall Mall the Blest. Merton kept straying with one guest or another into a corner of the balcony. He hinted that there was a thing in prospect. Would the guest hold himself, or herself, ready at need? Next morning, if the promise was given, the guest might awake to peace of conscience. The scheme was beneficent, and, incidentally, cheerful.

To some he mentioned retainers; money down, to speak grossly. Most accepted on the strength of Merton's assurances that their services must always be ready. There were difficulties with Miss Willoughby and Miss Markham. The former lady (who needed it most) flatly refused the arrangement. Merton pleaded in vain. Miss Markham, the girl known to her contemporaries as Milo, could not hazard her present engagement at Madame Claudine's. If she was needed by the scheme in the dead season she thought that she could be ready for whatever it was.

Nobody was told exactly what the scheme was. It was only made clear that nobody was to be employed without the full and exhaustive knowledge of the employers, for whom Merton and Logan were merely agents. If in doubt, the agents might apply for counsel to the lady patronesses, whose very names tranquilised the most anxious inquirers. The oath was commuted for a promise, on honour, of secrecy. And, indeed, little if anything was told that could be revealed. The thing was not political: spies on Russia or France were not being recruited. That was made perfectly clear. Anybody might withdraw, if the prospect, when beheld nearer, seemed undesirable. A mystified but rather merry gathering walked away to remote lodgings, Miss Maskelyne alone patronising a hansom.

On the day after the dinner Logan and Merton reviewed the event and its promise, taking Trevor into their counsels. They were not ill satisfied with the potential recruits.

'There was one jolly little thing in white,' said Trevor. 'So pretty and flowering! "Cherries ripe themselves do cry," a line in an old song, that's what her face reminded me of. Who was she?'

'She came with Miss Martin, the penny novelist,' said Logan. 'She is stopping with her. A country parson's daughter, come up to town to try to live by typewriting.'

'She will be of no use to us,' said Merton. 'If ever a young woman looked fancy-free it is that girl. What did you say her name is, Logan?'

'I did not say, but, though you won't believe it, her name is Miss Blossom, Miss Florry Blossom. Her godfathers and godmothers must bear the burden of her appropriate Christian name; the other, the surname, is a coincidence—designed or not.'

'Well, she is not suitable,' said Merton sternly. 'Misplaced affections she might distract, but then, after she had distracted them, she might reciprocate them. As a conscientious manager I cannot recommend her to clients.'

'But,' said Trevor, 'she may be useful for all that, as well as decidedly ornamental. Merton, you'll want a typewriter for your business correspondence, and Miss Blossom typewrites:

it is her profession.'

'Well,' said Merton, 'I am not afraid. I do not care too much for "that garden in her face," for your cherry-ripe sort of young person. If a typewriter is necessary I can bear with her as well as another.'

'I admire your courage and resignation,' said Trevor, 'so now let us go and take rooms for the Society.'

They found rooms, lordly rooms, which Trevor furnished in a stately manner, hanging a selection of his mezzotints on the walls—ladies of old years, after Romney, Reynolds, Hoppner, and the rest. A sober opulence and comfort characterised the chambers; a well-selected set of books in a Sheraton bookcase was intended to beguile the tedium of waiting clients. The typewriter (Miss Blossom accepted the situation) occupied an inner chamber, opening out of that which was to be sacred to consultations.

The firm traded under the title of Messrs. Gray and Graham. Their advertisement—in all the newspapers—addressed itself 'To Parents, Guardians, Children and others.' It set forth the sorrows and anxieties which beset families in the matter of undesirable matrimonial engagements and entanglements. The advertisers proposed, by a new method, to restore domestic peace and confidence. 'No private inquiries will, in any case, be made into the past of the parties concerned. The highest references will in every instance be given and demanded. Intending clients must in the first instance apply by letter to Messrs. Gray and Graham. No charge will be made for a first interview, which can only be granted after satisfactory references have been exchanged by letter.'

'If *that* does not inspire confidence,' said Merton, 'I don't know what will.'

'Nothing short of it will do,' said Logan.

'But the mezzotints will carry weight,' said Trevor, 'and a few good cloisonnes and enamelled snuff-boxes and bronzes will do no harm.'

So he sent in some weedings of his famous collection.

III

ADVENTURE OF THE FIRST CLIENTS

Merton was reading the newspaper in the office, expecting a client. Miss Blossom was typewriting in the inner chamber; the door between was open. The office boy knocked at Merton's outer door, and the sound of that boy's strangled chuckling was distinctly audible to his employer. There is something irritating in the foolish merriment of a youthful menial. No conduct could be more likely than that of the office boy to irritate the first client, arriving on business of which it were hard to exaggerate the delicate and anxious nature.

These reflections flitted through Merton's mind as he exclaimed 'Come in,' with a tone of admonishing austerity.

The office boy entered. His face was scarlet, his eyes goggled and ran water. Hastily and loudly exclaiming 'Mr. and Miss Apsley' (which ended with a crow) he stuffed his red pocket handkerchief into his mouth and escaped. At the sound of the names, Merton had turned towards the inner door, open behind him, whence came a clear and piercing trill of feminine laughter from Miss Blossom. Merton angrily marched to the inner door, and shut his typewriter in with a bang. His heart burned within him. Nothing could be so insulting to clients; nothing so ruinous to a nascent business. He wheeled round to greet his visitors with a face of apology; his eyes on the average level of the human countenance divine. There was no human countenance divine. There was no human countenance at that altitude. His eyes encountered the opposite wall, and a print of 'Mrs. Pelham Feeding Chickens.'

In a moment his eyes adjusted themselves to a lower elevation. In front of him were standing, hand in hand, a pair of small children, a boy of nine in sailor costume, but with bare knees not usually affected by naval officers, and a girl of seven with her finger in her mouth.

The boy bowed gravely. He was a pretty little fellow with a pale oval face, arched eyebrows, promise of an aquiline nose, and two large black eyes. 'I think, sir,' said the child, 'I have the pleasure of redressing myself to Mr. Gray or Mr. Graham?'

'Graham, at your service,' said Merton, gravely; 'may I ask you and Miss Apsley to be seated?'

There was a large and imposing arm-chair in green leather; the client's chair. Mr. Apsley lifted his little sister into it, and sat down beside her himself. She threw her arms round his neck, and laid her flaxen curls on his shoulder. Her blue eyes looked shyly at Merton out of her fleece of gold. The four shoes of the clients dangled at some distance above the carpet.

'You are the author of this article, I think, Mr. Graham?' said Mr. Apsley, showing his hand, which was warm, and holding out a little crumpled ball of paper, not precisely fresh.

Merton solemnly unrolled it; it contained the advertisement

of his firm.

'Yes,' he said, 'I wrote that.'

'You got our letters, for you answered them,' said Mr. Apsley, with equal solemnity. 'Why do you want Bats and me?'

'The lady's name is Bats?' said Merton, wondering why he was supposed to 'want' either of the pair.

'My name is Batsy. I like you: you are pretty,' said Miss Apsley.

Merton positively blushed: he was unaccustomed to compliments so frank from a member of the sex at an early stage of a business interview. He therefore kissed his fair client, who put up a pair of innocent damp lips, and then allowed her attention to be engrossed by a coin on his watch-chain.

'I don't quite remember your case, sir, or what you mean by saying I wanted you, though I am delighted to see you,' he said to Mr. Apsley. 'We have so many letters! With your permission I shall consult the letter book.'

'The article says "To Parents, Guardians, Children, and others." It was in print,' remarked Mr. Apsley, with a heavy stress on "children," 'and she said you wanted *us*.'

The mystified Merton, wondering who 'she' was, turned the pages of the letter book, mumbling, 'Abernethy, Applecombe, Ap. Davis, Apsley. Here we are,' he began to read the letter aloud. It was typewritten, which, when he saw his clients, not a little surprised him.

'Gentlemen,' the letter ran, 'having seen your advertisement in the *Daily Diatribe* of to-day, May 17, I desire to express my wish to enter into communication with you on a matter of pressing importance.—I am, in the name of my sister, Miss Josephine Apsley, and myself,

'Faithfully yours, 'THOMAS LLOYD APSLEY.'

'That's the letter,' said Mr. Apsley, 'and you wrote to us.'

'And what did I say?' asked Merton.

'Something about preferences, which we did not understand.'

'References, perhaps,' said Merton. 'Mr. Apsley, may I ask whether you wrote this letter yourself?'

'No; None-so-pretty printed it on a kind of sewing machine. *She* told us to come and see you, so we came. I called her None-so-pretty, out of a fairy story. She does not mind. Gran says she thinks she rather likes it.'

'I shouldn't wonder if she did,' said Merton. 'But what is her real name?'

'She made me promise not to tell. She was staying at the Home Farm when we were staying at Gran's.'

'Is Gran your grandmother?'

'Yes,' replied Mr. Apsley.

Hereon Bats remarked that she was 'velly hungalee.'

'To be sure,' said Merton. 'Luncheon shall be brought at once.' He rang the bell, and, going out, interpellated the office boy.

'Why did you laugh when my friends came to luncheon? You must learn manners.'

'Please, sir, the kid, the young gentleman I mean, said he came on business,' answered the boy, showing apoplectic symptoms.

'So he did; luncheon is his business. Go and bring luncheon for—five, and see that there are chicken, cutlets, tartlets, apricots, and ginger- beer.'

The boy departed and Merton reflected. 'A hoax, somebody's practical joke,' he said to himself. 'I wonder who Miss None-so-pretty is.' Then he returned, assured Batsy that luncheon was even at the doors, and leaving her to look at *Punch*, led Mr. Apsley aside. 'Tommy,' he said (having seen his signature), 'where do you live?'

The boy named a street on the frontiers of St. John's Wood.

'And who is your father?'

'Major Apsley, D.S.O.'

'And how did you come here?'

'In a hansom. I told the man to wait.'

'How did you get away?'

'Father took us to Lord's, with Miss Limmer, and there was a crowd, and Bats and I slipped out; for None-so-pretty said we ought to call on you.'

'Who is Miss Limmer?'

'Our governess.'

'Have you a mother?'

The child's brown eyes filled with tears, and his cheeks flushed. 'It was in India that she—'

'Yes, be a man, Tommy. I am looking the other way,' which Merton did for some seconds. 'Now, Tommy, is Miss Limmer kind to you?'

The child's face became strangely set and blank; his eyes looking vacant. 'Miss Limmer is very kind to us. She loves us and we love her dearly. Ask Batsy,' he said in a monotonous voice, as if he were repeating a lesson. 'Batsy, come here,' he said in the same voice. 'Is Miss Limmer kind to us?'

Batsy threw up her eyes—it was like a stage effect, 'We love Miss Limmer dearly, and she loves us. She is very, very kind to us, like our dear mamma.' Her voice was monotonous too. 'I never can say the last part,' said Tommy. 'Batsy knows it; about dear mamma.'

'Indeed!' said Merton. 'Tommy, *why* did you come here?'

'I don't know. I told you that None-so-pretty told us to. She did it after she saw *that* when we were bathing.' Tommy raised one of his little loose breeks that did not cover the knee.

That was not pleasant to look on: it was on the inside of the right thigh.

'How did you get hurt *there*?' asked Merton.

The boy's monotonous chant began again: his eyes were fixed and blank as before. 'I fell off a tree, and my leg hit a branch on the way down.'

'Curious accident,' said Merton; 'and None-so-pretty saw the mark?'

'Yes.'

'And asked you how you got it?'

'Yes, and she saw blue marks on Batsy, all over her arms.'

'And you told None-so-pretty that you fell off a tree?'

'Yes.'

'And she told you to come here?'

'Yes, she had read your printed article.'

'Well, here is luncheon,' said Merton, and bade the office boy call Miss Blossom from the inner chamber to share the meal. Batsy had as low a chair as possible, and was disposing her napkin to do the duty of a pinafore.

Miss Blossom entered from within with downcast eyes.

'None-so-pretty!'

'None-so-pretty!' shouted the children, while Tommy rushed to throw his arms round her neck, to meet which she stooped down, concealing a face of blushes. Batsy descended from her chair, waddled up, climbed another chair, and attacked the girl from the rear. The office boy was arranging luncheon. Merton called him to the writing-table, scribbled a note, and said, 'Take that to Dr. Maitland, with my compliments.'

Maitland had been one of the guests at the inaugural dinner. He was entirely devoid of patients, and was living on the anticipated gains of a great work on Clinical Psychology.

'Tell Dr. Maitland he will find me at luncheon if he comes instantly,' said Merton as the boy fled on his errand. 'I see that I need not introduce you to my young friends, Miss Blossom,' said Merton. 'May I beg you to help Miss Apsley to arrange her tucker?'

Miss Blossom, almost unbecomingly brilliant in her complexion, did as she was asked. Batsy had cold chicken, new potatoes, green peas, and two helpings of apricot tart. Tommy devoted himself to cutlets. A very mild shandygaff was compounded for him in an old Oriel pewter. Both children made love to Miss Blossom with their eyes. It was not at all what Merton felt inclined to do; the lady had entangled him in a labyrinth of puzzledom.

'None-so-pretty,' exclaimed Tommy, 'I am glad you told us to come here. Your friends are nice.'

Merton bowed to Tommy, 'I am glad too,' he said. 'Miss Blossom knew that we were kindred souls, same kind of chaps, I mean, you and me, you know, Tommy!'

Miss Blossom became more and more like the fabled peony, the crimson variety. Luckily the office boy ushered in Dr. Maitland, who, exchanging glances of surprise with Merton, over the children's heads, began to make himself agreeable. He had nearly as many tricks as Miss Maskelyne. He was doing the short-sighted man eating celery, and unable to find the salt because he is unable to find his eyeglass.

Merton, seeing his clients absorbed in mirth, murmured something vague about 'business,' and spirited Miss Blossom away to the inner chamber.

'Sit down, pray, Miss Blossom. There is no time to waste. What do you know about these children? Why did you send them here?'

The girl, who was pale enough now, said, 'I never thought they would come.'

'They are here, however. What do you know about them?'

'I went to stay, lately, at the Home Farm on their grand-mother's place. We became great friends. I found out that they were motherless, and that they were being cruelly ill-treated by their governess.'

'Miss Limmer?'

'Yes. But they both said they loved her dearly. They always said that when asked. I gathered from their grandmother, old Mrs. Apsley, that their father would listen to nothing against the governess. The old lady cried in a helpless way, and said he was capable of marrying the woman, out of obstinacy, if anybody interfered. I had your advertisement, and I thought you might disentangle him. It was a kind of joke. I only told them that you were a kind gentleman. I never dreamed of their really coming.'

'Well, you must take them back again presently, there is the address. You must see their father; you must wait till you see him. And how are you to explain this escapade? I can't have the children taught to lie.'

'They have been taught *that* lesson already.'

'I don't think they are aware of it,' said Merton.

Miss Blossom stared.

'I can't explain, but you must find a way of keeping them out of a scrape.'

'I think I can manage it,' said Miss Blossom demurely.

'I hope so. And manage, if you please, to see this Miss Limmer and observe what kind of person she is,' said Merton, with his hand on the door handle, adding, 'Please ask Dr. Maitland to come here, and do you keep the children amused for a moment.'

Miss Blossom nodded and left the room; there was laughter in the other chamber. Presently Maitland joined Merton.

'Look here,' said Merton, 'we must be rapid. These children are being cruelly ill-treated and deny it. Will you get into talk with the boy, and ask him if he is fond of his governess, say "Miss Limmer," and notice what he says and how he says it? Then we must pack them away.'

'All right,' said Maitland.

They returned to the children. Miss Blossom retreated to the inner room. Bats simplified matters by falling asleep in the client's chair. Maitland began by talking about schools. Was Tommy going to Eton?

Tommy did not know. He had a governess at home.

'Not at a preparatory school yet? A big fellow like you?'

Tommy said that he would like to go to school, but they would not send him.

'Why not?'

Tommy hesitated, blushed, and ended by saying that they didn't think it safe, as he walked in his sleep.

'You will soon grow out of that,' said Maitland, 'but it is not very safe at school. A boy I knew was found sound asleep on the roof at school.'

'He might have fallen off,' said Tommy.

'Yes. That's why your people keep you at home. But in a year or two you will be all right. Know any Latin yet?'

Tommy said that Miss Limmer taught him Latin.

'Are you and she great friends?'

Tommy's face and voice altered as before, while he mechanically repeated the tale of the mutual affection which linked him with Miss Limmer.

'*That's* all very jolly,' said Maitland.

'Now, Tommy,' said Merton, 'we must waken Batsy, and Miss Blossom is going to take you both home. Hope we shall often meet.'

He called Miss Blossom; Batsy kissed both of her new friends. Merton conducted the party to the cab, and settled, in spite of Tommy's remonstrances, with the cabman, who made a good thing of it, and nodded when told to drive away as soon as he had deposited his charges at their door. Then

Merton led Maitland upstairs and offered him a cigar.

'What do you think of it?' he asked.

'Common post-hypnotic suggestion by the governess,' said Maitland.

'I guessed as much, but can it really be worked like that? You are not chaffing?'

'Simplest thing to work in the world,' said Maitland. 'A lot of nonsense, however, that the public believes in can't be done. The woman could not sit down in St. John's Wood, and "will" Tommy to come to her if he was in the next room. At least she might "will" till she was black in the face, and he would know nothing about it. But she can put him to sleep, and make him say what he does not want to say, in answer to questions, afterwards, when he is awake.'

'You're sure of it?'

'It is as certain as anything in the world up to a certain point.'

'The girl said something that the boy did not say, more gushing, about his dead mother.'

'The hypnotised subject often draws a line somewhere.'

'The woman must be a fiend,' said Merton.

'Some of them are, now and then,' said the author of *Clinical Psychology.*

* * * * *

Miss Blossom's cab, the driver much encouraged by Tommy,

who conversed with him through the trap in the roof, dashed up to the door of a house close to Lord's. The horse was going fast, and nearly cannoned into another cab-horse, also going fast, which was almost thrown on its haunches by the driver. Inside the other hansom was a tall man with a pale face under the tan, who was nervously gnawing his moustache. Miss Blossom saw him, Tommy saw him, and cried 'Father!' Half-hidden behind a blind of the house Miss Blossom beheld a woman's face, expectant. Clearly she was Miss Limmer. All the while that they were driving Miss Blossom's wits had been at work to construct a story to account for the absence and return of the children. Now, by a flash of invention, she called to her cabman, 'Drive on— fast!' Major Apsley saw his lost children with their arms round the neck of a wonderfully pretty girl; the pretty girl waved her parasol to him with a smile, beckoning forwards; the children waved their arms, calling out 'A race! a race!'

What could a puzzled parent do but bid his cabman follow like the wind? Miss Blossom's cab flew past Lord's, dived into Regent's Park, leading by two lengths; reached the Zoological Gardens, and there its crew alighted, demurely waiting for the Major. He leaped from his hansom, and taking off his hat, strode up to Miss Blossom, as if he were leading a charge. The children captured him by the legs. 'What does this mean, Madam? What are you doing with my children? Who are you?'

'She's None-so-pretty,' said Tommy, by way of introduction.

Miss Blossom bowed with grace, and raising her head, shot two violet rays into the eyes of the Major, which were of a bistre hue. But they accepted the message, like a receiver in wireless telegraphy. No man, let be a Major, could have resisted None-so-pretty at that moment. 'Come into the gardens,' she said, and led the way. 'You would like a ride on the elephant, Tommy?' she asked Master Apsley. 'And you, Batsy?'

The children shouted assent.

'How in the world does she know them?' thought the bewildered officer.

The children mounted the elephant.

'Now, Major Apsley,' said Miss Blossom, 'I have found your children.'

'I owe you thanks, Madam; I have been very anxious, but—'

'It is more than your thanks I want. I want you to do something for me, a very little thing,' said Miss Blossom, with the air of a supplicating angel, the violet eyes dewy with tears.

'I am sure I shall be delighted to do anything you ask, but—'

'Will you *promise*? It is a very little thing indeed!' and her hands were clasped in entreaty. 'Please promise!'

'Well, I promise.'

'Then keep your word: it is a little thing! Take Tommy home this instant, let nobody speak to him or touch him—and— make him take a bath, and see him take it.'

'Take a bath!'

'Yes, at once, in your presence. Then ask him . . . any questions you please, but pay extreme attention to his answers and his face, and the sound of his voice. If that is not enough do the same with Batsy. And after that I think you had better not let the children out of your sight for a short time.'

'These are very strange requests.'

'And it was by a strange piece of luck that I met you driving home to see if the lost children were found, and secured your attention before it could be pre-engaged.'

'But where did you find them and why?'

Miss Blossom interrupted him, 'Here is the address of Dr. Maitland, I have written it on my own card; he can answer some questions you may want to ask. Later I will answer anything. And now in the name of God,' said the girl reverently, with sudden emotion, 'you will keep your promise to the letter?'

'I will,' said the Major, and Miss Blossom waved her parasol to the children. 'You must give the poor elephant a rest, he is tired,' she cried, and the tender-hearted Batsy needed no more to make her descend from the great earth-shaking beast. The children attacked her with kisses, and then walked off, looking back, each holding one of the paternal hands, and treading, after the manner of childhood, on the paternal toes.

Miss Blossom walked till she met an opportune omnibus.

About an hour later a four-wheeler bore a woman with blazing eyes, and a pile of trunks gaping untidily, from the Major's house in St. John's Wood Road.

The Honourable Company had won its first victory: Major Apsley, having fulfilled Miss Blossom's commands, had seen

Andrew Lang

what she expected him to see, and was disentangled from Miss Limmer.

The children still call their new stepmother None-so-pretty.

IV

ADVENTURE OF THE RICH UNCLE

'His God is his belly, Mr. Graham,' said the client, 'and if the text strikes you as disagreeably unrefined, think how it must pain me to speak thus of an uncle, if only by marriage.'

The client was a meagre matron of forty-five, or thereabouts. Her dark scant hair was smooth, and divided down the middle. Acerbity spoke in every line of her face, which was of a dusky yellow, where it did not rather verge on the faint hues of a violet past its prime. She wore thread gloves, and she carried a battered reticule of early Victorian days, in which Merton suspected that tracts were lurking. She had an anxious peevish mouth; in truth she was not the kind of client in whom Merton's heart delighted.

And yet he was sorry for her, especially as her rich uncle's cook was the goddess of the gentleman whose god had just been denounced in scriptural terms by the client, a Mrs. Gisborne. She was sad, as well she might be, for she was a struggler, with a large family, and great expectations from the polytheistic uncle who adored his cook and one of his nobler organs.

'What has his history been, this gentleman's—Mr. Fulton, I

Andrew Lang

think you called him?'

'He was a drysalter in the City, sir,' and across Merton's mind flitted a vision of a dark shop with Finnan haddocks, bacon, and tongues in the window, and smelling terribly of cheese.

'Oh, a drysalter?' he said, not daring to display ignorance by asking questions to corroborate his theory of the drysalting business.

'A drysalter, sir, and isinglass importer.'

Merton was conscious of vagueness as to isinglass, and was distantly reminded of a celebrated racehorse. However, it was clear that Mr. Fulton was a retired tradesman of some kind. 'He went out of isinglass—before the cheap scientific substitute was invented (it is made out of old quill pens)— with seventy-five thousand pounds. And it *ought* to come to my children. He has not another relation living but ourselves; he married my aunt. But we never see him: he said that he could not stand our Sunday dinners at Hampstead.'

A feeling not remote from sympathy with Mr. Fulton stole over Merton's mind as he pictured these festivals. 'Is his god very—voluminous?'

Mrs. Gisborne stared.

'Is he a very portly gentleman?'

'No, Mr. Graham, he is next door to a skeleton, though you would not expect it, considering.'

'Considering his devotion to the pleasures of the table?'

'Gluttony, shameful waste *I* call it. And he is a stumbling block and a cause of offence to others. He is a patron of the City and Suburban College of Cookery, and founded two scholarships there, for scholars learning how to pamper the—'

'The epicure,' said Merton. He knew the City and Suburban College of Cookery. One of his band, a Miss Frere, was a Fellow and Tutor of that academy.

'And about what age is your uncle?' he asked.

'About sixty, and not a white hair on his head.'

'Then he may marry his cook?'

'He will, sir.'

'And is very likely to have a family.'

Mrs. Gisborne sniffed, and produced a pocket handkerchief from the early Victorian reticule. She applied the handkerchief to her eyes in silence. Merton observed her with pity. 'We need the money so; there are so many of us,' said the lady.

'Do you think that Mr. Fulton is—passionately in love, with his domestic?'

'He only loves his meals,' said Mrs. Gisborne; '*he* does not want to marry her, but she has a hold over him through—his—'

'Passions, not of the heart,' said Merton hastily. He dreaded an anatomical reference.

'He is afraid of losing her. He and his cronies give each other dinners, jealous of each other they are; and he actually pays the woman two hundred a year.'

'And beer money?' said Merton. He had somewhere read or heard of beer money as an item in domestic finance.

'I don't know about that. The cruel thing is that she is a woman of strict temperance principles. So am I. I am sure it is an awful thing to say, Mr. Graham, but Satan has sometimes put it into my heart to wish that the woman, like too, too many of her sort, was the victim of alcoholic temptations. He has a fearful temper, and if once she was not fit for duty at one of his dinners, this awful gnawing anxiety would cease to ride my bosom. He would pack her off.'

'Very natural. She is free from the besetting sin of the artistic temperament?'

'If you mean drink, she is; and that is one reason why he values her. His last cook, and his last but one—' Here Mrs. Gisborne narrated at some length the tragic histories of these artists.

'Providential, I thought it, but now,' she said despairingly.

'She certainly seems a difficult woman to dislodge,' said Merton. 'A dangerous entanglement. Any followers allowed? Could anything be done through the softer emotions? Would a guardsman, for instance—?'

'She hates the men. Never one of them darkens her kitchen fire. Offers she has had by the score, but they come by post, and she laughs and burns them. Old Mr. Potter, one of his cronies, tried to get her away *that* way, but he is over seventy, and old at that, and she thought she had another chance to better herself. And she'll take it, Mr. Graham, if you can't do something: she'll take it.'

'Will you permit me to say that you seem to know a good deal about her! Perhaps you have some sort of means of intelligence in the enemy's camp?'

'The kitchen maid,' said Mrs. Gisborne, purpling a little, 'is the sister of our servant, and tells her things.'

'I see,' said Merton. 'Now can you remember any little weakness of this, I must frankly admit, admirable artist and exemplary woman?'

'You are not going to take her side, a scheming red-faced hussy, Mr. Graham?'

'I never betrayed a client, Madam, and if you mean that I am likely to help this person into your uncle's arms, you greatly misconceive me, and the nature of my profession.'

'I beg your pardon, sir, but I will say that your heart does not seem to be in the case.'

'It is not quite the kind of case with which we are accustomed to deal,' said Merton. 'But you have not answered my question. Are there any weak points in the defence? To Venus she is cold, of Bacchus she is disdainful.'

'I never heard of the gentlemen I am sure, sir, but as to her weaknesses, she has the temper of a—' Here Mrs. Gisborne paused for a comparison. Her knowledge of natural history and of mythology, the usual sources of parallels, failed to provide a satisfactory resemblance to the cook's temper.

'The temper of a Megaera,' said Merton, admitting to himself that the word was not, though mythological, what he

Andrew Lang

could wish.

'Of a Megaera as you know that creature, sir, and impetuous! If everything is not handy, if that poor girl is not like clockwork with the sauces, and herbs, and things, if a saucepan boils over, or a ham falls into the fire, if the girl treads on the tail of one of the cats—and the woman keeps a dozen—then she flies at her with anything that comes handy.'

'She is fond of cats?' said Merton; 'really this lady has sympathetic points:' and he patted the grey Russian puss, Kutuzoff, which was a witness to these interviews.

'She dotes on the nasty things: and you may well say "lady!" Her Siamese cat, a wild beast he is, took the first prize at the Crystal Palace Show. The papers said "Miss Blowser's *Rangoon*, bred by the exhibitor." Miss Blowser! I don't know what the world is coming to. He stands on the doorsteps, the cat, like a lynx, and as fierce as a lion. Why he got her into the police-court: flew at a dog, and nearly tore his owner, a clergyman, to pieces. There were articles about it in the papers.'

'I seem to remember it,' said Merton. '*Christianos ad Leones*'. In fact he had written this humorous article himself. 'But is there nothing else?' he asked. 'Only a temper, so natural to genius disturbed or diverted in the process of composition, and a passion for the *felidae*, such as has often been remarked in the great. There was Charles Baudelaire, Mahomet—'

'I don't know what you mean, sir, and,' said Mrs. Gisborne, rising, and snapping her reticule, 'I think I was a fool for answering your advertisement. I did not come here to be laughed at, and I think common politeness—'

'I beg a thousand pardons,' said Merton. 'I am most distressed at my apparent discourtesy. My mind was preoccupied by the circumstances of this very difficult case, and involuntarily glided into literary anecdote on the subject of cats and their owners. They are my passion—cats—and I regret that they inspire you with antipathy.' Here he picked up Kutuzoff and carried him into the inner room.

'It is not that I object to any of Heaven's creatures kept in their place,' said Mrs. Gisborne somewhat mollified, 'but you must make allowances, sir, for my anxiety. It sours a mother of nine. Friday is one of his gorging dinner-parties, and who knows what may happen if she pleases him? The kitchen maid says, I mean I hear, that she wears an engaged ring already.'

'That is very bad,' said Merton, with sympathy. 'The dinner is on Friday, you say?' and he made a note of the date.

'Yes, 15 Albany Grove, on the Regent's Canal.'

'You can think of nothing else—no weakness to work on?'

'No, sir, just her awful temper; I would save him from it, for *he* has another as bad. And besides hopes from him have kept me up so long, his only relation, and times are so hard, and schooling and boots, and everything so dear, and we so many in family.' Tears came into the poor lady's eyes.

'I'll give the case my very best attention,' he said, shaking hands with the client. To Merton's horror she tried, Heaven help her, to pass a circular packet, wrapped in paper, into his hand. He evaded it. It was a first interview, for which no charge was made. 'What can be done shall be done, though I confess that I do not see my way,' and he accompanied her downstairs to the street.

'I behaved like a cad with my chaff,' he said to himself, 'but hang me if I see how to help her. And I rather admire that cook.'

He went into the inner room, wakened the sleeping partner, Logan, on the sofa, and unfolded the case with every detail. 'What can we do, *que faire*!'

'There's an exhibition of modern, mediaeval, ancient, and savage cookery at Earl's Court, the Cookeries,' said Logan. 'Couldn't we seduce an artist like Miss Blowser there, I mean *thither* of course, the night before the dinner, and get her up into the Great Wheel and somehow stop the Wheel—and make her too late for her duties?'

'And how are you going to stop the Wheel?'

'Speak to the Man at the Wheel. Bribe the beggar.'

'Dangerous, and awfully expensive. Then think of all the other people on the Wheel! Logan, *vous chassez de race*. The old Restalrig blood is in your veins.'

'My ancestors nearly nipped off with a king, and why can't I carry off a cook? Hustle her into a hansom—'

'Oh, bah! these are not modern methods.'

'*Il n'y a rien tel que d'enlever*,' said Logan.

'I never shall stain the cause with police-courts,' said Merton. 'It would be fatal.'

'I've heard of a cook who fell on his sword when the fish did not come up to time. Now a raid on the fish? She might fall on her carving knife when they did not arrive, or leap into the flames of the kitchen fire, like OEnone, don't you know.'

'Bosh. Vatel was far from the sea, and he had not a fish-monger's shop round the corner. Be modern.'

Logan rumpled his hair, 'Can't I get her to lunch at a restaurant and ply her with the wines of Eastern France? No, she is Temperance personified. Can't we send her a forged telegram to say that her mother is dying? Servants seem to have such lots of mothers, always inconveniently, or conveniently, moribund.'

'I won't have forgery. Great heavens, how obsolete you are! Besides, that would not put her employer in a rage.'

'Could I go and consult—?' he mentioned a specialist. 'He is a man of ideas.'

'He is a man of the purest principles—and an uncommonly hard hitter.'

'It is his purity I want. My own mind is hereditarily lawless. I want something not immoral, yet efficacious. There was that parson, whom you say the woman's cat nearly devoured. Like Paul with beasts he fought the cat. Now, I wonder if that injured man is not meditating some priestly revenge that would do our turn and get rid of Miss Blowser?'

Merton shook his head impatiently. His own invention was busy, but to no avail. Miss Blowser seemed impregnable. Kutuzoff Hedzoff, the puss, stalked up to Logan and leaped on his knees. Logan stroked him, Kutuzoff purred and blinked, Logan sought inspiration in his topaz eyes. At last he spoke: 'Will you leave this affair to me, Merton? I think I have found out a way.'

'What way?'

'That's my secret. You are so beastly moral, you might object. One thing I may tell you—it does not compromise the Honourable Company of Disentanglers.'

'You are not going to try any detective work; to find out if she is a woman with a past, with a husband living? You are not going to put a live adder among the eels? I daresay drysalters eat eels. It is the reading of sensational novels that ruins our youth.'

'What a suspicious beggar you are. Certainly I am neither a detective nor a murderer *a la Montepin*!

'No practical jokes with the victuals?'

'Of course not.'

'No kidnapping Miss Blowser?'

'Certainly no kidnapping—Miss Blowser.'

'Now, honour bright, is your plan within the law? No police-court publicity?'

'No, the police will have no say or show in the matter; at least,' said Logan, 'as far as my legal studies inform me, they won't. But I can take counsel's opinion if you insist on it.'

'Then you are sailing near the wind?'

'Really I don't think so: not really what you call near.'

'I am sorry for that unlucky Mrs. Gisborne,' said Merton, musingly. 'And with two such tempers as the cook's and Mr.

Fulton's the match could not be a happy one. Well, Logan, I suppose you won't tell me what your game is?'

'Better not, I think, but, I assure you, honour is safe. I am certain that nobody can say anything. I rather expect to earn public gratitude, on the whole. *You* can't appear in any way, nor the rest of us. By-the- bye do you remember the address of the parson whose dog was hurt?'

'I think I kept a cutting of the police case; it was amusing,' said Merton, looking through a kind of album, and finding presently the record of the incident.

'It may come in handy, or it may not,' said Logan. He then went off, and had Merton followed him he might not have been reassured. For Logan first walked to a chemist's shop, where he purchased a quantity of a certain drug. Next he went to the fencing rooms which he frequented, took his fencing mask and glove, borrowed a fencing glove from a left- handed swordsman whom he knew, and drove to his rooms with this odd assortment of articles. Having deposited them, he paid a call at the dwelling of a fair member of the Disentanglers, Miss Frere, the lady instructress in the culinary art, at the City and Suburban College of Cookery, whereof, as we have heard, Mr. Fulton, the eminent drysalter, was a patron and visitor. Logan unfolded the case and his plan of campaign to Miss Frere, who listened with intelligent sympathy.

'Do you know the man by sight?' he asked.

'Oh yes, and he knows me perfectly well. Last year he distributed the prizes at the City and Suburban School of Cookery, and paid me the most extraordinary compliments.'

'Well deserved, I am confident,' said Logan; 'and now you

are sure that you know exactly what you have to do, as I have explained?'

'Yes, I am to be walking through Albany Grove at a quarter to four on Friday.'

'Be punctual.'

'You may rely on me,' said Miss Frere.

Logan next day went to Trevor's rooms in the Albany; he was the capitalist who had insisted on helping to finance the Disentanglers. To Trevor he explained the situation, unfolded his plan, and asked leave to borrow his private hansom.

'Delighted,' said Trevor. 'I'll put on an old suit of tweeds, and a seedy bowler, and drive you myself. It will be fun. Or should we take my motor car?'

'No, it attracts too much attention.'

'Suppose we put a number on my cab, and paint the wheels yellow, like pirates, you know, when they are disguising a captured ship. It won't do to look like a private cab.'

'These strike me as judicious precautions, Trevor, and worthy of your genius. That is, if we are not caught.'

'Oh, we won't be caught,' said Trevor. 'But, in the meantime, let us find that place you mean to go to on a map of London, and I'll drive you there now in a dog-cart. It is better to know the lie of the land.'

Logan agreed and they drove to his objective in the afternoon; it was beyond the border of known West

Hammersmith. Trevor reconnoitred and made judicious notes of short cuts.

On the following day, which was Thursday, Logan had a difficult piece of diplomacy to execute. He called at the rooms of the clergyman, a bachelor and a curate, whose dog and person had suffered from the assaults of Miss Blowser's Siamese favourite. He expected difficulties, for a good deal of ridicule, including Merton's article, *Christianos ad Leones*, had been heaped on this martyr. Logan looked forward to finding him crusty, but, after seeming a little puzzled, the holy man exclaimed, 'Why, you must be Logan of Trinity?'

'The same,' said Logan, who did not remember the face or name (which was Wilkinson) of his host.

'Why, I shall never forget your running catch under the scoring-box at Lord's,' exclaimed Mr. Wilkinson, 'I can see it now. It saved the match. I owe you more than I can say,' he added with deep emotion.

'Then be grateful, and do me a little favour. I want—just for an hour or two—to borrow your dog,' and he stooped to pat the animal, a fox-terrier bearing recent and glorious scars.

'Borrow Scout! Why, what can you want with him?'

'I have suffered myself through an infernal wild beast of a cat in Albany Grove,' said Logan, 'and I have a scheme—it is unchristian I own—of revenge.'

The curate's eyes glittered vindictively: 'Scout is no match for the brute,' he said in a tone of manly regret.

'Oh, Scout will be all right. There is not going to be a fight.

He is only needed to—give tone to the affair. You will be able to walk him safely through Albany Grove after to-morrow.'

'Won't there be a row if you kill the cat? He is what they think a valuable animal. I never could stand cats myself.'

'The higher vermin,' said Logan. 'But not a hair of his whiskers shall be hurt. He will seek other haunts, that's all.'

'But you don't mean to steal him?' asked the curate anxiously. 'You see, suspicion might fall on me, as I am known to bear a grudge to the brute.'

'I steal him! Not I,' said Logan. 'He shall sleep in his owner's arms, if she likes. But Albany Grove shall know him no more.'

'Then you may take Scout,' said Mr. Wilkinson. 'You have a cab there, shall I drive to your rooms with you and him?'

'Do,' said Logan, 'and then dine at the club.' Which they did, and talked much cricket, Mr. Wilkinson being an enthusiast.

* * * * *

Next day, about 3.40 P.M., a hansom drew up at the corner of Albany Grove. The fare alighted, and sauntered past Mr. Fulton's house. Rangoon, the Siamese puss, was sitting in a scornful and leonine attitude, in a tree of the garden above the railings, outside the open kitchen windows, whence came penetrating and hospitable smells of good fare. The stranger passed, and as he returned, dropped something here and there on the pavement. It was valerian, which no cat can resist.

Miss Blowser was in a culinary crisis, and could not leave

the kitchen range. Her face was of a fiery complexion; her locks were in a fine disorder. 'Is Rangoon in his place, Mary?' she inquired of the kitchen maid.

'Yes, ma'am, in his tree,' said the maid.

In this tree Rangoon used to sit like a Thug, dropping down on dogs who passed by.

Presently the maid said, 'Ma'am, Rangoon has jumped down, and is walking off to the right, after a gentleman.'

'After a sparrow, I dare say, bless him,' said Miss Blowser. Two minutes later she asked, 'Has Rangy come back?'

'No, ma'am.'

'Just look out and see what he is doing, the dear.'

'He's walking along the pavement, ma'am, sniffing at something. And oh! there's that curate's dog.'

'Yelping little brute! I hope Rangy will give him snuff,' said Miss Blowser.

'He's flown at him,' cried the maid ambiguously, in much excitement. 'Oh, ma'am, the gentleman has caught hold of Rangoon. He's got a wire mask on his face, and great thick gloves, not to be scratched. He's got Rangoon: he's putting him in a bag,' but by this time Miss Blowser, brandishing a saucepan with a long handle, had rushed out of the kitchen, through the little garden, cannoned against Mr. Fulton, who happened to be coming in with flowers to decorate his table, knocked him against a lamp-post, opened the garden gate, and, armed and bareheaded as she was, had rushed forth. You might have deemed that you beheld Bellona speeding to the fray.

What Miss Blowser saw was a man disappearing into a hansom, whence came the yapping of a dog. Another cab was loitering by, empty; and this cabman had his orders. Logan had seen to *that*. To hail that cab, to leap in, to cry, 'Follow the scoundrel in front: a sovereign if you catch him,' was to the active Miss Blowser the work of a moment. The man whipped up his horse, the pursuit began, 'there was racing and chasing on Cannobie Lee,' Marylebone rang with the screams of female rage and distress. Mr. Fulton, he also, leaped up and rushed in pursuit, wringing his hands. He had no turn of speed, and stopped panting. He only saw Miss Blowser whisk into her cab, he only heard her yells that died in the distance. Mr. Fulton sped back into his house. He shouted for Mary: 'What's the matter with your mistress, with my cook?' he raved.

'Somebody's taken her cat, sir, and is off, in a cab, and her after him.'

'After her cat! D— her cat,' cried Mr. Fulton. 'My dinner will be ruined! It is the last she shall touch in *this* house. Out she packs—pack her things, Mary; no, don't—do what you can in the kitchen. I *must* find a cook. Her cat!' and with language unworthy of a drysalter Mr. Fulton clapped on his hat, and sped into the street, with a vague idea of hurrying to Fortnum and Mason's, or some restaurant, or a friend's house, indeed to any conceivable place where a cook might be recruited *impromptu*. 'She leaves this very day,' he said aloud, as he all but collided with a lady, a quiet, cool-looking lady, who stopped and stared at him.

'Oh, Miss Frere!' said Mr. Fulton, raising his hat, with a wild gleam of hope in the trouble of his eyes, 'I have had such a misfortune!'

'What has happened, Mr. Fulton?'

'Oh, ma'am, I've lost my cook, and me with a dinner-party on to-day.'

'Lost your cook? Not by death, I hope?'

'No, ma'am, she has run away, in the very crisis, as I may call it.'

'With whom?'

'With nobody. After her cat. In a cab. I am undone. Where can I find a cook? You may know of some one disengaged, though it is late in the day, and dinner at seven. Can't you help me?'

'Can you trust me, Mr. Fulton?'

'Trust you; how, ma'am?'

'Let me cook your dinner, at least till your cook catches her cat,' said Miss Frere, smiling.

'You, don't mean it, a lady!'

'But a professed cook, Mr. Fulton, and anxious to help so nobly generous a patron of the art . . . if you can trust me.'

'Trust you, ma'am!' said Mr. Fulton, raising to heaven his obsecrating hands. 'Why, you're a genius. It is a miracle, a mere miracle of good luck.'

By this time, of course, a small crowd of little boys and girls, amateurs of dramatic scenes, was gathering.

'We have no time to waste, Mr. Fulton. Let us go in, and let me get to work. I dare say the cook will be back before I have taken off my gloves.'

'Not her, nor does she cook again in my house. The shock might have killed a man of my age,' said Mr. Fulton, breathing heavily, and leading the way up the steps to his own door. 'Her cat, the hussy!' he grumbled.

Mr. Fulton kept his word. When Miss Blowser returned, with her saucepan and Rangoon, she found her trunks in the passage, corded by Mr. Fulton's own trembling hands, and she departed for ever.

Her chase had been a stern chase, a long chase, the cab driven by Trevor had never been out of sight. It led her, in the western wilds, to a Home for Decayed and Destitute Cats, and it had driven away before she entered the lane leading to the Home. But there she found Rangoon. He had just been deposited there, in a seedy old traveller's fur-lined sleeping bag, the matron of the Home averred, by a very pleasant gentleman, who said he had found the cat astray, lost, and thinking him a rare and valuable animal had deemed it best to deposit him at the Home. He had left money to pay for advertisements. He had even left the advertisement, typewritten (by Miss Blossom).

'FOUND. A magnificent Siamese Cat. Apply to the Home for Destitute and Decayed Cats, Water Lane, West Hammersmith.'

'Very thoughtful of the gentleman,' said the matron of the Home. 'No; he did not leave any address. Said something about doing good by stealth.'

'Stealth, why he stole my cat!' exclaimed Miss Blowser. 'He must have had the advertisement printed like that ready beforehand. It's a conspiracy,' and she brandished her saucepan.

The matron, who was prejudiced in favour of Logan, and his two sovereigns, which now need not be expended in advertisements, was alarmed by the hostile attitude of Miss Blowser. 'There's your cat,' she said drily; 'it ain't stealing a cat to leave it, with money for its board, and to pay for advertisements, in a well-conducted charitable institution, with a duchess for president. And he even left five shillings to pay for the cab of anybody as might call for the cat. There is your money.'

Miss Blowser threw the silver away.

'Take your old cat in the bag,' said the matron, slamming the door in the face of Miss Blowser.

* * * * *

After the trial for breach of promise of marriage, and after paying the very considerable damages which Miss Blowser demanded and received, old Mr. Fulton hardened his heart, and engaged a male *chef*.

The gratitude of Mrs. Gisborne, now free from all anxiety, was touching. But Merton assured her that he knew nothing whatever of the stratagem, scarcely a worthy one, he thought, as she reported it, by which her uncle was disentangled.

It was Logan's opinion, and it is mine, that he had not been guilty of theft, but perhaps of the wrongous detention or imprisonment of Rangoon. 'But,' he said, 'the Habeas Corpus Act has no clause about cats, and in Scottish law, which is good enough for *me*, there is no property in cats. You can't, legally, *steal* them.'

'How do you know?' asked Merton.

'I took the opinion of an eminent sheriff substitute.'

'What is that?'

'Oh, a fearfully swagger legal official: *you* have nothing like it.'

'Rum country, Scotland,' said Merton.

'Rum country, England,' said Logan, indignantly. '*You* have no property in corpses.'

Merton was silenced.

Neither could foresee how momentous, to each of them, the question of property in corpses was to prove. *O pectora caeca*!

* * * * *

Miss Blowser is now Mrs. Potter. She married her aged wooer, and Rangoon still wins prizes at the Crystal Palace.

V

THE ADVENTURE OF THE OFFICE SCREEN

It is not to be supposed that all the enterprises of the Company of Disentanglers were fortunate. Nobody can command success, though, on the other hand, a number of persons, civil and military, are able to keep her at a distance with surprising uniformity. There was one class of business which Merton soon learned to renounce in despair, just as some sorts of maladies defy our medical science.

'It is curious, and not very creditable to our chemists,' Merton said, 'that love philtres were once as common as seidlitz powders, while now we have lost that secret. The wrong persons might drink love philtres, as in the case of Tristram and Iseult. Or an unskilled rural practitioner might send out the wrong drug, as in the instance of Lucretius, who went mad in consequence.'

'Perhaps,' remarked Logan, 'the chemist was voting at the Comitia, and it was his boy who made a mistake about the mixture.'

'Very probably, but as a rule, the love philtres *worked*. Now, with all our boasted progress, the secret is totally lost. Nothing but a love philtre would be of any use in some cases. There is Lord Methusalem, eighty if he is a day.'

'Methusalem has been unco "wastefu' in wives"!' said Logan.

'His family have been consulting me—the women in tears. He *will* marry his grandchildren's German governess, and there is nothing to be done. In such cases nothing is ever to be done. You can easily distract an aged man's volatile affections, and attach them to a new charmer. But she is just as ineligible as the first; marry he *will*, always a young woman. Now if a respectable virgin or widow of, say, fifty, could hand him a love philtre, and gain his heart, appearances would, more or less, be saved. But, short of philtres, there is nothing to be done. We turn away a great deal of business of that sort.'

The Society of Disentanglers, then, reluctantly abandoned dealings in this class of affairs.

In another distressing business, Merton, as a patriot, was obliged to abandon an attractive enterprise. The Marquis of Seakail was serving his country as a volunteer, and had been mentioned in despatches. But, to the misery of his family, he had entangled himself, before his departure, with a young lady who taught in a high school for girls. Her character was unimpeachable, her person graceful; still, as her father was a butcher, the duke and duchess were reluctant to assent to the union. They consulted Merton, and assured him that they would not flinch from expense. A great idea flashed across Merton's mind. He might send out a stalwart band of Disentanglers, who, disguised as the enemy, might capture Seakail, and carry him off prisoner to some retreat where the fairest of his female staff (of course with a suitable chaperon), would await him in the character of a daughter of the hostile race. The result would probably be to detach Seakail's heart from his love in England. But on reflection,

Merton felt that the scheme was unworthy of a patriot.

Other painful cases occurred. One lady, a mother, of resolute character, consulted Merton on the case of her son. He was betrothed to an excitable girl, a neighbour in the country, who wrote long literary letters about Mr. George Meredith's novels, and (when abroad) was a perfect Baedeker, or Murray, or Mr. Augustus Hare: instructing through correspondence. So the matron complained, but this was not the worst of it. There was an unhappy family history, of a kind infinitely more common in fiction than in real life. To be explicit, even according to the ideas of the most abject barbarians, the young people, unwittingly, were too near akin for matrimony.

'There is nothing for it but to tell both of them the truth,' said Merton. 'This is not a case in which we can be concerned.'

The resolute matron did not take his counsel. The man was told, not the girl, who died in painful circumstances, still writing. Her letters were later given to the world, though obviously not intended for publication, and only calculated to waken unavailing grief among the sentimental, and to make the judicious tired. There was, however, a case in which Merton may be said to have succeeded by a happy accident. Two visitors, ladies, were ushered into his consulting room; they were announced as Miss Baddeley and Miss Crofton.

Miss Baddeley was attired in black, wore a thick veil, and trembled a good deal. Miss Crofton, whose dress was a combination of untoward but decisive hues, and whose hat was enormous and flamboyant, appeared to be the other young lady's *confidante*, and conducted the business of the interview.

'My dear friend, Miss Baddeley,' she began, when Miss Baddeley took her hand, and held it, as if for protection and sympathy. 'My dear friend,' repeated Miss Crofton, 'has asked me to accompany her, and state her case. She is too highly strung to speak for herself.'

Miss Baddeley wrung Miss Crofton's hand, and visibly quivered.

Merton assumed an air of sympathy. 'The situation is grave?' he asked.

'My friend,' said Miss Crofton, thoroughly enjoying herself, 'is the victim of passionate and unavailing remorse, are you not, Julia?' Julia nodded.

'Deeply as I sympathise,' said Merton, 'it appears to me that I am scarcely the person to consult. A mother now—'

'Julia has none.'

'Or a father or sister?'

'But for me, Julia is alone in the world.'

'Then,' said Merton, 'there are many periodicals especially intended for ladies. There is *The Woman of the World*, *The Girl's Guardian Angel*, *Fashion and Passion*, and so on. The Editors, in their columns, reply to questions in cases of conscience. I have myself read the replies to *Correspondents*, and would especially recommend those published in a serial conducted by Miss Annie Swan.'

Miss Crofton shook her head.

'Miss Baddeley's social position is not that of the people who are answered in periodicals.'

'Then why does she not consult some discreet and learned person, her spiritual director? Remorse (entirely due, no doubt, to a conscience too delicately sensitive) is not in our line of affairs. We only advise in cases of undesirable matrimonial engagements.'

'So we are aware,' said Miss Crofton. 'Dear Julia *is* engaged, or rather entangled, in—how many cases, dear?'

Julia shook her head and sobbed behind her veil.

'Is it one, Julia—nod when I come to the exact number—two? three? four?'

At the word 'four' Julia nodded assent.

Merton very much wished that Julia would raise her veil. Her figure was excellent, and with so many sins of this kind on her remorseful head, her face, Merton thought, must be worth seeing. The case was new. As a rule, clients wanted to disentangle their friends and relations. *This* client wanted to disentangle herself.

'This case,' said Merton, 'will be difficult to conduct, and the expenses would be considerable. I can hardly advise you to incur them. Our ordinary method is to throw in the way of one or other of the engaged, or entangled persons, some one who is likely to distract their affections; of course,' he added, 'to a more eligible object. How can I hope to find an object more eligible, Miss Crofton, than I must conceive your interesting friend to be?'

Miss Crofton caressingly raised Julia's veil. Before the victim of remorse could bury her face in her hands, Merton had time to see that it was a very pretty one. Julia was dark, pale, with 'eyes like billiard balls' (as a celebrated amateur once remarked), with a beautiful mouth, but with a somewhat wildly enthusiastic expression.

'How can I hope?' Merton went on, 'to find a worthier and more attractive object? Nay, how can I expect to secure the services not of one, but of *four*—'

'Three would do, Mr. Merton,' explained Miss Crofton. 'Is it not so, Julia dearest?'

Julia again nodded assent, and a sob came from behind the veil, which she had resumed.

'Even three,' said Merton, gallantly struggling with a strong inclination to laugh, 'present difficulties. I do not speak the idle language of compliment, Miss Crofton, when I say that our staff would be overtaxed by the exigencies of this case. The expense also, even of three—'

'Expense is no object,' said Miss Crofton.

'But would it not, though I seem to speak against my own interests, be the wisest, most honourable, and infinitely the least costly course, for Miss Baddeley openly to inform her suitors, three out of the four at least, of the actual posture of affairs? I have already suggested that, as the lady takes the matter so seriously to heart, she should consult her director, or, if of the Anglican or other Protestant denomination, her clergyman, who I am sure will agree with me.'

Miss Crofton shook her head. 'Julia is unattached,' she said.

'I had gathered that to one of the four Miss Baddeley was— not indifferent,' said Merton.

'I meant,' said Miss Crofton severely, 'that Miss Baddeley is a Christian unattached. My friend is sensitive, passionate, and deeply religious, but not a member of any recognised denomination. The clergy—'

'They never leave one alone,' said Julia in a musical voice. It was the first time that she had spoken. 'Besides—' she added, and paused.

'Besides, dear Julia *is*—entangled with a young clergyman whom, almost in despair, she consulted on her case—at a picnic,' said Miss Crofton, adding, 'he is prepared to seek a martyr's fate, but he insists that she must accompany him.'

'How unreasonable!' murmured Merton, who felt that this recalcitrant clergyman was probably not the favourite out of the field of four.

'That is what *I* say,' remarked Miss Crofton. 'It is unreasonable to expect Julia to accompany him when she has so much work to overtake in the home field. But that is the way with all of them.'

'All of them!' exclaimed Merton. 'Are all the devoted young men under vows to seek the crown of martyrdom? Does your friend act as recruiting sergeant, if you will pardon the phrase, for the noble army of martyrs?'

'*Three* of them have made the most solemn promises.'

'And the fourth?'

'*He* is not in holy orders.'

'Am I to understand that all the three admirers about whom Miss Baddeley suffers remorse are clerics?'

'Yes. Julia has a wonderful attraction for the Church,' said Miss Crofton, 'and that is what causes her difficulties. She *can't* write to *them*, or communicate to *them* in personal interviews (as you advised), that her heart is no longer—'

'Theirs,' said Merton. 'But why are the clergy more privileged than the laity? I have heard of such things being broken to laymen. Indeed it has occurred to many of us, and we yet live.'

'I have urged the same facts on Julia myself,' said Miss Crofton. 'Indeed I *know*, by personal experience, that what you say of the laity is true. They do not break their hearts when disappointed. But Julia replies that for her to act as you and I would advise might be to shatter the young clergymen's ideals.'

'To shatter the ideals of three young men in holy orders!' said Merton.

'Yes, for Julia *is* their ideal—Julia and Duty,' said Miss Crofton, as if she were naming a firm. 'She lives only,' here Julia twisted the hand of Miss Crofton, 'she lives only to do good. Her fortune, entirely under her own control, enables her to do a great deal of good.'

Merton began to understand that the charms of Julia were not entirely confined to her *beaux yeux*.

'She is a true philanthropist. Why, she rescued *me* from the snares and temptations of the stage,' said Miss Crofton.

'Oh, *now* I understand,' said Merton; 'I knew that your face and voice were familiar to me. Did you not act in a revival of *The Country Wife*?'

'Hush,' said Miss Crofton.

'And Lady Teazle at an amateur performance in the Canterbury week?'

'These are days of which I do not desire to be reminded,' said Miss Crofton. 'I was trying to explain to you that Julia lives to do good, and has a heart of gold. No, my dear, Mr. Merton will much misconceive you unless you let me explain everything.' This remark was in reply to the agitated gestures of Julia. 'Thrown much among the younger clergy in the exercise of her benevolence, Julia naturally awakens in them emotions not wholly brotherly. Her sympathetic nature carries her off her feet, and she sometimes says "Yes," out of mere goodness of heart, when it would be wiser for her to say "No"; don't you, Julia?'

Merton was reminded of one of M. Paul Bourget's amiable married heroines, who erred out of sheer goodness of heart, but he only signified his intelligence and sympathy.

'Then poor Julia,' Miss Crofton went on hurriedly, 'finds that she has misunderstood her heart. Recently, ever since she met Captain Lestrange—of the Guards—'

'The fourth?' asked Merton.

Miss Crofton nodded. 'She has felt more and more certain that she *had* misread her heart. But on each occasion she *has* felt this—after meeting the—well, the next one.'

'I see the awkwardness,' murmured Merton.

'And then Remorse has set in, with all her horrors. Julia has wept, oh! for nights, on my shoulder.'

Andrew Lang

'Happy shoulder,' murmured Merton.

'And so, as she *dare* not shatter their ideals, and perhaps cause them to plunge into excesses, moral or doctrinal, this is what she has done. She has said to each, that what the Church, any Church, needs is martyrs, and that if they will go to benighted lands, where the crown of martyrdom may still be won, *then*, if they return safe in five years, then she— will think of naming a day. You will easily see the attractions of this plan for Julia, Mr. Merton. No ideals were shattered, the young men being unaware of the circum- stances. They *might* forget her—'

'Impossible,' cried Merton.

'They might forget her, or, perhaps they—'

Miss Crofton hesitated.

'Perhaps they might never—?' asked Merton.

'Yes,' said Miss Crofton; 'perhaps they might *not*. That would be all to the good for the Church; no ideals would be shattered—the reverse—and dear Julia would—'

'Cherish their pious memories,' said Merton.

'I see that you understand me,' said Miss Crofton.

Merton did understand, and he was reminded of the wicked lady, who, when tired of her lovers, had them put into a sack, and dropped into the Seine.

'But,' he asked, 'has this ingenious system failed to work? I should suppose that each young man, on distant and on deadly shores, was far from causing inconvenience.'

'The defect of the system,' said Miss Crofton, 'is that none of them has gone, or seems in a hurry to go. The first—that was Mr. Bathe, Julia?'

Julia nodded.

'Mr. Bathe was to have gone to Turkey during the Armenian atrocities, and to have *forced* England to intervene by taking the Armenian side and getting massacred. Julia was intensely interested in the Armenians. But Mr. Bathe first said that he must lead Julia to the altar before he went; and then the massacres fell off, and he remains at Cheltenham, and is very tiresome. And then there is Mr. Clancy, *he* was to go out to China, and denounce the gods of the heathen Chinese in the public streets. But *he* insisted that Julia should first be his, and he is at Leamington, and not a step has he taken to convert the Boxers.'

Merton knew the name of Clancy. Clancy had been his fag at school, and Merton thought it extremely improbable that the Martyr's crown would ever adorn his brow.

'Then—and this is the last of them, of the clergy, at least— Mr. Brooke: he was to visit the New Hebrides, where the natives are cannibals, and utterly unawakened. He is as bad as the others. He won't go alone. Now, Julia is obliged to correspond with all of them in affectionate terms (she keeps well out of their way), and this course of what she feels to be duplicity is preying terribly on her conscience.'

Here Julia sobbed hysterically.

'She is afraid, too, that by some accident, though none of them know each other, they may become aware of the state of affairs, or Captain Lestrange, to whom she is passionately attached, may find it out, and then, not only may their ideals be wrecked, but—'

'Yes, I see,' said Merton; 'it is awkward, very.'

The interview, an early one, had lasted for some time.
Merton felt that the hour of luncheon had arrived, and, after
luncheon, it had been his intention to go up to the University
match. He also knew, from various sounds, that clients were
waiting in the ante-chamber. At this moment the door
opened, and the office boy, entering, laid three cards before
him.

'The gentlemen asked when you could see them, sir. They
have been waiting some time. They say that their
appointment was at one o'clock, and they wish to go back to
Lord's.'

'So do I,' thought Merton sadly. He looked at the cards,
repressed a whistle, and handed them silently to Miss
Crofton, bidding the boy go, and return in three minutes.

Miss Crofton uttered a little shriek, and pressed the cards on
Julia's attention. Raising her veil, Julia scanned them, wrung
her hands, and displayed symptoms of a tendency to faint.
The cards bore the names of the Rev. Mr. Bathe, the Rev.
Mr. Brooke, and the Rev. Mr. Clancy.

'What is to be done?' asked Miss Crofton in a whisper. 'Can't
you send them away?'

'Impossible,' said Merton firmly.

'If we go out they will know me, and suspect Julia.'

Miss Crofton looked round the room with eyes of desperate
scrutiny. They at once fell on a large old-fashioned screen,

covered with engravings, which Merton had picked up for the sake of two or three old mezzotints, barbarously pasted on to this article of furniture by some ignorant owner.

'Saved! we are saved! Hist, Julia, hither!' said Miss Crofton in a stage whisper. And while Merton murmured 'Highly unprofessional,' the skirts of the two ladies vanished behind the screen.

Miss Crofton had not played Lady Teazle for nothing.

'Ask the gentlemen to come in,' said Merton, when the boy returned.

They entered: three fair young curates, nervous and inclined to giggle. Shades of difference of ecclesiastical opinion declared themselves in their hats, costume, and jewellery.

'Be seated, gentlemen,' said Merton, and they sat down on three chairs, in identical attitudes.

'We hope,' said the man on the left, 'that we are not here inconveniently. We would have waited, but, you see, we have all come up for the match.'

'How is it going?' asked Merton anxiously.

'Cambridge four wickets down for 115, but—' and the young man stared, 'it must be, it is Pussy Merton!'

'And you, Clancy Minor, why are you not converting the Heathen Chinee? You deserve a death of torture.'

'Goodness! How do you know that?' asked Clancy.

'I know many things,' answered Merton. 'I am not sure which

of you is Mr. Bathe.'

Clancy presented Mr. Bathe, a florid young evangelist, who blushed.

'Armenia is still suffering, Mr. Bathe; and Mr. Brooke,' said Merton, detecting him by the Method of Residues, 'the oven is still hot in the New Hebrides. What have you got to say for yourselves?'

The curates shifted nervously on their chairs.

'We see, Merton,' said Clancy, 'that you know a good deal which we did not know ourselves till lately. In fact, we did not know each other till the Church Congress at Leamington. Then the other men came to tea at my rooms, and saw—'

'A portrait of a lady; each of you possessed a similar portrait,' said Merton.

'How the dev—I mean, how do you know *that*?'

'By a simple deductive process,' said Merton. 'There were also letters,' he said. Here a gurgle from behind the screen was audible to Merton.

'We did not read each others' letters,' said Clancy, blushing.

'Of course not,' said Merton.

'But the handwriting on the envelopes was identical,' Clancy went on.

'Well, and what can our Society do for you?'

'Why, we saw your advertisements, never guessed they were

yours, of course, Pussy, and—none of us is a man of the world—'

'I congratulate you,' said Merton.

'So we thought we had better take advice: it seemed rather a lark, too, don't you know? The fact is—you appear to have divined it somehow—we find that we are all engaged to the same lady. We can't fight, and we can't all marry her.'

'In Thibet it might be practicable: martyrdom might also be secured there,' said Merton.

'Martyrdom is not good enough,' said Clancy.

'Not half,' said Bathe.

'A man has his duties in his own country,' said Brooke.

'May I ask whether in fact your sorrows at this discovery have been intense?' asked Merton.

'I was a good deal cut up at first,' said Clancy, 'I being the latest recruit. Bathe had practically given up hope, and had seen some one else.' Mr. Bathe drooped his head, and blushed. 'Brooke laughed. Indeed we *all* laughed, though we felt rather foolish. But what are we to do? Should we write her a Round Robin? Bathe says he ought to be the man, because he was first man in, and I say *I* ought to be the man, because I am not out.'

'I would not build much on *that*,' said Merton, and he was sure that he heard a rustle behind the screen, and a slight struggle. Julia was trying to emerge, restrained by Miss Crofton.

'I knew,' said Clancy, 'that there was *something*—that there were other fellows. But that I learned, more or less, under the seal of confession, so to speak.'

'At a picnic,' said Merton.

At this moment the screen fell with a crash, and Julia emerged, her eyes blazing, while Miss Crofton followed, her hat somewhat crushed by the falling screen. The three young men in Holy Orders, all of them desirable young men, arose to their feet, trembling visibly.

'Apostates!' cried Julia, who had by far the best of the dramatic situation and pressed her advantage. 'Recreants! was it for such as *you* that I pointed to the crown of martyrdom? Was it for *your* shattered ideals that I have wept many a night on Serena's faithful breast?' She pointed to Miss Crofton, who enfolded her in an embrace. 'You!' Julia went on, aiming at them the finger of conviction. 'I am but a woman, weak I may have been, wavering I may have been, but I took you for men! I chose you to dare, perhaps to perish, for a Cause. But now, triflers that you are, boys, mere boys, back with you to your silly games, back to the thoughtless throng. I have done.'

Julia, attended by Miss Crofton, swept from the chamber, under her indignation (which was quite as real as any of her other emotions) the happiest woman in London. She had no more occasion for remorse, no ideals had she sensibly injured. Her entanglements were disentangled. She inhaled the fragrance of orange blossoms from afar, and heard the marriage music in the chapel of the Guards. Meanwhile the three curates and Merton felt as if they had been whipped.

'Trust a woman to have the best of it,' muttered Merton admiringly. 'And now, Clancy, may I offer a hasty luncheon to you and your friends before we go to Lord's? Your business has been rather rapidly despatched.'

The conversation at luncheon turned exclusively on cricket.

VI

A LOVER IN COCKY

It cannot be said that the bearers of the noblest names in the land flocked at first to the offices of Messrs. Gray and Graham. In fact the reverse, in the beginning, was the case. Members even of the more learned professions held aloof: indeed barristers and physicians never became eager clients. On the other hand, Messrs. Gray and Graham received many letters in such handwritings, such grammar, and such orthography, that they burned them without replying. A common sort of case was that of the young farmer whose widowed mother had set her heart on marriage with 'a bonny labouring boy,' a ploughman.

'We can do nothing with these people,' Merton remarked. 'We can't send down a young and elegant friend of ours to distract the affections of an elderly female agriculturist. The bonny labouring boy would punch the fashionable head; or, at all events, would prove much more attractive to the widow than our agent.'

'Then there are the members of the Hebrew community. They hate mixed marriages, and quite right too. I deeply sympathise. But if Leah has let her affections loose on young Timmins, an Anglo-Saxon and a Christian, what can we do?

How stop the mesalliance? We have not, in our little regiment, one fair Hebrew boy to smile away her maiden blame among the Hebrew mothers of Maida Vale, and to cut out Timmins. And of course it is as bad with the men. If young Isaacs wants to marry Miss Julia Timmins, I have no Rebecca to slip at him. The Semitic demand, though large and perhaps lucrative, cannot be met out of a purely Aryan supply.'

Business was pretty slack, and so Merton rather rejoiced over the application of a Mrs. Nicholson, from The Laburnums, Walton-on-Dove, Derbyshire. Mrs. Nicholson's name was not in Burke's 'Landed Gentry,' and The Laburnums could hardly be estimated as one of the stately homes of England. Still, the lady was granted an interview. She was what the Scots call 'a buddy;' that is, she was large, round, attired in black, between two ages, and not easily to be distinguished, by an unobservant eye, from buddies as a class. After greetings, and when enthroned in the client's chair, Mrs. Nicholson stated her case with simplicity and directness.

'It is my ward,' she said, 'Barbara Monypenny. I must tell you that she was left in my charge till she is twenty-six. I and her lawyers make her an allowance out of her property, which she is to get when she marries with my consent, at whatever age.'

'May I ask how old the lady is at present?' said Merton.

'She is twenty-two.'

'Your kindness in taking charge of her is not not wholly uncompensated?'

'No, an allowance is made to me out of the estate.'

'An allowance which ends on her marriage, if she marries with your consent?'

'Yes, it ends then. Her uncle trusted me a deal more than he trusted Barbara. She was strange from a child. Fond of the men,' as if that were an unusual and unbecoming form of philanthropy.

'I see, and she being an heiress, the testator was anxious to protect her youth and innocence?'

Mrs. Nicholson merely sniffed, but the sniff was affirmative, though sarcastic.

'Her property, I suppose, is considerable? I do not ask from impertinent curiosity, nor for exact figures. But, as a question of business, may we call the fortune considerable?'

'Most people do. It runs into six figures.'

Merton, who had no mathematical head, scribbled on a piece of paper. The result of his calculations (which I, not without some fever of the brow, have personally verified) proved that 'six figures' might be anything between 100,000*l*. and 999,000*l*. 19*s*. 11.75*d*.

'Certainly it is very considerable,' Merton said, after a few minutes passed in arithmetical calculation. 'Am I too curious if I ask what is the source of this opulence?'

'"Wilton's Panmedicon, or Heal All," a patent medicine. He sold the patent and retired.'

Merton shuddered.

'It would be Pammedicum if it could be anything,' he

thought, 'but it can't, linguistically speaking.'

'Invaluable as a subterfuge,' said Mrs. Nicholson, obviously with an indistinct recollection of the advertisement and of the properties of the drug.

Merton construed the word as 'febrifuge,' silently, and asked: 'Have you taken the young lady much into society: has she had many opportunities of making a choice? You are dissatisfied with the choice, I understand, which she has made?'

'I don't let her see anybody if I can help it. Fire and powder are better kept apart, and she is powder, a minx! Only a fisher or two comes to the Perch, that's the inn at Walton-on-Dove, and *they* are mostly old gentlemen, pottering with their rods and things. If a young man comes to the inn, I take care to trapes after her through the nasty damp meadows.'

'Is the young lady an angler?'

'She is—most unwomanly I call it.'

Merton's idea of the young lady rose many degrees. 'You said the young lady was "strange from a child, very strange. Fond of the men." Happily for our sex, and for the world, it is not so very strange or unusual to take pity on us.'

'She has always been queer.'

'You do not hint at any cerebral disequilibrium?' asked Merton.

'Would you mind saying that again?' asked Mrs. Nicholson.

'I meant nothing wrong *here*?' Merton said, laying his finger on his brow.

'No, not so bad as that,' said Mrs. Nicholson; 'but just queer. Uncommon. Tells odd stories about—nonsense. She is wearing with her dreams. She reads books on, I don't know how to call it—Tipsy-cake, Tipsicakical Search. Histories, *I* call it.'

'Yes, I understand,' said Merton; 'Psychical Research.'

'That's it, and Hyptonism,' said Mrs. Nicholson, as many ladies do.

'Ah, Hyptonism, so called from its founder, Hypton, the eminent Anglo- French chemist; he was burned at Rome, one of the latest victims of the Inquisition,' said Merton.

'I don't hold with Popery, sir, but it served *him* right.'

'That is all the queerness then!'

'That and general discontentedness.'

'Girls will be girls,' said Merton; 'she wants society.'

'Want must be her master then,' said Mrs. Nicholson stolidly.

'But about the man of her choice, have you anything against him?'

'No, but nothing *for* him: I never even saw him.'

'Then where did Miss Monypenny make his acquaintance?'

'Well, like a fool, I let her go to pass Christmas with some distant cousins of my own, who should have known better.

They stupidly took her to a dance, at Tutbury, and there she met him: just that once.'

'And they became engaged on so short an acquaintance?'

'Not exactly that. She was not engaged when she came home, and did not seem to mean to be. She did talk of him a lot. He had got round her finely: told her that he was going out to the war, and that they were sister spirits. He had dreamed of meeting her, he said, and that was why he came to the ball, for he did not dance. He said he believed they had met in a state of pre—something; meaning, if you understand me, before they were born, which could not be the case: she not being a twin, still less *his* twin.'

'That would be the only way of accounting for it, certainly,' said Merton. 'But what followed? Did they correspond?'

'He wrote to her, but she showed me the letter, and put it in the fire unopened. He had written his name, Marmaduke Ingles, on a corner of the envelope.'

'So far her conduct seems correct, even austere,' said Merton.

'It was at first, but then he wrote from South Africa, where he volunteered as a doctor. He was a doctor at Tutbury.'

'She opened that letter?'

'Yes, and showed it to me. He kept on with his nonsense, asking her never to forget him, and sending his photograph in cocky.'

'Pardon!' said Merton.

'In uniform. And if he fell, she would see his ghost, in cocky, crossing her room, he said. In fact he knew how to get round the foolish girl. I believe he went out there just to make himself interesting.'

'Did you try to find out what sort of character he had at home?'

'Yes, there was no harm in it, only he had no business to speak of, everybody goes to Dr. Younghusband.'

'Then, really, if he is an honest young man, as he seems to be a patriotic fellow, are you certain that you are wise in objecting?'

'I *do* object,' said Mrs. Nicholson, and indeed her motives for refusing her consent were only too obvious.

'Are they quite definitely engaged?' asked Merton.

'Yes they are now, by letter, and she says she will wait for him till I die, or she is twenty-six, if I don't give my consent. He writes every mail, from places with outlandish names, in Africa. And she keeps looking in a glass ball, like the labourers' women, some of them; she's sunk as low as *that*; so superstitious; and sometimes she tells me that she sees what he is doing, and where he is; and now and then, when his letters come, she shows me bits of them, to prove she was right. But just as often she's wrong; only she won't listen to *me*. She says it's Telly, Tellyopathy. I say it's flat nonsense.'

'I quite agree with you,' said Merton, with conviction. 'After all, though, honest, as far as you hear. . . .'

'Oh yes, honest enough, but that's all,' interrupted Mrs. Nicholson, with a hearty sneer.

'Though he bears a good character, from what you tell me he seems to be a very silly young man.'

'Silly Johnny to silly Jenny,' put in Mrs. Nicholson.

'A pair with ideas so absurd could not possibly be happy.' Merton reasoned. 'Why don't you take her into the world, and show her life? With her fortune and with *you* to take her about, she would soon forget this egregiously foolish romance.'

'And me to have her snapped up by some whipper-snapper that calls himself a lord? Not me, Mr. Graham,' said Mrs. Nicholson. 'The money that her uncle made by the Panmedicon is not going to be spent on horses, and worse, if I can help it.'

'Then,' said Merton, 'all I can do for you is by our ordinary method—to throw some young man of worth and education in the way of your ward, and attempt to—divert her affections.'

'And have *him* carry her off under my very nose? Not much, Mr. Graham. Why where do *I* come in, in this pretty plan?'

'Do not suppose me to suggest anything so—detrimental to your interests, Mrs. Nicholson. Is your ward beautiful?'

'A toad!' said Mrs. Nicholson with emphasis.

'Very well. There is no danger. The gentleman of whom I speak is betrothed to one of the most beautiful girls in England. They are deeply attached, and their marriage is only deferred for prudential reasons.'

'I don't trust one of them,' said Mrs. Nicholson.

'Very well, madam,' answered Merton severely; 'I have done all that experience can suggest. The gentleman of whom I speak has paid especial attention to the mental delusions under which your ward is labouring, and has been successful in removing them in some cases. But as you reject my suggestion'—he rose, so did Mrs. Nicholson—'I have the honour of wishing you a pleasant journey back to Derbyshire.'

'A bullet may hit him,' said Mrs. Nicholson with much acerbity. 'That's my best hope.'

Then Merton bowed her out.

'The old woman will never let the girl marry anybody, except some adventurer, who squares her by giving her the full value of her allowance out of the estate,' thought Merton, adding 'I wonder how much it is! Six figures is anything between a hundred thousand and a million!'

The man he had thought of sending down to divert Miss Monypenny's affections from the young doctor was Jephson, the History coach, at that hour waiting for a professorship to enable him to marry Miss Willoughby.

However, he dismissed Mrs. Nicholson and her ward from his mind. About a fortnight later Merton received a letter directed in an uneducated hand. 'Another of the agricultural classes,' he thought, but, looking at the close of the epistle, he saw the name of Eliza Nicholson. She wrote:

'Sir,—Barbara has been at her glass ball, and seen him being carried on board a ship. If she is right, and she is not always wrong, he is on his way home. Though I will never give my consent, this spells botheration for me. You can send down your young man that cures by teleopathy, a thing that has come up since my time. He can stay at the Perch, and take a fishing rod, then they are safe to meet. I trust him no more than the rest, but she may fall between two stools, if the doctor does come home.

'Your obedient servant,

'Eliza Nicholson.'

'Merely to keep one's hand in,' thought Merton, 'in the present disappointing slackness of business, I'll try to see Jephson. I don't like or trust him. I don't think he is the man for Miss Willoughby. So, if he ousts the doctor, and catches the heiress, why "there was more lost at Shirramuir," as Logan says.'

Merton managed to go up to Oxford, and called on Jephson. He found him anxious about a good, quiet, cheap place for study.

'Do you fish?' asked Merton.

'When I get the chance,' said Jephson.

He was a dark, rather clumsy, but not unprepossessing young don, with a very slight squint.

'If you fish did you ever try the Perch—I mean an inn, not the fish of the same name—at Walton-on-Dove? A pretty quiet place, two miles of water, local history perhaps interesting. It is not very far from Tutbury, where Queen Mary was kept, I think.'

'It sounds well,' said Jephson; 'I'll write to the landlord and ask about terms.'

'You could not do better,' said Merton, and he took his leave.

'Now, am I,' thought Merton as he walked down the Broad, 'to put Jephson up to it? If I don't, of course I can't "reap the benefit of one single pin" for the Society: Jephson not being a member. But the money, anyhow, would come from that old harpy out of the girl's estate. *Olet!* I don't like the fragrance of that kind of cash. But if the girl really is plain, "a toad," nothing may happen. On the other hand, Jephson is sure to hear about her position from local gossip—that she is rich, and so on. Perhaps she is not so very plain. They are sure to meet, or Mrs. Nicholson will bring them together in her tactful way. She has not much time to lose if the girl's glass ball yarn is true, and it *may* be true by a fluke. Jephson is rather bitten by a taste for all that "teleopathy" business, as the old Malaprop calls it. On the whole, I shall say no more to him, but let him play the game, if he goes to Walton, off his own bat.'

Presently Merton received a note from Jephson dated 'The Perch, Walton-on- Dove.' Jephson expressed his gratitude; the place suited his purpose very well. He had taken a brace and a half of trout, 'bordering on two pounds' ('one and a quarter,' thought Merton). 'And, what won't interest *you*,' his letter said, 'I have run across a curiously interesting subject, what *you* would call *hysterical*. But what, after all, is hysteria?' &c., &c.

'*L'affaire est dans le sac*!' said Merton to himself. 'Jephson and Miss Monypenny have met!'

Weeks passed, and one day, on arriving at the office, Merton found Miss Willoughby there awaiting his arrival. She was the handsome Miss Willoughby, Jephson's betrothed, a learned young lady who lived but poorly by verifying references and making researches at the Record Office.

Merton at once had a surmise, nor was it mistaken. The usual greetings had scarcely passed, when the girl, with cheeks on fire and eyes aflame, said:

'Mr. Merton, do you remember a question, rather unconventional, which you put to me at the dinner party you and Mr. Logan gave at the restaurant?'

'I ought not to have said it,' said Merton, 'but then it was an unconventional gathering. I asked if you—'

'Your words were "Had I a spark of the devil in me?" Well, I have! Can I—'

'Turn it to any purpose? You can, Miss Willoughby, and I shall have the honour to lay the method before you, of course only for your consideration, and under seal of secrecy. Indeed I was just about to write to you asking for an interview.'

Merton then laid the circumstances in which he wanted Miss Willoughby's aid before her, but these must be reserved for the present. She listened, was surprised, was clearly ready for more desperate adventures; she came into his views, and departed.

'Jephson *has* played the game off his own bat—and won it,' thought Merton to himself. 'What a very abject the fellow is! But, after all, I have disentangled Miss Willoughby; she was infinitely too good for the man, with his squint.'

As Merton indulged in these rather Pharisaical reflections, Mrs. Nicholson was announced. Merton greeted her, and gave orders that no other client was to be admitted. He was himself rather nervous. Was Mrs. Nicholson in a rage? No, her eyes beamed friendly; geniality clothed her brow.

'He has squared her,' thought Merton.

Indeed, the lady had warmly grasped his hand with both of her own, which were imprisoned in tight new gloves, while her bonnet spoke of regardlessness of expense and recent prodigality. She fell back into the client's chair.

'Oh, sir,' she said, 'when first we met we did not part, or *I* did not—*you* were quite the gentleman—on the best of terms. But now, how can I speak of your wise advice, and how much don't I owe you?'

Merton answered very gravely: 'You do not owe me anything, Madam. Please understand that I took absolutely no professional steps in your affair.'

'What?' cried Mrs. Nicholson. 'You did not send down that blessed young man to the Perch?'

'I merely suggested that the inn might suit a person whom I knew, who was looking for country quarters. Your name never crossed my lips, nor a word about the business on which you did me the honour to consult me.'

'Then I owe you nothing?'

'Nothing at all.'

'Well, I do call this providential,' said Mrs. Nicholson, with devout enthusiasm.

'You are not in my debt to the extent of a farthing, but if you think I have accidentally been—'

'An instrument?' said Mrs. Nicholson.

'Well, an unconscious instrument, perhaps you can at least tell me why you think so. What has happened?'

'You really don't know?'

'I only know that you are pleased, and that your anxieties seem to be relieved.'

'Why, he saved her from being burned, and the brave,' said Mrs. Nicholson, 'deserve the fair, not that *she* is a beauty.'

'Do tell me all that happened.'

'And tell you I can, for that precious young man took me into his confidence. First, when I heard that he had come to the Perch, I trampled about the damp riverside with Barbara, and sure enough they met, he being on the Perch's side of the fence, and Barbara's line being caught high up in a tree on ours, as often happens. Well, I asked him to come over the fence and help her to get her line clear, which he did very civilly, and then he showed her how to fish, and then I asked him to tea and left them alone a bit, and when I came back they were talking about teleopathy, and her glass ball, and all that nonsense. And he seemed interested, but not to believe in it quite. I could not understand half their tipsycakical lingo. So of course they often met again at the river, and he often came to tea, and she seemed to take to him—she was always one for the men. And at last a very queer thing happened, and gave him his chance.

'It was a very hot day in July, and she fell asleep on a seat under a tree with her glass ball in her lap; she had been staring at it, I suppose. Any way she slept on, till the sun went round and shone full on the ball; and just as he, Mr. Jephson, that is, came into the gate, the glass ball began to act like a burning glass and her skirt began to smoke. Well, he waited a bit, I think, till the skirt blazed a little, and then he rushed up and threw his coat over her skirt, and put the fire out. And so he saved her from being a Molochaust, like you read about in the bible.'

Merton mentally disengaged the word 'Molochaust' into 'Moloch' and 'holocaust.'

'And there she was, when I happened to come by, a-crying and carrying on, with her head on his shoulder.'

'A pleasing group, and so they were engaged on the spot?' asked Merton.

'Not she! She held off, and thanked her preserver; but she would be true, she said, to her lover in cocky. But before that Mr. Jephson had taken me into his confidence.'

'And you made no objection to his winning your ward, if he could?'

'No, sir, I could trust that young man: I could trust him with Barbara.'

'His arguments,' said Merton, 'must have been very cogent?'

'He understood my situation if she married, and what I deserved,' said Mrs. Nicholson, growing rather uncomfortable, and fidgeting in the client's chair.

Merton, too, understood, and knew what the sympathetic arguments of Jephson must have been.

'And, after all,' Merton asked, 'the lover has prospered in his suit?'

'This is how he got round her. He said to me that night, in private: "Mrs. Nicholson," said he, "your niece is a very interesting historical subject. I am deeply anxious, apart from my own passion for her, to relieve her from a singular but not very uncommon delusion."

'"Meaning her lover in cocky," I said.

'"There is no lover in cocky," says he.

'"No Dr. Ingles!" said I.

'"Yes, there *is* a Dr. Ingles, but he is not her lover, and your niece never met him. I bicycled to Tutbury lately, and, after examining the scene of Queen Mary's captivity, I made a few inquiries. What I had always suspected proved to be true. Dr. Ingles was not present at that ball at the Bear at Tutbury."

'Well,' Mrs. Nicholson went on, 'you might have knocked me down with a feather! I had never asked my second cousins the question, not wanting them to guess about my affairs. But down I sat, and wrote to Maria, and got her answer. Barbara never saw Dr. Ingles! only heard the girls mention him, and his going to the war. And then, after that, by Mr. Jephson's advice, I went and gave Barbara my mind. She should marry Mr. Jephson, who saved her life, or be the laughing stock of the country. I showed her up to herself, with her glass ball, and her teleopathy, and her sham love-letters, that she wrote herself, and all her humbug. She cried, and she fainted, and she carried on, but I went at her whenever she could listen to reason. So she said "Yes," and I am the happy woman.'

'And Mr. Jephson is to be congratulated on so sensible and veracious a bride,' said Merton.

'Oh, he says it is by no means an uncommon case, and that he has effected a complete cure, and they will be as happy as idiots,' said Mrs. Nicholson, as she rose to depart.

She left Merton pensive, and not disposed to overrate human nature. 'But there can't be many fellows like Jephson,' he said. 'I wonder how much the six figures run to?' But that question was never answered to his satisfaction.

VII

THE ADVENTURE OF THE EXEMPLARY EARL

I

The Earl's Long-Lost Cousin

'A jilt in time saves nine,' says the proverbial wisdom of our forefathers, adding, 'One jilt makes many.' In the last chapter of the book of this chronicle, we told how the mercenary Mr. Jephson proved false to the beautiful Miss Willoughby, who supported existence by her skill in deciphering and transcribing the manuscript records of the past. We described the consequent visit of Miss Willoughby to the office of the Disentanglers, and how she reminded Merton that he had asked her once 'if she had a spark of the devil in her.' She had that morning received, in fact, a letter, crawling but explicit, from the unworthy Jephson, her lover. Retired, he said, to the rural loneliness of Derbyshire, he had read in his own heart, and what he there deciphered convinced him that, as a man of honour, he had but one course before him: he must free Miss Willoughby from her engagement. The lady was one of those who suffer in silence. She made no moan, and no reply to Jephson's letter; but she did visit Merton, and, practically, gave him to understand that she was ready to start as a Corsair on the seas of amorous adventure. She had nailed the black flag to the mast: unhappy herself, she was apt to have no mercy on the sentiments and affections of others.

Merton, as it chanced, had occasion for the services of a lady in this mood; a lady at once attractive, and steely-hearted; resolute to revenge, on the whole of the opposite sex, the baseness of a Fellow of his College. Such is the frenzy of an injured love—illogical indeed (for we are not responsible for the errors of isolated members of our sex), but primitive, natural to women, and even to some men, in Miss Willoughby's position.

The occasion for such services as she would perform was provided by a noble client who, on visiting the office, had found Merton out and Logan in attendance. The visitor was the Earl of Embleton, of the North. Entering the rooms, he fumbled with the string of his eyeglass, and, after capturing it, looked at Logan with an air of some bewilderment. He was a tall, erect, slim, and well-preserved patrician, with a manner really shy, though hasty critics interpreted it as arrogant. He was 'between two ages,' a very susceptible period in the history of the individual.

'I think we have met before,' said the Earl to Logan. 'Your face is not unfamiliar to me.'

'Yes,' said Logan, 'I have seen you at several places;' and he mumbled a number of names.

'Ah, I remember now—at Lady Lochmaben's,' said Lord Embleton. 'You are, I think, a relation of hers. . . .'

'A distant relation: my name is Logan.'

'What, of the Restalrig family?' said the Earl, with excitement.

'A far-off kinsman of the Marquis,' said Logan, adding, 'May I ask you to be seated?'

'This is really very interesting to me—surprisingly interesting,' said the Earl. 'What a strange coincidence! How small the world is, how brief are the ages! Our ancestors, Mr. Logan, were very intimate long ago.'

'Indeed?' said Logan.

'Yes. I would not speak of it to everybody; in fact, I have spoken of it to no one; but recently, examining some documents in my muniment-room, I made a discovery as interesting to me as it must be to you. Our ancestors three hundred years ago—in 1600, to be exact—were fellow conspirators.'

'Ah, the old Gowrie game, to capture the King?' asked Logan, who had once kidnapped a cat.

His knowledge of history was mainly confined to that obscure and unexplained affair, in which his wicked old ancestor is thought to have had a hand.

'That is it,' said the visitor—'the Gowrie mystery! You may remember that an unknown person, a friend of your ancestor, was engaged?'

'Yes,' said Logan; 'he was never identified. Was his name Harris?'

The peer half rose to his feet, flushed a fine purple, twiddled the obsolete little grey tuft on his chin, and sat down again.

'I think I said, Mr. Logan, that the hitherto unidentified associate of your ancestor was *a member of my own family.*

Our name is *not* Harris—a name very honourably borne—
our family name is Guevara. My ancestor was a cousin of the
brave Lord Willoughby.'

'Most interesting! You must pardon me, but as nobody ever
knew what you have just found out, you will excuse my
ignorance,' said Logan, who, to be sure, had never heard of
the brave Lord Willoughby.

'It is I who ought to apologise,' said the visitor. 'Your
mention of the name of Harris appeared to me to indicate a
frivolity as to matters of the past which, I must confess, is
apt to make me occasionally forget myself. *Noblesse oblige*,
you know: we respect ourselves—in our progenitors.'

'Unless he wants to prevent someone from marrying his
great-grandmother, I wonder what he is doing with his Tales
of a Grandfather *here*,' thought Logan, but he only smiled,
and said, 'Assuredly—my own opinion. I wish I could
respect *my* ancestor!'

'The gentleman of whom I speak, the associate of your own
distant progenitor, was the founder of our house, as far as
mere titles are concerned. We were but squires of
Northumbria, of ancient Celtic descent, before the time of
Queen Elizabeth. My ancestor at that time—'

'Oh bother his pedigree!' thought Logan.

'—was a young officer in the English garrison of Berwick, and
he, I find, was *your* ancestor's unknown correspondent. I am
not skilled in reading old hands, and I am anxious to secure a
trustworthy person—really trustworthy—to transcribe the
manuscripts which contain these exciting details.'

Logan thought that the office of the Disentanglers was hardly the place to come to in search of an historical copyist. However, he remembered Miss Willoughby, and said that he knew a lady of great skill and industry, of good family too, upon whom his client might entirely depend. 'She is a Miss Willoughby,' he added.

'Not one of the Willoughbys of the Wicket, a most worthy, though unfortunate house, nearly allied, as I told you, to my own, about three hundred years ago?' said the Earl.

'Yes, she is a daughter of the last squire.'

'Ruined in the modern race for wealth, like so many!' exclaimed the peer, and he sat in silence, deeply moved; his lips formed a name familiar to Law Courts.

'Excuse my emotion, Mr. Logan,' he went on. 'I shall be happy to see and arrange with this lady, who, I trust will, as my cousin, accept my hospitality at Rookchester. I shall be deeply interested, as you, no doubt, will also be, in the result of her researches into an affair which so closely concerns both you and me.'

He was silent again, musing deeply, while Logan marvelled more and more what his real original business might be. All this affair of the documents and the muniment-room had arisen by the merest accident, and would not have arisen if the Earl had found Merton at home. The Earl obviously had a difficulty in coming to the point: many clients had. To approach a total stranger on the most intimate domestic affairs (even if his ancestor and yours were in a big thing together three hundred years ago) is, to a sensitive patrician, no easy task. In fact, even members of the middle class were, as clients, occasionally affected by shyness.

'Mr. Logan,' said the Earl, 'I am not a man of to-day. The

Andrew Lang

cupidity of our age, the eagerness with which wealthy aliens are welcomed into our best houses and families, is to me, I may say, distasteful. Better that our coronets were dimmed than that they should be gilded with the gold eagles of Chicago or blazing with the diamonds of Kimberley. My feelings on this point are unusually—I do not think that they are unduly—acute.'

Logan murmured assent.

'I am poor,' said the Earl, with all the expansiveness of the shy; 'but I never held what is called a share in my life.'

'It is long,' said Logan, with perfect truth, 'since anything of that sort was in my own possession. In that respect my 'scutcheon, so to speak, is without a stain.'

'How fortunate I am to have fallen in with one of sentiments akin to my own, unusual as they are!' said the Earl. 'I am a widower,' he went on, 'and have but one son and one daughter.'

'He is coming to business *now*,' thought Logan.

'The former, I fear, is as good almost as affianced—is certainly in peril of betrothal—to a lady against whom I have not a word to say, except that she is inordinately wealthy, the sole heiress of—' Here the Earl gasped, and was visibly affected. 'You may have heard, sir,' the patrician went on, 'of a commercial transaction of nature unfathomable to myself—I have not sought for information,' he waved his hand impatiently, 'a transaction called a Straddle?'

Logan murmured that he was aware of the existence of the phrase, though unconscious of its precise meaning.

'The lady's wealth is based on a successful Straddle, operated by her only known male ancestor, in—Bristles—Hogs' Bristles and Lard,' said the Earl.

'Miss Bangs!' exclaimed Logan, knowing the name, wealth, and the source of the wealth of the ruling Chicago heiress of the day.

'I am to be understood to speak of Miss Bangs—as her name has been pronounced between us—with all the respect due to youth, beauty, and an amiable disposition,' said the peer; 'but Bristles, Mr. Logan, Hogs' Bristles and Lard. And a Straddle!'

'Lucky devil, Scremerston,' thought Logan, for Scremerston was the only son of Lord Embleton, and he, as it seemed, had secured that coveted prize of the youth of England, the heart of the opulent Miss Bangs. But Logan only sighed and stared at the wall as one who hears of an irremediable disaster.

'If they really were betrothed,' said Lord Embleton, 'I would have nothing to say or do in the way of terminating the connection, however unwelcome. A man's word is his word. It is in these circumstances of doubt (when the fortunes of a house ancient, though titularly of mere Tudor *noblesse*, hang in the balance) that, despairing of other help, I have come to you.'

'But,' asked Logan, 'have things gone so very far? Is the disaster irremediable? I am acquainted with your son, Lord Scremerston; in fact, he was my fag at school. May I speak quite freely?'

'Certainly; you will oblige me.'

'Well, by the candour of early friendship, Scremerston was

Andrew Lang

called the Arcadian, an allusion to a certain tenderness of heart allied with—h'm—a rather confident and sanguine disposition. I think it may console you to reflect that perhaps he rather overestimates his success with the admirable young lady of whom we spoke. You are not certain that she has accepted him?'

'No,' said the Earl, obviously relieved. 'I am sure that he has not positively proposed to her. He knows my opinion: he is a dutiful son, but he did seem very confident—seemed to think that his honour was engaged.'

'I think we may discount that a little,' said Logan, 'and hope for the best.'

'I shall try to take that view,' said the Earl. 'You console me infinitely, Mr. Logan.'

Logan was about to speak again, when his client held up a gently deprecating hand.

'That is not all, Mr. Logan. I have a daughter—'

Logan chanced to be slightly acquainted with the daughter, Lady Alice Guevara, a very nice girl.

'Is she attached to a South African Jew?' Logan thought.

'In this case,' said the client, 'there is no want of blood; Royal in origin, if it comes to that. To the House of Bourbon I have no objection, in itself, that would be idle affectation.'

Logan gasped.

Was this extraordinary man anxious to reject a lady 'multimillionaire' for his son, and a crown of some sort or other for his daughter?

'But the stain of ill-gotten gold—silver too—is ineffaceable.'

'It really cannot be Bristles this time,' thought Logan.

'And a dynasty based on the roulette-table, . . . '

'Oh, the Prince of Scalastro!' cried Logan.

'I see that you know the worst,' said the Earl.

Logan knew the worst fairly well. The Prince of Scalastro owned a percentage of two or three thousand which Logan had dropped at the tables licensed in his principality.

'To the Prince, personally, I bear no ill-will,' said the Earl. 'He is young, brave, scientific, accomplished, and this unfortunate attachment began before he inherited his—h'm— dominions. I fear it is, on both sides, a deep and passionate sentiment. And now, Mr. Logan, you know the full extent of my misfortunes: what course does your experience recommend? I am not a harsh father. Could I disinherit Scremerston, which I cannot, the loss would not be felt by him in the circumstances. As to my daughter—'

The peer rose and walked to the window. When he came back and resumed his seat, Logan turned on him a countenance of mournful sympathy. The Earl silently extended his hand, which Logan took. On few occasions had a strain more severe been placed on his gravity, but, unlike a celebrated diplomatist, he 'could command his smile.'

'Your case,' he said, 'is one of the most singular, delicate, and distressing which I have met in the course of my experience. There is no objection to character, and poverty is not the impediment: the reverse. You will permit me, no doubt, to consult my partner, Mr. Merton; we have naturally no secrets between us, and he possesses a delicacy of touch and a power of insight which I can only regard with admiring envy. It was he who carried to a successful issue that difficult case in the family of the Sultan of Mingrelia (you will observe that I use a fictitious name). I can assure you, Lord Embleton, that polygamy presents problems almost insoluble; problems of extreme delicacy—or indelicacy.'

'I had not heard of that affair,' said the Earl. 'Like Eumaeus in Homer and in Mr. Stephen Phillips, I dwell among the swine, and come rarely to the city.'

'The matter never went beyond the inmost diplomatic circles,' said Logan. 'The Sultan's favourite son, the Jam, or Crown Prince, of Mingrelia (*Jamreal*, they called him), loved four beautiful Bollachians, sisters—again I disguise the nationality.'

'Sisters!' exclaimed the peer; 'I have always given my vote against the Deceased Wife's Sister Bill; but *four*, and all alive!'

'The law of the Prophet, as you are aware, is not mono-gamous,' said Logan; 'and the Eastern races are not averse to connections which are reprobated by our Western ideas. The real difficulty was that of religion.

'Oh, why from the heretic girl of my soul
Should I fly, to seek elsewhere an orthodox kiss?'

hummed Logan, rather to the surprise of Lord Embleton. He went on: 'It is not so much that the Mingrelians object to mixed marriages in the matter of religion, but the Bollachians, being Christians, do object, and have a horror of polygamy. It was a cruel affair. All four girls, and the Jamreal himself, were passionately attached to each other. It was known, too, that, for political reasons, the maidens had received a dispensation from the leading Archimandrite, their metropolitan, to marry the proud Paynim. The Mingrelian Sultan is suzerain of Bollachia; his native subjects are addicted to massacring the Bollachians from religious motives, and the Bollachian Church (Nestorians, as you know) hoped that the four brides would convert the Jamreal to their creed, and so solve the Bollachian question. The end, they said, justified the means.'

'Jesuitical,' said the Earl, shaking his head sadly.

'That is what my friend and partner, Mr. Merton, thought,' said Logan, 'when we were applied to by the Sultan. Merton displayed extraordinary tact and address. All was happily settled, the Sultan and the Jamreal were reconciled, the young ladies met other admirers, and learned that what they had taken for love was but a momentary infatuation.'

The Earl sighed, '*Renovare dolorem*! My family,' said he, 'is, and has long been—ever since the Gunpowder Plot—firmly, if not passionately, attached to the Church of England. The Prince of Scalastro is a Catholic.'

'Had we a closer acquaintance with the parties concerned!' murmured Logan.

'You must come and visit us at Rookchester,' said the Earl. 'In any case I am most anxious to know better one whose ancestor was so closely connected with my own. We shall examine my documents under the tuition of the lady you mentioned, Miss Willoughby, if she will accept the hospitality of a kinsman.'

Andrew Lang

Logan murmured acquiescence, and again asked permission to consult Merton, which was granted. The Earl then shook hands and departed, obviously somewhat easier in his mind.

This remarkable conversation was duly reported by Logan to Merton.

'What are we to do next?' asked Logan.

'Why you can do nothing but reconnoitre. Go down to Rookchester. It is in Northumberland, on the Coquet—a pretty place, but there is no fishing just now. Then we must ask Lord Embleton to meet Miss Willoughby. The interview can be here: Miss Willoughby will arrive, chaperoned by Miss Blossom, after the Earl makes his appearance.'

'That will do, as far as his bothering old manuscripts are concerned; but how about the real business—the two undesirable marriages?'

'We must first see how the land lies. I do not know any of the lovers. What sort of fellow is Scremerston?'

'Nothing remarkable about him—good, plucky, vain little fellow. I suppose he wants money, like the rest of the world: but his father won't let him be a director of anything, though he is in the House and his name would look well on a list.'

'So he wants to marry dollars?'

'I suppose he has no objection to them; but have you seen Miss Bangs?'

'I don't remember her,' said Merton.

'Then you have not seen her. She is beautiful, by Jove; and, I fancy, clever and nice, and gives herself no airs.'

'And she has all that money, and yet the old gentleman objects!'

'He can not stand the bristles and lard,' said Logan.

'Then the Prince of Scalastro—him I have come across. You would never take him for a foreigner,' said Merton, bestowing on the Royal youth the highest compliment which an Englishman can pay, but adding, 'only he is too intelligent and knows too much.'

'No; there is nothing the matter with *him*,' Logan admitted—'nothing but happening to inherit a gambling establishment and the garden it stands in. He is a scientific character—a scientific soldier. I wish we had a few like him.'

'Well, it is a hard case,' said Merton. 'They all seem to be very good sort of people. And Lady Alice Guevara? I hardly know her at all; but she is pretty enough—tall, yellow hair, brown eyes.'

'And as good a girl as lives,' added Logan. 'Very religious, too.'

'She won't change her creed?' asked Merton.

'She would go to the stake for it,' said Logan. 'She is more likely to convert the Prince.'

'That would be one difficulty out of the way,' said Merton. 'But the gambling establishment? There is the rub! And the usual plan won't work. You are a captivating person, Logan, but I do not think that you could attract Lady Alice's affections and disentangle her in that way. Besides, the

Prince would have you out. Then Miss Bangs' dollars, not to mention herself, must have too strong a hold on Scremerston. It really looks too hard a case for us on paper. You must go down and reconnoitre.'

Logan agreed, and wrote asking Lord Embleton to come to the office, where he could see Miss Willoughby and arrange about her visit to him and his manuscripts. The young lady was invited to arrive rather later, bringing Miss Blossom as her companion.

On the appointed day Logan and Merton awaited Lord Embleton. He entered with an air unwontedly buoyant, and was introduced to Merton. The first result was an access of shyness. The Earl hummed, began sentences, dropped them, and looked pathetically at Logan. Merton understood. The Earl had taken to Logan (on account of their hereditary partnership in an ancient iniquity), and it was obvious that he would say to him what he would not say to his partner. Merton therefore withdrew to the outer room (they had met in the inner), and the Earl delivered himself to Logan in a little speech.

'Since we met, Mr. Logan,' said he, 'a very fortunate event has occurred. The Prince of Scalastro, in a private interview, has done me the honour to take me into his confidence. He asked my permission to pay his addresses to my daughter, and informed me that, finding his ownership of the gambling establishment distasteful to her, he had determined not to renew the lease to the company. He added that since his boyhood, having been educated in Germany, he had entertained scruples about the position which he would one day occupy, that he had never entered the rooms (that haunt of vice), and that his acquaintance with my daughter had greatly increased his objections to gambling, though his scruples were not approved of by his confessor, a very learned priest.'

'That is curious,' said Logan.

'Very,' said the Earl. 'But as I expect the Prince and his confessor at Rookchester, where I hope you will join us, we may perhaps find out the reasons which actuate that no doubt respectable person. In the meantime, as I would constrain nobody in matters of religion, I informed the Prince that he had my permission to—well, to plead his cause for himself with Lady Alice.'

Logan warmly congratulated the Earl on the gratifying resolve of the Prince, and privately wondered how the young people would support life, when deprived of the profits from the tables.

It was manifest, however, from the buoyant air of the Earl, that this important question had never crossed his mind. He looked quite young in the gladness of his heart, 'he smelled April and May,' he was clad becomingly in summer raiment, and to Logan it was quite a pleasure to see such a happy man. Some fifteen years seemed to have been taken from the age of this buxom and simple-hearted patrician.

He began to discuss with Logan all conceivable reasons why the Prince's director had rather discouraged his idea of closing the gambling-rooms for ever.

'The Father, Father Riccoboni, is a Jesuit, Mr. Logan,' said the Earl gravely. 'I would not be uncharitable, I hope I am not prejudiced, but members of that community, I fear, often prefer what they think the interests of their Church to those of our common Christianity. A portion of the great wealth of the Scalastros was annually devoted to masses for the souls of the players—about fifteen per cent. I believe—who yearly shoot themselves in the gardens of the establishment.'

'No more suicides, no more subscriptions, I suppose,' said Logan; 'but the practice proved that the reigning Princes of Scalastro had feeling hearts.'

While the Earl developed this theme, Miss Willoughby, accompanied by Miss Blossom, had joined Merton in the outer room. Miss Blossom, being clad in white, with her blue eyes and apple-blossom complexion, looked like the month of May. But Merton could not but be struck by Miss Willoughby. She was tall and dark, with large grey eyes, a Greek profile, and a brow which could, on occasion, be thunderous and lowering, so that Miss Willoughby seemed to all a remarkably fine young woman; while the educated spectator was involuntarily reminded of the beautiful sister of the beautiful Helen, the celebrated Clytemnestra. The young lady was clad in very dark blue, with orange points, so to speak, and compared with her transcendent beauty, Miss Blossom, as Logan afterwards remarked, seemed a

'Wee modest crimson-tippit beastie,'

he intending to quote the poet Burns.

After salutations, Merton remarked to Miss Blossom that her well-known discretion might prompt her to take a seat near the window while he discussed private business with Miss Willoughby. The good-humoured girl retired to contemplate life from the casement, while Merton rapidly laid the nature of Lord Embleton's affairs before the other lady.

'You go down to Rookchester as a kinswoman and a guest, you understand, and to do the business of the manuscripts.'

'Oh, I shall rather like that than otherwise,' said Miss

Willoughby, smiling.

'Then, as to the regular business of the Society, there is a Prince who seems to be thought unworthy of the daughter of the house; and the son of the house needs disentangling from an American heiress of great charm and wealth.'

'The tasks might satisfy any ambition,' said Miss Willoughby. 'Is the idea that the Prince and the Viscount should *both* neglect their former flames?'

'And burn incense at the altar of Venus Verticordia,' said Merton, with a bow.

'It is a large order,' replied Miss Willoughby, in the simple phrase of a commercial age: but as Merton looked at her, and remembered the vindictive feeling with which she now regarded his sex, he thought that she, if anyone, was capable of executing the commission. He was not, of course, as yet aware of the moral resolution lately arrived at by the young potentate of Scalastro.

'The manuscripts are the first thing, of course,' he said, and, as he spoke, Logan and Lord Embleton re-entered the room.

Merton presented the Earl to the ladies, and Miss Blossom soon retired to her own apartment, and wrestled with the correspondence of the Society and with her typewriting-machine.

The Earl proved not to be nearly so shy where ladies were concerned. He had not expected to find in his remote and long-lost cousin, Miss Willoughby, a magnificent being like Persephone on a coin of Syracuse, but it was plain that he was prepossessed in her favour, and there was a touch of the affectionate in his courtesy. After congratulating himself on recovering a kinswoman of a long-separated branch of his family, and after a good deal of genealogical disquisition, he explained the nature of the lady's historical tasks, and engaged her to visit him in the country at an early date. Miss Willoughby then said farewell, having an engagement at the Record Office, where, as the Earl gallantly observed, she would 'make a sunshine in a shady place.'

When she had gone, the Earl observed, '*Bon sang ne peut pas mentir*! To think of that beautiful creature condemned to waste her lovely eyes on faded ink and yellow papers! Why, she is, as the modern poet says, "a sight to make an old man young."'

He then asked Logan to acquaint Merton with the new and favourable aspect of his affairs, and, after fixing Logan's visit to Rookchester for the same date as Miss Willoughby's, he went off with a juvenile alertness.

'I say,' said Logan, 'I don't know what will come of this, but *something* will come of it. I had no idea that girl was such a paragon.'

'Take care, Logan,' said Merton. 'You ought only to have eyes for Miss Markham.'

Miss Markham, the precise student may remember, was the lady once known as the Venus of Milo to her young companions at St. Ursula's. Now mantles were draped on her stately shoulders at Madame Claudine's, and Logan and she were somewhat hopelessly attached to each other.

'Take care of yourself at Rookchester,' Merton went on, 'or the Disentangler may be entangled.'

'I am not a viscount and I am not an earl,' said Logan, with a reminiscence of an old popular song, 'nor I am not a prince, but a shade or two *wuss*; and I think that Miss Willoughby will find other marks for the artillery of her eyes.'

'We shall have news of it,' said Merton.

II

The Affair of the Jesuit

Trains do not stop at the little Rookchester station except when the high and puissant prince the Earl of Embleton or his visitors, or his ministers, servants, solicitors, and agents of all kinds, are bound for that haven. When Logan arrived at the station, a bowery, flowery, amateur-looking depot, like one of the 'model villages' that we sometimes see off the stage, he was met by the Earl, his son Lord Scremerston, and Miss Willoughby. Logan's baggage was spirited away by menials, who doubtless bore it to the house in some ordinary conveyance, and by the vulgar road. But Lord Embleton explained that as the evening was warm, and the woodland path by the river was cool, they had walked down to welcome the coming guest.

The walk was beautiful indeed along the top of the precipitous red sandstone cliffs, with the deep, dark pools of the Coquet sleeping far below. Now and then a heron poised, or a rock pigeon flew by, between the river and the cliff-top. The opposite bank was embowered in deep green wood, and the place was very refreshing after the torrid bricks and distressing odours of the July streets of London.

The path was narrow: there was room for only two abreast.

Miss Willoughby and Scremerston led the way, and were soon lost to sight by a turn in the path. As for Lord Embleton, he certainly seemed to have drunk of that fountain of youth about which the old French poet Pontus de Tyard reports to us, and to be going back, not forward, in age. He looked very neat, slim, and cool, but that could not be the only cause of the miracle of rejuvenescence. Closely regarding his host in profile, Logan remarked that he had shaved off his moustache and the little, obsolete, iron-grey chin-tuft which, in moments of perplexity, he had been wont to twiddle. Its loss was certainly a very great improvement to the clean-cut features of this patrician.

'We are a very small party,' said Lord Embleton, 'only the Prince, my daughter, Father Riccoboni, Miss Willoughby, my sister, Scremerston, and you and I. Miss Willoughby came last week. In the mornings she and I are busy with the manuscripts. We have found most interesting things. When their plot failed, your ancestor and mine prepared a ship to start for the Western seas and attack the treasure-ships of Spain. But peace broke out, and they never achieved that adventure. Miss Willoughby is a cousin well worth discovering, so intelligent, and so wonderfully attractive.'

'So Scremerston seems to think,' was Logan's idea, for the further he and the Earl advanced, the less, if possible, they saw of the pair in front of them; indeed, neither was visible again till the party met before dinner.

However, Logan only said that he had a great esteem for Miss Willoughby's courage and industry through the trying years of poverty since she left St. Ursula's.

'The Prince we have not seen very much of,' said the Earl, 'as is natural; for you will be glad to know that everything seems most happily arranged, except so far as the religious difficulty goes. As for Father Riccoboni, he is a quiet intelligent man, who passes most of his time in the library, but makes himself very agreeable at meals. And now here we are arrived.'

They had reached the south side of the house—an eighteenth-century building in the red sandstone of the district, giving on a grassy terrace. There the host's maiden sister, Lady Mary Guevara, was seated by a tea-table, surrounded by dogs—two collies and an Aberdeenshire terrier. Beside her were Father Riccoboni, with a newspaper in his hand, Lady Alice, with whom Logan had already some acquaintance, and the Prince of Scalastro. Logan was presented, and took quiet notes of the assembly, while the usual chatter about the weather and his journey got itself transacted, and the view of the valley of the Coquet had justice done to its charms.

Lady Mary was very like a feminine edition of the Earl, refined, shy, and with silvery hair. Lady Alice was a pretty, quiet type of the English girl who is not up to date, with a particularly happy and winning expression. The Prince was of a Teutonic fairness; for the Royal caste, whatever the nationality, is to a great extent made in Germany, and retains the physical characteristics of that ancient forest people whom the Roman historian (never having met them) so lovingly idealised. The Prince was tall, well-proportioned, and looked 'every inch a soldier.' There were a great many inches.

As for Father Riccoboni, the learned have remarked that there are two chief clerical types: the dark, ascetic type, to be found equally among Unitarians, Baptists, Anglicans, Presbyterians, and Catholics, and the burly, well-fed, genial type, which 'cometh eating and drinking.' The Father was of this second kind; a lusty man—not that you could call him a sensual-looking man, still less was he a noisy humourist; but he had a considerable jowl, a strong jaw, a wide, firm mouth, and large teeth, very white and square. Logan thought that he, too, had the makings of a soldier, and also felt almost certain that he had seen him before. But where?—for Logan's acquaintance with the clergy, especially the foreign clergy, was not extensive. The Father spoke English very well, with a slight German accent and a little hoarseness; his voice, too, did not sound unfamiliar to Logan. But he delved in his subconscious memory in vain; there was the Father, a man with whom he certainly had some associations, yet he could not place the man.

A bell jangled somewhere without as they took tea and tattled; and, looking towards the place whence the sound came, Logan saw a little group of Italian musicians walking down the avenue which led through the park to the east side of the house and the main entrance. They entered, with many obeisances, through the old gate of floreated wrought iron, and stopping there, about forty yards away, they piped, while a girl, in the usual *contadina* dress, clashed her cymbals and danced not ungracefully. The Father, who either did not like music or did not like it of that sort, sighed, rose from his seat, and went into the house by an open French window. The Prince also rose, but he went forward to the group of Italians, and spoke to them for a few minutes. If he did not like that sort of music, he took the more excellent way, for the action of his elbow indicated a movement of his hand towards his waistcoat-pocket. He returned to the party on the terrace, and the itinerant artists, after more obeisances, walked slowly back by the way they had come.

'They are Genoese,' said the Prince, 'tramping north to Scotland for the holiday season.'

'They will meet strong competition from the pipers,' said

Andrew Lang

Logan, while the Earl rose, and walked rapidly after the musicians.

'I do not like the pipes myself,' Logan went on, 'but when I hear them in a London street my heart does warm to the skirl and the shabby tartans.'

'I feel with you,' said the Prince, 'when I see the smiling faces of these poor sons of the South among—well, your English faces are not usually joyous—if one may venture to be critical.'

He looked up, and, his eyes meeting those of Lady Alice, he had occasion to learn that every rule has its exceptions. The young people rose and wandered off on the lawn, while the Earl came back and said that he had invited the foreigners to refresh themselves.

'I saw Father Riccoboni in the hall, and asked him to speak to them a little in their own lingo,' he added, 'though he does not appear to be partial to the music of his native land.'

'He seems to be of the Romansch districts,' Logan said; 'his accent is almost German.'

'I daresay he will make himself understood,' said the Earl. 'Do you understand this house, Mr. Logan? It looks very modern, does it not?'

'Early Georgian, surely?' said Logan.

'The shell, at least on this side, is early Georgian—I rather regret it; but the interior, northward, except for the rooms in front here, is of the good old times. We have secret stairs— not that there is any secret about them—and odd cubicles, in the old Border keep, which was re-faced about 1750; and we have a priest's hole or two, in which Father Riccoboni might have been safe, but would have been very uncomfortable, three hundred years ago. I can show you the places to-morrow; indeed, we have very little in the way of amusement to offer you. Do you fish?'

'I always take a trout rod about with me, in case of the best,' said Logan, 'but this is "soolky July," you know, and the trout usually seem sound asleep.'

'Their habits are dissipated here,' said Lord Embleton. 'They begin to feed about ten o'clock at night. Did you ever try night fishing with the bustard?'

'The bustard?' asked Logan.

'It is a big fluffy fly, like a draggled mayfly, fished wet, in the dark. I used to be fond of it, but age,' sighed the Earl, 'and fear of rheumatism have separated the bustard and me.'

'I should like to try it very much,' said Logan. 'I often fished Tweed and Whitadder, at night, when I was a boy, but we used a small dark fly.'

'You must be very careful if you fish at night here,' said Lady Mary. 'It is so dark in the valley under the woods, and the Coquet is so dangerous. The flat sandstone ledges are like the floor of a room, and then a step may land you in water ten feet deep, flowing in a narrow channel. I am always anxious when anyone fishes here at night. You can swim?'

Logan confessed that he was not destitute of that accomplishment, and that he liked, of all things, to be by a darkling river, where you came across the night side of nature in the way of birds, beasts, and fishes.

'Mr. Logan can take very good care of himself, I am sure,' said Lord Embleton, 'and Fenwick knows every inch of the water, and will go with him. Fenwick is the water-keeper, Mr. Logan, and represents man in the fishing and shooting stage. His one thought is the destruction of animal life. He is a very happy man.'

'I never knew but one keeper who was not,' said Logan. 'That was in Galloway. He hated shooting, he hated fishing. My impression is that he was what we call a "Stickit Minister."'

'Nothing of that about Fenwick,' said the Earl. 'I daresay you would like to see your room?'

Thither Logan was conducted, through a hall hung with pikes, and guns, and bows, and clubs from the South Seas, and Zulu shields and assegais, while a few empty figures in tilting armour, lance in hand, stood on pedestals. Thence up a broad staircase, along a little gallery, up a few steps of an old 'turnpike' staircase, Logan reached his room, which looked down through the trees of the cliff to the Coquet.

Dinner passed in the silver light of the long northern day, that threw strange blue reflections, softer than sapphire, on the ancient plate—the ambassadorial plate of a Jacobean ancestor.

'It should all have gone to the melting-pot for King Charles's service,' said the Earl, with a sigh, 'but my ancestor of that day stood for the Parliament.'

Logan's position at dinner was better for observation than for entertainment. He sat on the right hand of Lady Mary, where the Prince ought to have been seated, but Lady Alice sat on her father's left, and next her, of course, the Prince. 'Love rules the camp, the court, the grove,' and Love deranged the accustomed order, for the Prince sat between Lady Alice and Logan. Opposite Logan, and at Lady Mary's left, was the Jesuit, and next him, Scremerston, beside whom was Miss Willoughby, on the Earl's right. Inevitably the conversation of the Prince and Lady Alice was mainly directed to each other—so much so that Logan did not once perceive the princely eyes attracted to Miss Willoughby opposite to him, though it was not easy for another to look at anyone else. Logan, in the pauses of his rather conventional entertainment by Lady Mary, *did* look, and he was amazed no less by the beauty than by the spirits and gaiety of the young lady so recently left forlorn by the recreant Jephson. This flower of the Record Office and of the British Museum was obviously not destined to blush unseen any longer. She manifestly dazzled Scremerston, who seemed to remember Miss Bangs, her charms, and her dollars no more than Miss Willoughby appeared to remember the treacherous Don.

Scremerston was very unlike his father: he was a small, rather fair man, with a slight moustache, a close-clipped beard, and little grey eyes with pink lids. His health was not good: he had been invalided home from the Imperial Yeomanry, after a slight wound and a dangerous attack of enteric fever, and he had secured a pair for the rest of the Session. He was not very clever, but he certainly laughed sufficiently at what Miss Willoughby said, who also managed to entertain the Earl with great dexterity and *aplomb*. Meanwhile Logan and the Jesuit amused the excellent Lady Mary as best they might, which was not saying much. Lady Mary, though extremely amiable, was far from brilliant, and never having met a Jesuit before, she regarded Father Riccoboni with a certain hereditary horror, as an animal of a rare species, and, of habits perhaps startling and certainly perfidious. However, the lady was philan-thropic in a rural way, and Father Riccoboni enlightened her as to the reasons why his enterprising countrymen leave their smiling land, and open small ice-shops in little English towns, or, less ambitious, invest their slender capital in a monkey and a barrel-organ.

'I don't so very much mind barrel-organs myself,' said Logan; 'I don't know anything prettier than to see the little girls dancing to the music in a London side street.'

'But do not the musicians all belong to that dreadful Camorra?' asked the lady.

'Not if they come from the North, madam,' said the Jesuit. 'And do not all your Irish reapers belong to that dreadful Land League, or whatever it is called?'

'They are all Pap—' said Lady Mary, who then stopped, blushed, and said, with some presence of mind, 'paupers, I fear, but they are quite safe and well-behaved on this side of the Irish Channel.'

'And so are our poor people,' said the Jesuit. 'If they occasionally use the knife a little—*naturam expellas furca*, Mr. Logan, but the knife is a different thing—it is only in a homely war among themselves that they handle it in the East-end of London.'

'*Coelum non animum*,' said Logan, determined not to be outdone in classical felicities; and, indeed, he thought his own quotation the more appropriate.

At this moment a great silvery-grey Persian cat, which had sat hitherto in a stereotyped Egyptian attitude on the arm of the Earl's chair, leaped down and sprang affectionately on the shoulder of the Jesuit. He shuddered strongly and obviously repressed an exclamation with difficulty, as he gently removed the cat.

'Fie, Meriamoun!' said the Earl, as the puss resumed her Egyptian pose beside him. 'Shall I send the animal out of the room? I know some people cannot endure a cat,' and he mentioned the gallant Field Marshal who is commonly supposed to share this infirmity.

'By no means, my lord,' said the Jesuit, who looked strangely pale. 'Cats have an extraordinary instinct for caressing people who happen to be born with exactly the opposite instinct. I am like the man in Aristotle who was afraid of the cat.'

'I wish we knew more about that man,' said Miss Willoughby, who was stroking Meriamoun. 'Are *you* afraid of cats, Lord Scremerston?—but you, I suppose, are afraid of nothing.'

'I am terribly afraid of all manner of flying things that buzz and bite,' said Scremerston.

'Except bullets,' said Miss Willoughby—Beauty rewarding Valour with a smile and a glance so dazzling that the good little Yeoman blushed with pleasure.

'It is a shame!' thought Logan. 'I don't like it now I see it.'

'As to horror of cats,' said the Earl, 'I suppose evolution can explain it. I wonder how they would work it out in *Science Jottings*. There is a great deal of electricity in a cat.'

'Evolution can explain everything,' said the Jesuit demurely, 'but who can explain evolution?'

'As to electricity in the cat,' said Logan, 'I daresay there is as much in the dog, only everybody has tried stroking a cat in the dark to see the sparks fly, and who ever tried stroking a dog in the dark, for experimental purposes?—did you, Lady Mary?'

Lady Mary never had tried, but the idea was new to her, and she would make the experiment in winter.

'Deer skins, stroked, do sparkle,' said Logan, 'I read that in a book. I daresay horses do, only nobody tries. I don't think electricity is the explanation of why some people can't bear cats.'

'Electricity is the modern explanation of everything—love, faith, everything,' remarked the Jesuit; 'but, as I said, who shall explain electricity?'

Lady Mary, recognising the orthodoxy of these sentiments, felt more friendly towards Father Riccoboni. He might be a Jesuit, but he was *bien pensant*.

'What I am afraid of is not a cat, but a mouse,' said Miss Willoughby, and the two other ladies admitted that their own terrors were of the same kind.

'What I am afraid of,' said the Prince, 'is a banging door, by day or night. I am not, otherwise, of a nervous constitution, but if I hear a door bang, I *must* go and hunt for it, and stop the noise, either by shutting the door, or leaving it wide open. I am a sound sleeper, but, if a door bangs, it wakens me at once. I try not to notice it. I hope it will leave off. Then it does leave off—that is the artfulness of it—and, just as you are falling asleep, *knock* it goes! A double knock, sometimes. Then I simply *must* get up, and hunt for that door, upstairs or downstairs—'

'Or in my—' interrupted Miss Willoughby, and stopped, thinking better of it, and not finishing the quotation, which passed unheard.

'That research has taken me into some odd places,' the Prince ended; and Logan reminded the Society of the Bravest of the Brave. What *he* was afraid of was a pair of tight boots.

These innocent conversations ended, and, after dinner, the company walked about or sat beneath the stars in the fragrant evening air, the Earl seated by Miss Willoughby, Scremerston smoking with Logan; while the white dress of Lady Alice flitted ghost-like on the lawn, and the tip of the Prince's cigar burned red in the neighbourhood. In the drawing-room Lady Mary was tentatively conversing with the Jesuit, that mild but probably dangerous animal. She had the curiosity which pious maiden ladies feel about the member of a community which they only know through novels. Certainly this Jesuit was very unlike Aramis.

'And who *is* he like?' Logan happened to be asking Scremerston at that moment. 'I know the face—I know the voice; hang it!—where have I seen the man?'

'Now you mention it,' said Scremerston, '*I* seem to remember him too. But I can't place him. What do you think of a game of billiards, father?' he asked, rising and addressing Lord Embleton. 'Rosamond—Miss Willoughby, I mean—'

'Oh, we are cousins, Lord Embleton says, and you may call me Rosamond. I have never had any cousins before,' interrupted the young lady.

'Rosamond,' said Scremerston, with a gulp, 'is getting on wonderfully well for a beginner.'

'Then let us proceed with her education: it is growing chilly, too,' said the Earl; and they all went to billiards, the Jesuit marking with much attention and precision. Later he took a cue, and was easily the master of every man there, though better acquainted, he said, with the foreign game. The late

Pope used to play, he said, nearly as well as Mr. Herbert Spencer. Even for a beginner, Miss Willoughby was not a brilliant player; but she did not cut the cloth, and her arms were remarkably beautiful—an excellent but an extremely rare thing in woman. She was rewarded, finally, by a choice between bedroom candles lit and offered by her younger and her elder cousins, and, after a momentary hesitation, accepted that of the Earl.

'How is this going to end?' thought Logan, when he was alone. 'Miss Bangs is out of the running, that is certain: millions of dollars cannot bring her near Miss Willoughby with Scremerston. The old gentleman ought to like that—it relieves him from the bacon and lard, and the dollars, and the associations with a Straddle; and then Miss Willoughby's family is all right, but the girl is reckless. A demon has entered into her: she used to be so quiet. I'd rather marry Miss Bangs without the dollars. Then it is all very well for Scremerston to yield to Venus Verticordia, and transfer his heart to this new enchantress. But, if I am not mistaken, the Earl himself is much more kind than kin. The heart has no age, and he is a very well-preserved peer. You might take him for little more than forty, though he quite looked his years when I saw him first. Well, *I* am safe enough, in spite of Merton's warning: this new Helen has no eyes for me, and the Prince has no eyes for her, I think. But who is the Jesuit?'

Logan fought with his memory till he fell asleep, but he recovered no gleam of recollection about the holy man.

It did not seem to Logan, next day, that he was in for a very lively holiday. His host carried off Miss Willoughby to the muniment-room after breakfast; that was an advantage he had over Scremerston, who was decidedly restless and ill at ease. He took Logan to see the keeper, and they talked about fish and examined local flies, and Logan arranged to go and try the trout with the bustard some night; and then they pottered about, and ate cherries in the garden, and finally the Earl found them half asleep in the smoking-room. He routed the Jesuit out of the library, where he was absorbed in a folio containing the works of the sainted Father Parsons, and then the Earl showed Logan and Father Riccoboni over the house. From a window of the gallery Scremerston could be descried playing croquet with Miss Willoughby, an apparition radiant in white.

The house was chiefly remarkable for queer passages, which, beginning from the roof of the old tower, above the Father's chamber, radiated about, emerging in unexpected places. The priests' holes had offered to the persecuted clergy of old times the choice between being grilled erect behind a chimney, or of lying flat in a chamber about the size of a coffin near the roof, where the martyr Jesuits lived on suction, like the snipe, absorbing soup from a long straw passed through a wall into a neighbouring garret.

'Those were cruel times,' said Father Riccoboni, who presently, at luncheon, showed that he could thoroughly appreciate the tender mercies of the present or Christian era. Logan watched him, and once when, something that interested him being said, the Father swept the table with his glance without raising his head, a memory for a fraction of a moment seemed to float towards the surface of Logan's consciousness. Even as when an angler, having hooked a salmon, a monster of the stream, long the fish bores down impetuous, seeking the sunken rocks, disdainful of the steel, and the dark wave conceals him; then anon is beheld a gleam of silver, and again is lost to view, and the heart of the man rejoices—even so fugitive a glimpse had Logan of what he sought in the depths of memory. But it fled, and still he was puzzled.

Logan loafed out after luncheon to a seat on the lawn in the shade of a tree. They were all to be driven over to an Abbey not very far away, for, indeed, in July, there is little for a man to do in the country. Logan sat and mused. Looking up he saw Miss Willoughby approaching, twirling an open parasol on her shoulder. Her face was radiant; of old it had often looked as if it might be stormy, as if there were thunder behind those dark eyebrows. Logan rose, but the lady sat down on the garden seat, and he followed her example.

'This is better than Bloomsbury, Mr. Logan, and cocoa *pour tout potage*: singed cocoa usually.'

'The *potage* here is certainly all that heart can wish,' said Logan.

'The chrysalis,' said Miss Willoughby, 'in its wildest moments never dreamed of being a butterfly, as the man said in the sermon; and I feel like a butterfly that remembers being a chrysalis. Look at me now!'

'I could look for ever,' said Logan, 'like the sportsman in Keats's *Grecian Urn*: "For ever let me look, and thou be fair!"'

'I am so sorry for people in town,' said Miss Willoughby. 'Don't you wish dear old Milo was here?'

Milo was the affectionate nickname—a tribute to her charms—borne by Miss Markham at St. Ursula's.

'How can I wish that anyone was here but you?' asked Logan. 'But, indeed, as to her being here, I should like to know in what capacity she was a guest.'

The Clytemnestra glance came into Miss Willoughby's grey

eyes for a moment, but she was not to be put out of humour.

'To be here as a kinswoman, and an historian, with a maid—fancy me with a maid!—and everything handsome about me, is sufficiently excellent for me, Mr. Logan; and if it were otherwise, do you disapprove of the proceedings of your own Society? But there is Lord Scremerston calling to us, and a four-in-hand waiting at the door. And I am to sit on the box-seat. Oh, this is better than the dingy old Record Office all day.'

With these words Miss Willoughby tripped over the sod as lightly as the Fairy Queen, and Logan slowly followed. No; he did *not* approve of the proceedings of his Society as exemplified by Miss Willoughby, and he was nearly guilty of falling asleep during the drive to Winderby Abbey. Scremerston was not much more genial, for his father was driving and conversing very gaily with his fair kinswoman.

'Talk about a distant cousin!' thought Logan, who in fact felt ill-treated. However deep in love a man may be, he does not like to see a fair lady conspicuously much more interested in other members of his sex than in himself.

The Abbey was a beautiful ruin, and Father Riccoboni did not conceal from Lady Mary the melancholy emotions with which it inspired him.

'When shall our prayers be heard?' he murmured. 'When shall England return to her Mother's bosom?'

Lady Mary said nothing, but privately trusted that the winds would disperse the orisons of which the Father spoke. Perhaps nuns had been bricked up in these innocent-looking mossy walls, thought Lady Mary, whose ideas on this matter were derived from a scene in the poem of *Marmion*. And deep in Lady Mary's heart was a half-formed wish that, if there was to be any bricking up, Miss Willoughby might be the interesting victim. Unlike her brother the Earl, she was all for the Bangs alliance.

Scremerston took the reins on the homeward way, the Earl being rather fatigued; and, after dinner, *two* white robes flitted ghost-like on the lawn, and the light which burned red beside one of them was the cigar-tip of Scremerston. The Earl had fallen asleep in the drawing-room, and Logan took a lonely stroll, much regretting that he had come to a house where he felt decidedly 'out of it.' He wandered down to the river, and stood watching. He was beside the dark-brown water in the latest twilight, beside a long pool with a boat moored on the near bank. He sat down in the boat pensively, and then—what was that? It was the sound of a heavy trout rising. '*Plop, plop*!' They were feeding all round him.

'By Jove! I'll try the bustard to-morrow night, and then I'll go back to town next day,' thought Logan. 'I am doing no good here, and I don't like it. I shall tell Merton that I have moral objections to the whole affair. Miserable, mercenary fraud!' Thus, feeling very moral and discontented, Logan walked back to the house, carefully avoiding the ghostly robes that still glimmered on the lawn, and did not re-enter the house till bedtime.

The following day began as the last had done; Lord Embleton and Miss Willoughby retiring to the muniment-room, the lovers vanishing among the walks. Scremerston later took Logan to consult Fenwick, who visibly brightened at the idea of night-fishing.

'You must take one of those long landing-nets, Logan,' said Scremerston. 'They are about as tall as yourself, and as stout as lance-shafts. They are for steadying you when you wade, and feeling the depth of the water in front of you.'

Scremerston seemed very pensive. The day was hot; they wandered to the smoking-room. Scremerston took up a novel, which he did not read; Logan began a letter to Merton—a gloomy epistle.

'I say, Logan,' suddenly said Scremerston, 'if your letter is not very important, I wish you would listen to me for a moment.'

Logan turned round. 'Fire away,' he said; 'my letter can wait.'

Scremerston was in an attitude of deep dejection. Logan lit a cigarette and waited.

'Logan, I am the most miserable beggar alive.'

'What is the matter? You seem rather in-and-out in your moods,' said Logan.

'Why, you know, I am in a regular tight place. I don't know how to put it. You see, I can't help thinking that—that—I have rather committed myself—it seems a beastly conceited thing to say—that there's a girl who likes me, I'm afraid.'

'I don't want to be inquisitive, but is she in this country?' asked Logan.

'No; she's at Homburg.'

'Has it gone very far? Have you *said* anything?' asked Logan.

'No; my father did not like it. I hoped to bring him round.'

'Have you *written* anything? Do you correspond?'

'No, but I'm afraid I have *looked* a lot.'

As the Viscount Scremerston's eyes were by no means fitted to express with magnetic force the language of the affections, Logan had to command his smile.

'But why have you changed your mind, if you liked her?' he asked.

'Oh, *you* know very well! Can anybody see her and not love her?' said Scremerston, with a vagueness in his pronouns, but referring to Miss Willoughby.

Logan was inclined to reply that he could furnish, at first hand, an exception to the rule, but this appeared tactless.

'No one, I daresay, whose affections were not already engaged, could see her without loving her; but I thought yours had been engaged to a lady now at Homburg?'

'So did I,' said the wretched Scremerston, 'but I was mistaken. Oh, Logan, you don't know the difference! *This* is genuine biz,' remarked the afflicted nobleman with much simplicity. He went on: 'Then there's my father—you know him. He was against the other affair, but, if he thinks I have committed myself and then want to back out, why, with his ideas, he'd rather see me dead. But I can't go on with the other thing now: I simply can *not*. I've a good mind to go out after rabbits, and pot myself crawling through a hedge.'

'Oh, nonsense!' said Logan; 'that is stale and superfluous. For all that I can see, there is no harm done. The young lady, depend upon it, won't break her heart. As a matter of fact, they don't—*we* do. You have only to sit tight. You are no more committed than I am. You would only make both of you wretched if you went and committed yourself now, when you don't want to do it. In your position I would certainly sit tight: don't commit yourself—either here or there, so to speak; or, if you can't sit tight, make a bolt for it. Go to Norway. I am very strongly of opinion that the second plan is the best. But, anyhow, keep up your pecker. You are all right—I give you my word that I think you are all right.'

'Thanks, old cock,' said Scremerston. 'Sorry to have bored you, but I *had* to speak to somebody.'

* * * * * *

'Best thing you could do,' said Logan. 'You'll feel ever so much better. That kind of worry comes of keeping things to oneself, till molehills look mountains. If you like I'll go with you to Norway myself.'

'Thanks, awfully,' said Scremerston, but he did not seem very keen. Poor little Scremerston!

Logan 'breasted the brae' from the riverside to the house. His wading- boots were heavy, for he had twice got in over the tops thereof; heavy was his basket that Fenwick carried behind him, but light was Logan's heart, for the bustard had slain its dozens of good trout. He and the keeper emerged from the wood on the level of the lawn. All the great mass of the house lay dark before them. Logan was to let himself in by the locked French window; for it was very late—about two in the morning. He had the key of the window-door in his pocket. A light moved through the long gallery: he saw it pass each window and vanish. There was dead silence: not a leaf stirred. Then there rang out a pistol-shot, or was it two pistol-shots? Logan ran for the window, his rod, which he had taken down after fishing, in his hand.

'Hurry to the back door, Fenwick!' he said; and Fenwick,

throwing down the creel, but grasping the long landing-net, flew to the back way. Logan opened the drawing-room window, took out his matchbox, with trembling fingers lit a candle, and, with the candle in one hand, the rod in the other, sped through the hall, and along a back passage leading to the gunroom. He had caught a glimpse of the Earl running down the main staircase, and had guessed that the trouble was on the ground floor. As he reached the end of the long dark passage, Fenwick leaped in by the back entrance, of which the door was open. What Logan saw was a writhing group—the Prince of Scalastro struggling in the arms of three men: a long white heap lay crumpled in a corner. Fenwick, at this moment, threw the landing-net over the head of one of the Prince's assailants, and with a twist, held the man half choked and powerless. Fenwick went on twisting, and, with the leverage of the long shaft of the net, dragged the wretch off the Prince, and threw him down. Another of the men turned on Logan with a loud guttural oath, and was raising a pistol. Logan knew the voice at last—knew the Jesuit now. '*Rien ne va plus!*' he cried, and lunged, with all the force and speed of an expert fencer, at the fellow's face with the point of the rod. The metal joints clicked and crashed through the man's mouth, his pistol dropped, and he staggered, cursing through his blood, against the wall. Logan picked up the revolver as the Prince, whose hands were now free, floored the third of his assailants with an upper cut. Logan thrust the revolver into the Prince's hand. 'Keep them quiet with that,' he said, and ran to where the Earl, who had entered unseen in the struggle, was kneeling above the long, white, crumpled heap.

It was Scremerston, dead, in his night dress: poor plucky little Scremerston.

* * * * * *

Afterwards, before the trial, the Prince told Logan how matters had befallen. 'I was wakened,' he said—'you were very late, you know, and we had all gone to bed—I was wakened by a banging door. If you remember, I told you all, on the night of your arrival at Rookchester, how I hated that sound. I tried not to think of it, and was falling asleep when it banged again—a double knock. I was nearly asleep, when it clashed again. There was no wind, my window was open and I looked out: I only heard the river murmuring and the whistle of a passing train. The stillness made the abominable recurrent noise more extraordinary. I dressed in a moment in my smoking-clothes, lit a candle, and went out of my room, listening. I walked along the gallery—'

'It was your candle that I saw as I crossed the lawn,' said Logan.

'When a door opened,' the Prince went on—'the door of one of the rooms on the landing—and a figure, all in white,—it was Scremerston,—emerged and disappeared down the stairs. I followed at the top of my speed. I heard a shot, or rather two pistols that rang out together like one. I ran through the hall into the long back passage at right-angles to it, down the passage to the glimmer of light through the partly glazed door at the end of it. Then my candle was blown out and three men set on me. They had nearly pinioned me when you and Fenwick took them on both flanks. You know the rest. They had the boat unmoored, a light cart ready on the other side, and a steam-yacht lying off Warkworth. The object, of course, was to kidnap me, and coerce or torture me into renewing the lease of the tables at Scalastro. Poor Scremerston, who was a few seconds ahead of me, not carrying a candle, had fired in the dark, and missed. The answering fire, which was simultaneous, killed him. The shots saved me, for they brought you and Fenwick to the rescue. Two of the fellows whom we damaged were—'

'The Genoese pipers, of course,' said Logan.

'And you guessed, from the cry you gave, who my confessor (*he* banged the door, of course to draw me) turned out to be?'

'Yes, the head croupier at Scalastro years ago; but he wore a beard and blue spectacles in the old time, when he raked in a good deal of my patrimony,' said Logan. 'But how was he planted on *you*?'

'My old friend, Father Costa, had died, and it is too long a tale of forgery and fraud to tell you how this wretch was forced on me. He *had* been a Jesuit, but was unfrocked and expelled from Society for all sorts of namable and unnamable offences. His community believed that he was dead. So he fell to the profession in which you saw him, and, when the gambling company saw that I was disinclined to let that hell burn any longer on my rock, ingenious treachery did the rest.'

'By Jove!' said Logan.

* * * * *

The Prince of Scalastro, impoverished by his own generous impulse, now holds high rank in the Japanese service. His beautiful wife is much admired in Yokohama.

The Earl was nursed through the long and dangerous illness which followed the shock of that dreadful July night, by the unwearying assiduity of his kinswoman, Miss Willoughby. On his recovery, the bride (for the Earl won her heart and hand) who stood by him at the altar looked fainter and more ghostly than the bridegroom. But her dark hour of levity was passed and over. There is no more affectionate pair than the Earl and Countess of Embleton. Lady Mary, who lives with them, is once more an aunt, and spoils, it is to be feared, the young Viscount Scremerston, a fine but mischievous little boy. On the fate of the ex-Jesuit we do not dwell: enough to say that his punishment was decreed by the laws of our country, not of that which he had disgraced.

The manuscripts of the Earl have been edited by him and the Countess for the Roxburghe Club.

VIII

THE ADVENTURE OF THE LADY PATRONESS

'I cannot bring myself to refuse my assent. It would break the dear child's heart. She has never cared for anyone else, and, oh, she is quite wrapped up in him. I have heard of your wonderful cures, Mr. Merton, I mean successes, in cases which everyone has given up, and though it seems a very strange step to me, I thought that I ought to shrink from no remedy'—

'However unconventional,' said Merton, smiling. He felt rather as if he were being treated like a quack doctor, to whom people (if foolish enough) appeal only as the last desperate resource.

The lady who filled, and amply filled, the client's chair, Mrs. Malory, of Upwold in Yorkshire, was a widow, obviously, a widow indeed. 'In weed' was an unworthy *calembour* which flashed through Merton's mind, since Mrs. Malory's undying regret for her lord (a most estimable man for a coal owner) was explicitly declared, or rather was blazoned abroad, in her costume. Mrs. Mallory, in fact, was what is derisively styled 'Early Victorian'—'Middle' would have been, historically, more accurate. Her religion was mildly Evangelical; she had been brought up on the Memoirs of the Fairchild Family, by

Mrs. Sherwood, tempered by Miss Yonge and the Waverley Novels. On these principles she had trained her family. The result was that her sons had not yet brought the family library, and the family Romneys and Hoppners, to Christie's. Not one of them was a director of any company, and the name of Malory had not yet been distinguished by decorating the annals of the Courts of Bankruptcy or of Divorce. In short, a family more deplorably not 'up to date,' and more 'out of the swim' could scarcely be found in England.

Such, and of such connections, was the lady, fair, faded, with mildly aquiline features, and an aspect at once distinguished and dowdy, who appealed to Merton. She sought him in what she, at least, regarded as the interests of her eldest daughter, an heiress under the will of a maternal uncle. Merton had met the young lady, who looked like a portrait of her mother in youth. He knew that Miss Malory, now 'wrapped up in' her betrothed lover, would, in a few years, be equally absorbed in 'her boys.' She was pretty, blonde, dull, good, and cast by Providence for the part of one of the best of mothers, and the despair of what man soever happened to sit next her at a dinner party. Such women are the safeguards of society—though sneered at by the frivolous as 'British Matrons.'

'I have laid the case before the—where I always take my troubles,' said Mrs. Malory, 'and I have not felt restrained from coming to consult you. When I permitted my daughter's engagement (of course after carefully examining the young man's worldly position) I was not aware of what I know now. Matilda met him at a visit to some neighbours—he really is very attractive, and very attentive—and it was not till we came to London for the season that I heard the stories about him. Some of them have been pointed out to me, in print, in the dreadful French newspapers, others came to me in anonymous letters. As far as a mother may, I tried to warn

Matilda, but there are subjects on which one can hardly speak to a girl. The Vidame, in fact,' said Mrs. Malory, blushing, 'is celebrated—I should say infamous—both in France and Italy, Poland too, as what they call *un homme aux bonnes fortunes*. He has caused the break-up of several families. Mr. Merton, he is a rake,' whispered the lady, in some confusion.

'He is still young; he may reform,' said Merton, 'and no doubt a pure affection will be the saving of him.'

'So Matilda believes, but, though a Protestant—his ancestors having left France after the Revocation of the Edict of Nancy—Nantes I mean—I am certain that he is *not* under conviction.'

'Why does he call himself Vidame, "the Vidame de la Lain"?' asked Merton.

'It is an affectation,' said Mrs. Malory. 'None of his family used the title in England, but he has been much on the Continent, and has lands in France; and, I suppose, has romantic ideas. He is as much French as English, more I am afraid. The wickedness of that country! And I fear it has affected ours. Even now—I am not a scandal-monger, and I hope for the best—but even last winter he was talked about,' Mrs. Malory dropped her voice, 'with a lady whose husband is in America, Mrs. Brown- Smith.'

'A lady for whom I have the very highest esteem,' said Merton, for, indeed, Mrs. Brown-Smith was one of his references or Lady Patronesses; he knew her well, and had a respect for her character, *au fond*, as well as an admiration for her charms.

'You console me indeed,' said Mrs. Malory. 'I had heard—'

'People talk a great deal of ill-natured nonsense,' said Merton warmly. 'Do you know Mrs. Brown-Smith?'

'We have met, but we are not in the same set; we have exchanged visits, but that is all.'

'Ah!' said Merton thoughtfully. He remembered that when his enterprise was founded Mrs. Brown-Smith had kindly offered her practical services, and that he had declined them for the moment. 'Mrs. Malory,' he went on, after thinking awhile, 'may I take your case into my consideration—the marriage is not till October, you say, we are in June—and I may ask for a later interview? Of course you shall be made fully aware of every detail, and nothing shall be done without your approval. In fact all will depend on your own co-operation. I don't deny that there may be distasteful things, but if you are quite sure about this gentleman's—'

'Character?' said Mrs. Malory. 'I am *so* sure that it has cost me many a wakeful hour. You will earn my warmest gratitude if you can do anything.'

'Almost everything will depend on your own energy, and tolerance of our measures.'

'But we must not do evil that good may come,' said Mrs. Malory nervously.

'No evil is contemplated,' said Merton. But Mrs. Malory, while consenting, so far, did not seem quite certain that her estimate of 'evil' and Merton's would be identical.

She had suffered poignantly, as may be supposed, before she set the training of a lifetime aside, and consulted a professional expert. But the urbanity and patience of Merton, with the high and unblemished reputation of his Association, consoled her. 'We must yield where we innocently may,' she assured herself, 'to the changes of the times. Lest one good order' (and ah, how good the Early Victorian order had been!) 'should corrupt the world.' Mrs. Malory knew that line of poetry. Then she remembered that Mrs. Brown-Smith was on the list of Merton's references, and that reassured her, more or less.

As for Merton, he evolved a plan in his mind, and consulted Bradshaw's invaluable Railway Guide.

On the following night Merton was fortunate or adroit enough to find himself seated beside Mrs. Brown-Smith in a conservatory at a party given by the Montenegrin Ambassador. Other occupants of the fairy-like bower of blossoms, musical with all the singing of the innumerable fountains, could not but know (however preoccupied) that Mrs. Brown-Smith was being amused. Her laughter 'rang merry and loud,' as the poet says, though not a word of her whispered conversation was audible. Conservatories (in novels) are dangerous places for confidences, but the pale and angry face of Miss Malory did *not* suddenly emerge from behind a grove of gardenias, and startle the conspirators. Indeed, Miss Malory was not present; she and her sister had no great share in the elegant frivolities of the metropolis.

'It all fits in beautifully,' said Mrs. Brown-Smith. 'Just let me look at the page of Bradshaw again.' Merton handed to her a page of closely printed matter. '9.17 P.M., 9.50 P.M.' read Mrs. Brown-Smith aloud; 'it gives plenty of time in case of delays. Oh, this is too delicious! You are sure that these trains won't be altered. It might be awkward.'

'I consulted Anson,' said Merton. Anson was famous for his mastery of time-tables, and his prescience as to railway arrangements.

'Of course it depends on the widow,' said Mrs. Brown-Smith, 'I shall see that Johnnie is up to time. He hopes to undersell the opposition soap' (Mr. Brown-Smith was absent in America, in the interests of that soap of his which is familiar to all), 'and he is in the best of humours. Then their grouse! We have disease on our moors in Perthshire; I was in despair. But the widow needs delicate handling.'

'You won't forget—I know how busy you are—her cards for your party?'

'They shall be posted before I sleep the sleep of conscious innocence.'

'And real benevolence,' said Merton.

'And revenge,' added Mrs. Brown-Smith. 'I have heard of his bragging, the monster. He has talked about *me*. And I remember how he treated Violet Lebas.'

At this moment the Vidame de la Lain, a tall, fair young man, vastly too elegant, appeared, and claimed Mrs. Brown-Smith for a dance. With a look at Merton, and a sound which, from less perfect lips, might have been described as a suppressed giggle, Mrs. Brown-Smith rose, then turning, 'Post the page to me, Mr. Merton,' she said. Merton bowed, and, folding up the page of the time-table, he consigned it to his cigarette case.

* * * * * *

Mrs. Malory received, with a blending of emotions, the invitation to the party of Mrs. Brown-Smith. The social popularity and the wealth of the hostess made such invitations acceptable. But the wealth arose from trade, in soap, not in coal, and coal (like the colza bean) is 'a product of the soil,' the result of creative forces which, in the geological past, have worked together for the good of landed families. Soap, on the other hand, is the result of human artifice, and is certainly advertised with more of emphasis and of ingenuity than of delicacy. But, by her own line of descent, Mrs. Brown-Smith came from a Scottish house of ancient standing, historically renowned for its assassins, traitors, and time- servers. This partly washed out the stain of soap. Again, Mrs. Malory had heard the name of Mrs. Brown-Smith taken in vain, and that in a matter nearly affecting her Matilda's happiness. On the other side, Merton had given the lady a valuable testimonial to character. Moreover, the Vidame would be at her party, and Mrs. Malory told herself that she could study the ground. Above all, the girls were so anxious to go: they seldom had such a chance. Therefore, while the Early Victorian moralist hesitated, the mother accepted.

They were all glad that they went. Susan, the younger Miss Malory, enjoyed herself extremely. Matilda danced with the Vidame as often as her mother approved. The conduct of Mrs. Brown-Smith was correctness itself. She endeared herself to the girls: invited them to her place in Perthshire, and warmly congratulated Mrs. Malory on the event approaching in her family. The eye of maternal suspicion could detect nothing amiss. Thanks mainly to Mrs. Brown-Smith, the girls found the season an earthly Paradise: and Mrs. Malory saw much more of the world than she had ever done before. But she remained vigilant, and on the alert. Before the end of July she had even conceived the idea of inviting Mrs. Brown-Smith, fatigued by her toils, to inhale the bracing air of Upwold in the moors. But she first consulted Merton, who expressed his warm approval.

'It is dangerous, though she has been so kind,' sighed Mrs. Malory. 'I have observed nothing to justify the talk which I have heard, but I am in doubt.'

'Dangerous! it is safety,' said Merton.

'How?'

Merton braced himself for the most delicate and perilous part of his enterprise.

'The Vidame de la Lain will be staying with you?'

'Naturally,' said Mrs. Malory. 'And if there *is* any truth in what was whispered—'

'He will be subject to temptation,' said Merton.

'Mrs. Brown-Smith is so pretty and so amusing, and dear Matilda; she takes after my dear husband's family, though the best of girls, Matilda has not that flashing manner.'

'But surely no such thing as temptation should exist for a man so fortunate as de la Lain! And if it did, would his conduct not confirm what you have heard, and open the eyes of Miss Malory?'

'It seems so odd to be discussing such things with—so young a man as you—not even a relation,' sighed Mrs. Malory.

'I can withdraw at once,' said Merton.

'Oh no, please don't speak of that! I am not really at all happy yet about my daughter's future.'

'Well, suppose the worst by way of argument; suppose that you saw, that Miss Malory saw—'

'Matilda has always refused to see or to listen, and has spoken of the reforming effects of a pure affection. She would be hard, indeed, to convince that anything was wrong, but, once certain—I know Matilda's character—she would never forgive the insult, never.'

'And you would rather that she suffered some present distress?'

'Than that she was tied for life to a man who could cause it? Certainly I would.'

'Then, Mrs. Malory, as it *is* awkward to discuss these intimate matters with me, might I suggest that you should have an interview with Mrs. Brown-Smith herself? I assure you that you can trust her, and I happen to know that her view of the man about whom we are talking is exactly your own. More I could say as to her reasons and motives, but we entirely decline to touch on the past or to offer any opinion about the characters of our patients—the persons about whose engagements we are consulted. He might have murdered his grandmother or robbed a church, but my lips would be sealed.'

'Do you not think that Mrs. Brown-Smith would be very much surprised if I consulted her?'

'I know that she takes a sincere interest in Miss Malory, and that her advice would be excellent—though perhaps rather startling,' said Merton.

'I dislike it very much. The world has altered terribly since I was Matilda's age,' said Mrs. Malory; 'but I should never forgive myself if I neglected any precaution, and I shall take your advice. I shall consult Mrs. Brown-Smith.'

Merton thus retreated from what even he regarded as a difficult and delicate affair. He fell back on his reserves; and Mrs. Brown-Smith later gave an account of what passed between herself and the representative of an earlier age:

'She first, when she had invited me to her dreary place, explained that we ought not, she feared, to lead others into temptation. "If you think that man, de la Lain's temptation is to drag my father's name, and my husband's, in the dust," I answered, "let me tell you that *I* have a temptation also."

'"Dear Mrs. Brown-Smith," she answered, "this is indeed honourable candour. Not for the world would I be the occasion—"

'I interrupted her, "*My* temptation is to make him the laughing stock of his acquaintance, and, if he has the impudence to give me the opportunity, I *will*!" And then I told her, without names, of course, that story about this Vidame Potter and Violet Lebas.'

'I did *not*,' said Merton. 'But why Vidame Potter?'

'His father was a Mr. Potter; his grandfather married a Miss Lalain—I know all about it—and this creature has wormed out, or invented, some story of a Vidameship, or whatever it is, hereditary in the female line, and has taken the title. And this is the man who has had the impertinence to talk about *me*, a Ker of Graden.'

'But did not the story you speak of make her see that she must break off her daughter's engagement?'

'No. She was very much distressed, but said that her daughter Matilda would never believe it.'

'And so you are to go to Upwold?'

'Yes, it is a mournful place; I never did anything so good-natured. And, with the widow's knowledge, I am to do as I please till the girl's eyes are opened. I think it will need that stratagem we spoke of to open them.'

'You are sure that you will be in no danger from evil tongues?'

'They say, What say they? Let them say,' answered Mrs. Brown-Smith, quoting the motto of the Keiths.

The end of July found Mrs. Brown-Smith at Upwold, where it is to be hoped that the bracing qualities of the atmosphere made up for the want of congenial society. Susan Malory had been discreetly sent away on a visit. None of the men of the family had arrived. There was a party of local neighbours, who did not feel the want of anything to do, but lived in dread of flushing the Vidame and Matilda out of a window seat whenever they entered a room.

As for the Vidame, being destitute of all other entertainment, he made love in a devoted manner.

But at dinner, after Mrs. Brown-Smith's arrival, though he sat next Matilda, Mrs. Malory saw that his eyes were mainly bent on the lady opposite. The ping-pong of conversation, even, was played between him and Mrs. Brown-Smith across the table: the county neighbours were quite lost in their endeavours to follow the flight of the ball. Though the drawing-room window, after dinner, was open on the fragrant lawn, though Matilda sat close by it, in her wonted place, the Vidame was hanging over the chair of the visitor, and later, played billiards with her, a game at which Matilda did not excel. At family prayers next morning (the service was conducted by Mrs. Malory) the Vidame appeared with a white rosebud in his buttonhole, Mrs. Brown-Smith wearing its twin sister. He took her to the stream in the park where she fished, Matilda following in a drooping manner. The Vidame was much occupied in extracting the flies from the hair of Mrs. Brown-Smith, in which they were frequently entangled. After luncheon he drove with the two ladies and Mrs. Malory to the country town, the usual resource of ladies in the country, and though he sat next Matilda, Mrs. Brown-Smith was beaming opposite, and the pair did most of the talking. While Mrs. Malory and her daughter shopped, it was the Vidame who took Mrs. Brown-Smith to inspect the ruins of the Abbey. The county neighbours had left in the morning, a new set arrived, and while Matilda had to entertain them, it was Mrs Brown-Smith whom the Vidame entertained.

This kind of thing went on; when Matilda was visiting her cottagers it was the Vidame and Mrs. Brown-Smith whom visitors flushed in window seats. They wondered that Mrs. Malory had asked so dangerous a woman to the house: they marvelled that she seemed quite radiant and devoted to her lively visitor. There was a school feast: it was the Vidame who arranged hurdle-races for children of both sexes (so improper!), and who started the competitors.

Meanwhile Mrs. Malory, so unusually genial in public, held frequent conventicles with Matilda in private. But Matilda declined to be jealous; they were only old friends, she said, these flagitious two; Dear Anne (that was the Vidame's Christian name) was all that she could wish.

'You know the place is *so* dull, mother,' the brave girl said. 'Even grandmamma, who was a saint, says so in her *Domestic Outpourings*' (religious memoirs privately printed in 1838). 'We cannot amuse Mrs. Brown-Smith, and it is so kind and chivalrous of Anne.'

'To neglect you?'

'No, to do duty for Tom and Dick,' who were her brothers, and who would not greatly have entertained the fair visitor had they been present.

Matilda was the kind of woman whom we all adore as represented in the characters of Fielding's Amelia and Sophia. Such she was, so gracious and yielding, in her overt demeanour, but, alas, poor Matilda's pillow was often wet with her tears. She was loyal; she would not believe evil: she crushed her natural jealousy 'as a vice of blood, upon the threshold of the mind.'

Mrs. Brown-Smith was nearly as unhappy as the girl. The more she hated the Vidame—and she detested him more deeply every day—the more her heart bled for Matilda. Mrs. Brown-Smith also had her secret conferences with Mrs. Malory.

'Nothing will shake her belief in that man,' said Mrs. Malory.

'Your daughter is the best girl I ever met,' said Mrs. Brown-Smith. 'The best tempered, the least suspicious, the most loyal. And I am doing my worst to make her hate me. Oh, I can't go on!' Here Mrs. Brown-Smith very greatly surprised her hostess by bursting into tears.

'You must not desert us now,' said the elder lady. 'The better you think of poor Matilda—and she *is* a good girl—the more you ought to help her.'

It was the 8th of August, no other visitors were at the house, a shooting party was expected to arrive on the 11th. Mrs.

Brown-Smith dried her tears. 'It must be done,' she said, 'though it makes me sick to think of it.'

Next day she met the Vidame in the park, and afterwards held a long conversation with Mrs. Malory. As for the Vidame, he was in feverish high spirits, he devoted himself to Matilda, in fact Mrs. Brown-Smith had insisted on such dissimulation, as absolutely necessary at this juncture of affairs. So Matilda bloomed again, like a rose that had been 'washed, just washed, in a shower.' The Vidame went about humming the airs of the country which he had honoured by adopting it as the cradle of his ancestry.

On the morning of the following day, while the Vidame strayed with Matilda in the park, Mrs. Brown-Smith was closeted with Mrs. Malory in her boudoir.

'Everything is arranged,' said Mrs. Brown-Smith. 'I, guilty and reckless that I am, have only to sacrifice my character, and all my things. But I am to retain Methven, my maid. That concession I have won from his chivalry.'

'How do you mean?' asked Mrs. Malory.

'At seven he will get a telegram summoning him to Paris on urgent business. He will leave in your station brougham in time to catch the 9.50 up train at Wilkington. Or, rather, so impatient is he, he will leave half an hour too early, for fear of accidental delays. I and my maid will accompany him. I have thought honesty the best policy, and told the truth, like Bismarck, "and the same,"' said Mrs. Brown-Smith hysterically, '"with intent to deceive." I have pointed out to him that my best plan is to pretend to you that I am going to meet my husband, who really arrives at Wilkington from Liverpool by the 9.17, though the Vidame thinks that is an invention of mine. So, you see, I leave without any secrecy, or fuss, or luggage, and, when my husband comes here, he will find me flown, and will have to console himself with my luggage and jewels. He—this Frenchified beast, I mean—has written a note for your daughter, which he will give to her maid, and, of course, the maid will hand it to *you*. So he will have burned his boats. And then you can show it to Matilda, and so,' said Mrs. Brown-Smith, 'the miracle of opening her eyes will be worked. Johnnie, my husband, and I will be hungry when we return about half-past ten. And I think you had better telegraph that there is whooping cough, or bubonic plague, or something in the house, and put off your shooting party.'

'But that would be an untruth,' said Mrs. Malory.

'And what have I been acting for the last ten days?' asked Mrs. Brown- Smith, rather tartly. 'You must settle your excuse with your conscience.'

'The cook's mother really is ill,' said Mrs. Malory, 'and she wants dreadfully to go and see her. That would do.'

'All things work together for good. The cook must have a telegram also,' said Mrs. Brown-Smith.

The day, which had been extremely hot, clouded over. By five it was raining: by six there was a deluge. At seven, Matilda and the Vidame were evicted from their dusky window seat by the butler with a damp telegraph envelope. The Vidame opened it, and handed it to Matilda. His presence at Paris was instantly demanded. The Vidame was desolated, but his absence could not be for more than five days. Bradshaw was hunted for, and found: the 9.50 train was opportune. The Vidame's man packed his clothes. Mrs. Brown-Smith was apprised of these occurrences in the drawing-room before dinner.

'I am very sorry for dear Matilda,' she cried. 'But it is an ill wind that blows nobody good. I will drive over with the Vidame and astonish my Johnnie by greeting him at the station. I must run and change my dress.'

She ran, she returned in morning costume, she heard from Mrs. Malory of the summons by telegram calling the cook to her moribund mother. 'I must send her over to the station in a dog-cart,' said Mrs. Malory.

'Oh no,' cried Mrs. Brown-Smith, with impetuous kindness, 'not on a night like this; it is a cataclysm. There will be plenty of room for the cook as well as for Methven and me, and the Vidame, in the brougham. Or *he* can sit on the box.'

The Vidame really behaved very well. The introduction of the cook, to quote an old novelist, 'had formed no part of his profligate scheme of pleasure.' To elope from a hospitable roof, with a married lady, accompanied by her maid, might be an act not without precedent. But that a cook should come to form *une partie carree*, on such an occasion, that a lover should be squeezed with three women in a brougham, was a trying novelty.

The Vidame smiled, 'An artist so excellent,' he said, 'deserves a far greater sacrifice.'

So it was arranged. After a tender and solitary five minutes with Matilda, the Vidame stepped, last, into the brougham. The coachman whipped up the horses, Matilda waved her kerchief from the porch, the guilty lovers drove away. Presently Mrs. Malory received, from her daughter's maid, the letter destined by the Vidame for Matilda. Mrs. Malory locked it up in her despatch box.

The runaways, after a warm and uncomfortable drive of

three-quarters of an hour, during which the cook wept bitterly and was very unwell, reached the station. Contrary to the Vidame's wish, Mrs. Brown-Smith, in an ulster and a veil, insisted on perambulating the platform, buying the whole of Mr. Hall Caine's works as far as they exist in sixpenny editions. Bells rang, porters stationed themselves in a line, like fielders, a train arrived, the 9.17 from Liverpool, twenty minutes late. A short stout gentleman emerged from a smoking carriage, Mrs. Brown-Smith, starting from the Vidame's side, raised her veil, and threw her arms round the neck of the traveller.

'You didn't expect *me* to meet you on such a night, did you, Johnnie?' she cried with a break in her voice.

'Awfully glad to see you, Tiny,' said the short gentleman. 'On such a night!'

After thus unconsciously quoting the *Merchant of Venice*, Mr. Brown-Smith turned to his valet. 'Don't forget the fishing-rods,' he said.

'I took the opportunity of driving over with a gentleman from Upwold,' said Mrs. Brown-Smith. 'Let me introduce him. Methven,' to her maid, 'where is the Vidame de la Lain?'

'I heard him say that he must help Mrs. Andrews, the cook, to find a seat, Ma'am,' said the maid.

'He really *is* kind,' said Mrs. Brown-Smith, 'but I fear we can't wait to say good-bye to him.'

Three-quarters of an hour later, Mr. Brown-Smith and his wife were at supper at Upwold.

Next day, as the cook's departure had postponed the shooting party, they took leave of their hostess, and returned to their moors in Perthshire.

Weeks passed, with no message from the Vidame. He did not answer a letter which Mrs. Malory allowed Matilda to write. The mother never showed to the girl the note which he had left with her maid. The absence and the silence of the lover were enough. Matilda never knew that among the four packed in the brougham on that night of rain, one had been eloping with a married lady—who returned to supper.

The papers were 'requested to state that the marriage announced between the Vidame de la Lain and Miss Malory will not take place.' Why it did not take place was known only to Mrs. Malory, Mrs. Brown-Smith, and Merton.

Matilda thought that her lover had been kidnapped and arrested, by the Secret Police of France, for his part in a scheme to restore the Royal House, the White Flag, the Lilies, the children of St. Louis. At Mrs. Brown-Smith's place in Perthshire, in the following autumn, Matilda met Sir Aylmer Jardine. Then she knew that what she had taken for love (in the previous year) had been,

'Not love, but love's first flush in youth.'

They always do make that discovery, bless them! Lady Jardine is now wrapped up in her baby boy. The mother of the cook recovered her health.

IX

ADVENTURE OF THE LADY NOVELIST
AND THE VACCINATIONIST

'Mr. Frederick Warren'—so Merton read the card presented to him on a salver of Limoges enamel by the office-boy.

'Show the gentleman in.'

Mr. Warren entered. He was a tall and portly person, with a red face, red whiskers, and a tightly buttoned frock-coat, which more expressed than hid his goodly and prominent proportions. He bowed, and Merton invited him to be seated. It struck Merton as a singular circumstance that his visitor wore on each arm the crimson badge of the newly vaccinated.

Mr. Warren sat down, and, taking a red silk handkerchief out of the crown of his hat, he wiped his countenance. The day was torrid, and Mr. Merton hospitably offered an effervescent draught.

'Without the whisky, if you please, sir,' said Mr. Warren, in a provincial accent. He pointed to a blue ribbon in the buttonhole of his coat, indicating that he was conscientiously opposed to the use of alcoholic refreshment in all its forms.

'Two glasses of Apollinaris water,' said Merton to the office-boy; and the innocent fluid was brought, while Merton silently admired his client's arrangement in blue and crimson. When the thirst of that gentleman had been assuaged, he entered upon business thus:

'Sir, I am a man of principle!'

Merton congratulated him; the age was lax, he said, and principle was needed. He wondered internally what he was going to be asked to subscribe to, or whether his vote only was required.

'Sir, have you been vaccinated?' asked the client earnestly.

'Really,' said Merton, 'I do not quite understand your interest in a matter so purely personal.'

'Personal, sir? Not at all. It is the first of public duties—the debt that every man, woman, and child owes to his or her country. Have you been vaccinated, sir?'

'Why, if you insist on knowing,' said Merton, 'I have, though I do not see—'

'Recently?' asked the visitor.

'Yes, last month; but I cannot conjecture why—'

'Enough, sir,' said Mr. Warren. 'I am a man of principle. Had you not done your duty in this matter by your country, I should have been compelled to seek some other practitioner in your line.'

'I was not aware that my firm had any competitors in our line of business,' said Merton. 'But perhaps you have come here under some misapprehension. There is a firm of family solicitors on the floor above, and next them are the offices of a company interested in a patent explosive. If your affairs, or your political ideas, demand a legal opinion, or an outlet in an explosive which is widely recommended by the Continental Press—'

'For what do you take me, sir?' asked Mr. Warren.

'For a Temperance Anarchist,' Merton would have liked to reply, 'judging by your colours'; but he repressed this retort, and mildly answered, 'Perhaps it would be as much to the purpose to ask, for what do you take *me*?'

'For the representative of Messrs. Gray & Graham, the specialists in matrimonial affairs,' answered the client; and Merton said that he would be happy if Mr. Warren would enter into the details of his business.

'I am the ex-Mayor of Bulcester,' said Mr. Warren, 'and, as I told you, a man of principle. My attachment to the Temperance cause'—and he fingered his blue ribbon—'procured for me the honour of a defeat at the last general election, but endeared me to the consciences of the Nonconformist element in the constituency. Yet, sir, I am at this moment the most unpopular man in Bulcester; but I shall fight it out—I shall fight it to my latest breath.'

'Is Bulcester, then, such an intemperate constituency? I had understood that the Nonconformist interest was strong there,' said Merton.

'So it is, sir, so it is; but the interest is now bound to the chariot wheels of the truckling Toryism of our time—to the sycophants who basely made vaccination permissive, and paltered with the Conscientious Objector. These badges, sir'—the client pointed to his own crimson decorations—'proclaim that I have been vaccinated on *both* arms, as a testimony to the immortal though, in Bulcester, maligned discovery of the great Jenner. Sir, I am hooted in the public streets of my native town, where Anti-vaccinationism is a frenzy. Mr. Rider Haggard, the author of *Dr. Therne*, has been burned in effigy for his thrilling and manly protest to which I owe my own conversion.'

'Then the conversion is relatively recent?' asked Merton.

'It dates since my reading of that powerful argument, sir; that appeal to reason which overcame my prejudice, for I was a prominent A. V.'

'*Ave?*' asked Merton.

'A. V., sir—Anti-Vaccinationist. A. C. D. A. too, and always,' he added proudly; but Merton did not think it prudent to ask for further explanations.

'An A. V. I was, an A. V. I am no longer; and I defy popular clamour, accompanied by brickbats, to shake my principles.'

'*Justum et tinacem propositi virum,*' murmured Merton, adding, 'All that is very interesting, but, my dear sir, while I admire the tenacity of your principles, will you permit me to ask, what has vaccination to do with the special business of our firm?'

'Why, sir, I have a family, and my eldest son—'

'Does he decline to be vaccinated?' asked Merton, in a sympathetic voice.

'No, sir, or he would never darken my doorway,' exclaimed

this more than Roman father. 'But he is engaged, and I can never give my consent; and if he marries that girl, the firm ceases to be "Warren & Son, wax-cloth manufacturers." That's all, sir—that's all.'

Mr. Warren again applied his red handkerchief to his glowing features.

'And what, may I ask, are the grounds of your objection to this engagement? Social inequality?' asked Merton.

'No, the young lady is the daughter of one of our leading ministers, Mr. Truman—author of *The Bishops to the Block*—but principles are concerned.'

'You cannot mean that the young lady is excessively addicted to the—wine cup?' asked Merton gravely. 'In melancholy cases of that kind Mr. Hall Caine, in a romance, has recommended hypnotic treatment, but we do not venture to interfere.'

'You misunderstand me, sir,' replied Mr. Warren, frowning. 'The young woman, on principle, as they call it, has never been vaccinated. Like most of our prominent citizens, her father (otherwise an excellent man) objects to what he calls "The Worship of the Calf" on grounds of conscience.'

'Conscience! It is a hard thing to constrain the conscience,' murmured Merton, quoting a remark of Queen Mary to John Knox.

'What is conscience without knowledge, sir?' asked the client, using—without knowing it—the very argument of Mr. Knox to the Queen.

'You have no other objections to the alliance?' asked Merton.

'None whatever, sir. She is a good and good-looking girl. On most important points we are thoroughly agreed. She won a prize essay on Bacon's authorship of Shakespeare's plays. Of course Shakespeare could not have written them—a thoroughly uneducated man, who never could have passed the fourth standard. But look at the plays! There are things in them that, with all our modern advantages, are beyond me. I admit they are beyond me. "To be, and to do, and to suffer,"' declaimed Mr. Warren, apparently under the impression that this is part of Hamlet's soliloquy—'Shakespeare could never have written *that*. Where did *he* learn grammar?'

'Where, indeed?' replied Merton. 'But as the lady is in all other respects so suitable a match, cannot this one difficulty be got over?'

'Impossible, sir; my son could not slice the sleeve in her dress and inflict this priceless boon on her with affectionate violence. Even the hero of *Dr. Therne* failed there—'

'And rather irritated his pretty Jane,' added Merton, who remembered this heroic adventure. 'It is a very hard case,' he went on, 'but I fear that our methods are powerless. The only chance would be to divert young Mr. Warren's affections into some other more enlightened channel. That expedient has often been found efficacious. Is he very deeply enamoured? Would not the society of another pretty and intelligent girl perhaps work wonders?'

'Perhaps it might, sir, but I don't know where to find any one that would attract my James. Except for political meetings, and a literary lecture or two, with a magic-lantern and a piano, we have not much social relaxation at Bulcester. We object to promiscuous dancing, on grounds of conscience. Also, of course, to the stage.'

'Ah, so you *do* allow for the claims of conscience, do you?'

'For what do you take me, sir? Only, of course the conscience must be enlightened,' said Mr. Warren, as other earnest people usually do.

'Certainly, certainly,' said Merton; 'nothing so dangerous as the unenlightened conscience. Why, in this very matter of marriage the conscience of the Mormons leads them to singular aberrations, while that of the Arunta tribe—but I should only pain you if I pursued the subject. You said that your Society indulged in literary lectures: is your programme for the season filled up?'

'I am President of the Bulcester Literary Society,' said Mr. Warren, 'and I ought to know. We have a vacancy for Friday week; but why do you inquire? In fact I want a lecturer on "The Use and Abuse of Novels," now you ask. Our people, somehow, always want their literary lectures to be about novels. I try to make the lecturers take a lofty moral tone, and usually entertain them at my house, where I probe their ideas, and warn them that we must have nothing loose. Once, sir, we had a lecturer on "The Oldest Novel in the World." He gave us a terrible shock, sir! I never saw so many red cheeks in a Bulcester audience. And the man seemed quite unaware of the effect he was producing.'

'Short-sighted, perhaps?' said Merton.

'Ever since we have been very careful. But, sir, we seem to have got away from the subject.'

'It is only seeming,' said Merton. 'I have an idea which may be of service to you.'

'Thank you, most kindly,' said Mr. Warren. 'But as how?'

'Does your Society ever employ lady lecturers?'

'We prefer them; we are all for enlarging the sphere of woman's activity—virtuous activity, I mean.'

'That is fortunate,' remarked Merton. 'You said just now that to try the plan of a counter-attraction was difficult, because there was little of social relaxation in your Society, and you knew no lady who had the opportunities necessary for presenting an agreeable alternative to the charms of Miss Truman. A young man's fancy is often caught merely by the juxtaposition of a single member of the opposite sex, with whom he contracts a custom of walking home from chapel.'

'That's mostly the way at Bulcester,' said Mr. Warren.

'Well,' Merton went on, 'you are in the habit of entertaining the lecturers at your house. Now, I know a young lady—one of our staff, in fact—who is very well qualified to lecture on "The Use and Abuse of Novels." She is a novelist herself; one of the most serious and improving of our younger writers. In her works virtue (after struggles) is always rewarded, and vice (especially if gilded) is held up to execration, though never allowed to display itself in colours which would bring a blush to the cheek of—a white rabbit. Here is her portrait,' said Merton, taking up a family periodical, *The Young Girl*. This blameless journal was publishing a serial story by Miss Martin, one of the ladies who had been enlisted at the dinner given by Logan and Merton when they founded their Society. A photograph of Miss Martin, in white and in a large shadowy hat, was published in *The Young Girl*, and certainly no one could have recognised in this conscientiously innocent and domestic portrait the fair author of romances of social adventure and unimagined crime. 'There you see our young friend,' said Merton; 'and the magazine, to which she is a regular contributor, is a voucher for her character as an author.'

Mr. Warren closely scrutinised the portrait, which displayed loveliness and candour in a very agreeable way, and arranged in the extreme of modest simplicity.

'That is a young woman who bears her testimonials in her face,' said Mr. Warren. 'She is one whom a father can trust— but has she been vaccinated?'

'Early and often,' answered Merton reassuringly. 'Girls with faces like hers do not care to run any risks.'

'Jane Truman does, though my son has put it to her, I know, on the ground of her looks. "*Nothing*," she said, "will ever induce me to submit to that filthy, that revolting operation."'

'"Conscience doth make cowards of us all," as Bacon says,' replied Merton, 'or at least of such of us as are unenlightened. But to come to business. What do you think of asking our young friend down to lecture—on Friday week, I think you said—on the Use and Abuse of Novels? You could easily persuade her, I dare say, to stay over Sunday—longer if necessary—and then young Mr. Warren would at least find out that there is more than one young woman in the world.'

'I shall be delighted to see your friend,' answered Mr. Warren. 'At Bulcester we welcome intellect, and a real novelist of moral tendencies would make quite a sensation in our midst.'

'They are but too scarce at present,' Merton answered— 'novelists of high moral tone.'

'She is not a Christian Scientist?' asked Mr. Warren anxiously.

'They reject vaccination, like all other means appointed, and rely on miracles, which ceased with the Apostolic age, being no longer necessary.'

'The lady, I can assure you, is not a Christian Scientist,' said Merton 'but comes of an Evangelical family. Shall I give you her address? In my opinion it would be best to write to her from Bulcester, on the official paper of the Literary Society.' For Merton wished to acquaint Miss Martin with the nature of her mission, lecturing being an art which she had never cultivated.

'There is just one thing,' remarked Mr. Warren hesitatingly. 'This young lady, if our James lets his affections loose on her—how would *that* be, sir?'

Merton smiled.

'Why, no great harm would be done, Mr. Warren. You need not fear any complication: any new matrimonial difficulty. The affection would be all on one side, and that side would not be the lady lecturer's. I happen to know that she has a prior attachment.'

'Vaccinated!' cried Mr. Warren, letting a laugh out of him.

'Exactly,' said Merton.

Mr. Warren now gladly concurred in the plan of his adviser, after which the interview was concerned with financial details. Merton usually left these vague, but in Mr. Warren he saw a client who would feel more confidence if everything was put on a strictly business footing. The client retired in a hopeful frame of mind, and Merton went to look for Miss Martin at her club, where she was usually to be found at the hour of tea.

He was fortunate enough to find her, dressed by no means after the style of her portrait in *The Young Girl*, but still very well dressed. She offered him the refreshment of tea and toast—very good toast, Merton thought—and he asked how her craft as a novelist was prospering. Friends of Miss Martin were obliged to ask, for they did not read *The Young Girl*, or the other and less domestic serials in which her works appeared.

'I am doing very well, thank you,' said Miss Martin. 'My tale *The Curate's Family* has raised the circulation of *The Young Girl*; and, mind you, it is no easy thing for a novelist to raise the circulation of any periodical. For example, if *The Quarterly Review* published a new romance, even by Mr. Thomas Hardy, I doubt if the end would justify the proceedings.'

'It would take about four years to get finished in a quarterly,' said Merton.

'And the nonagenarians who read quarterlies,' said Miss Martin, with the flippancy of youth, 'would go to their graves without knowing whether the heroine found a lenient jury or not. I have six heroines in *The Curate's Family*, and I own their love affairs tend to get a little mixed. I have rigged up a small stage, with puppets in costume to represent the characters, and keep them straight in my mind; but Ethelinda, who is engaged to the photographer, as nearly as possible eloped with the baronet last week.'

'Anything else on?' asked Merton.

'An up-to-date story, all heredity and evolution,' said Miss Martin. 'The father has his legs bitten off by a shark, and it gets on the nerves of his wife, the Marchioness, and two of the girls are born like mermaids. They have immense popularity at bathing-places on the French coast, but it is not easy for them to go into general society.'

'What nonsense!' exclaimed Merton.

'Not worse than other stuff that is highly recommended by eminent reviewers,' said Miss Martin.

'Anything else?'

'Oh, yes; there is "The Pope's Poisoner, a Tale of the Borgias." That is a historical romance, I got it up out of Histories of the Renaissance. The hero (Lionardo da Vinci) is the Pope's bravo, and in love with Lucrezia Borgia.'

'Are the dates all right?' asked Merton.

'Oh, bother the dates! Of course he is a bravo *pour le bon motif*, and frustrates the pontifical designs.'

'I want you,' said Merton, 'you have such a fertile imagination, to take part in a little plot of our own. Beneficent, of course, but I admit that my fancy is baffled. Could we find a room less crowded? This is rather private business.'

'There is never anybody in the smoking-room at the top of the house,' said Miss Martin, 'because—to let out a secret—none of us ever smoke, except at public dinners to give tone. But *you* may.'

She led Merton to a sepulchral little chamber upstairs, and he told her all the story of Mr. Warren, his son, and the daughter of the minister.

'Why don't they elope?' asked Miss Martin.

'The Nonconformist conscience is unfriendly to elopements, and the young man has no accomplishment by which he could support his bride except the art of making oilcloth.'

'Well, what do you want me to do?'

Merton unfolded the scheme of the lady lecturer, and prepared Miss Martin to receive an invitation from Mr. Warren.

'Can you write a lecture on "The Use and Abuse of Novels" before Friday week?' he asked.

'Say seven thousand words? I could do it by to-morrow morning,' said Miss Martin.

'You know you must be very careful?'

'Style of answers to correspondents in *The Young Girl*,' said Miss Martin. 'I know my way about.'

'Then you really will essay the adventure?'

'Like a bird,' answered the lady. 'It will be great fun. I shall pick up copy about the habits of the middle classes in the Midlands.'

'They won't recognise you as the author of your more criminal romances?'

'How can they? I sign them "Passion Flower" and "Nightshade," and "La Tofana," and so on.'

'You will dress as in your photograph in *The Young Girl*?'

'I will, and take a *fichu* to wear in the evening. They always wear *fichus* in evening dress. But, look here, do you want a happy ending to this romance?'

'How can it be happy if you are to be successful? Miss Jane Truman will be miserable, and Mr. James Warren will die of remorse and a broken heart, when you—'

'Fail to crown his flame, and Jane has too much pride to welcome back the wanderer?'

'I'm afraid that, or something like that, will be the end of it,' said Merton, 'and, perhaps, on reflection, we had better drop the affair.'

'But suppose I could manage a happy ending? Suppose I reconcile Mr. Warren to the union? I am all for happy endings myself. I drink to King Charles II., who declared that while *he* was king all tragedies should end happily.'

'You don't mean that you can persuade Jane to be vaccinated?'

'One never knows till one tries. You'll find that I shall make a happy conclusion to my Borgia novel, and *that* is not so easy. You see Lionardo goes to the Pope's jeweller and exchanges the—'

Miss Martin paused and remained absorbed in thought.

Suddenly she danced round the room with much grace and *abandon*, while Merton, smoking in an arm-chair that had lost a castor, gently applauded the performance.

'You have your idea?' he asked.

'I have it. Happy ending! Hurrah!'

Miss Martin spun round like a dancing Dervish, and finally fell into another arm-chair, overcome by the heat and the intoxication of genius.

'We owe a candle to Saint Alexander Borgia!' she said, when she recovered her breath.

'Miss Martin,' said Merton gravely, 'this is a serious matter. You are not going, I trust, to poison the lemons for the elder Mr. Warren's lemon squash? He is strictly Temperance, you know.'

'Poison the lemons? With a hypodermic syringe?' asked Miss Martin. 'No; that is good business. I have made one of my villains do *that*, but that is not my idea. Perfectly harmless, my idea.'

'But sensational, I fear?' asked Merton.

'Some very cultured critics might think so,' the lady admitted. 'But I am sure to succeed, and I hear the merry, merry wedding bells of the Bulcester tabernacle ringing a peal for the happy pair.'

'Well, what is the plan?'

'That is my secret.'

'But I *must* know. I am responsible. Tell me, or I telegraph to Mr. Warren: "Lecturer never vaccinated; sorry for my mistake."'

'That would not be true,' said Miss Martin.

'A noble falsehood,' said Merton.

'But I assure you that if my plan fails no harm can possibly be caused or suspected. And if it succeeds then the thing is done: either Mr. Warren is reconciled to the marriage, or— the marriage is broken off, as he desires.'

'By whom?'

'By the Conscientious Objectrix, if that is the feminine of Objector—by Miss Jane Truman.'

'Why should Jane break it off if the old gentleman agrees?'

'Because Jane would be a silly girl. Mr. Merton, I will promise you one thing. The plan shall not be tried without the approval of the lover himself. None but he shall be concerned in the affair.'

'You won't hypnotise the girl and let him vaccinate her when she is in the hypnotic sleep?'

'No, nor even will I give her a post-hypnotic suggestion to vaccinate herself, or go to the doctor's and have it done when she is awake; though,' said Miss Martin, 'that is not bad business either. I must make a note of that. But I can't hypnotise anybody. I tried lots of girls when I was at St. Ursula's and nothing ever came of it. Thank you for the idea all the same. By the way, I first must sterilise the pontifical—' She paused.

'The what?'

'That is my secret! Don't you see how safe it is? None but the lover shall have his and her fate in his hands. *C'est a prendre ou a laisser.*'

Merton was young and adventurous.

'You give me your word that your idea is absolutely safe and harmless? It involves no crime?'

'None; and if you like,' said Miss Martin, 'I will bring you the highest professional opinion,' and she mentioned an eminent name in the craft of healing. 'He was our doctor when we were children,' said the lady, 'and we have always been friends.'

'Well,' Merton said, 'what is good enough for Sir Josiah Wilkinson is good enough for me. But you will bring me the document?'

'The day after to-morrow,' said Miss Martin, and with that assurance Merton had to be content.

Sir Josiah was almost equally famous in the world as a physician and, in a smaller but equally refined circle, as a virtuoso and collector of objects of art. His opinions about the beneficent effects of vaccination were known to be at the opposite pole from those of the intelligent population of Bulcester.

On the next day but one Miss Martin again entertained Merton at her club, and demurely presented him with three documents. These were Mr. Warren's invitation, her reply in acceptance, and a formal signed statement by Sir Josiah that her scheme was perfectly harmless, and commanded his admiring approval.

'Now!' said Miss Martin.

'I own that I don't like it,' said Merton. 'Logan thinks that it is all right, but Logan is a born conspirator. However, as you are set on it, and as Sir Josiah's opinion carries great weight, you may go. But be very careful. Have you written your lecture?'

'Here is the scenario,' said Miss Martin, handing a typewritten synopsis to Merton.

'USE AND ABUSE OF NOVELS.

'All good things capable of being abused. Alcohol not one of these; alcohol *always* pernicious. Fiction, on the other hand, a good thing. Antiquity of fiction. In early days couched in verse. Civilisation prefers prose. Fiction, from the earlier ages, intended to convey Moral Instruction. Opinion of Aristotle defended against that of Plato. Morality in mediaeval Romance. Criticism of Mr. Frederic Harrison. Opinion of Moliere. Yet French novels usually immoral, and why. Remarks on Popery. To be avoided. Morality of Richardson and of Sir Walter Scott. Impropriety re-introduced by Charlotte Bronte. Unwillingness of Lecturer to dwell on this Topic. The Novel is now the whole of Literature. The people have no time to read anything else. Responsibilities of the Novelist as a Teacher. The Novel the proper vehicle of Theological, Scientific, Social, and Political Instruction. Mr. Hall Caine, Miss Corelli. Fallacy of thinking that the Novel should Amuse. Abuse of the Novel as a source of mischievous and false Opinions. Case of *The Woman Who Did*. Sacredness of Marriage. Study of the Novel becomes an abuse if it leads to the Neglect of the Morning and Evening Newspapers. Sir Walter Besant on the Novel. None but the newest Novels ought to be read. Mr. W. D. Howells on this subject. Experience of the Lecturer as a Novelist. Gratifying letters from persons happily influenced by the Lecturer. Anecdotes. Case of Miss A— C—. Case of Mr. J— R—. Unhappy Endings demoralising. Marriage the true End of the Novel, but the beginning of the happy life. Lecturer wishes her audience happy Endings and true Beginnings. Conclusion.'

Andrew Lang

'Will *that* do?' asked Miss Martin anxiously.

'Yes, if you don't exceed your plan, or run into chaff.'

'I won't,' said Miss Martin. 'It is all chaff, but they won't see it.'

'I think I would drop that about Popery,' said Merton—'it may lead to letters in the newspapers; and *do* be awfully careful about impropriety in novels.'

'I'll put in "Vice to be Condemned, not Described,"' said Miss Martin, pencilling a note on the margin of her paper.

'That seems safe,' said Merton. 'But it cuts out some of our most powerful teachers.'

'Serve them right!' said Miss Martin. 'Teachers! the arrant humbugs.'

'You will report at once on your return?' said Merton. 'I shall be on tenter-hooks till I see you again. If I knew what you are really about, I'd take counsel's opinion. Medical opinion does not satisfy me: I want legal.'

'How nervous you are!' said Miss Martin. 'Counsel would be rather stuck up, I think; it is a new kind of case,' and the lady laughed in an irritating way. 'I'll tell you what I'll do,' she said. 'I'll telegraph to you on the Monday morning after the lecture. If everything goes well, I'll telegraph, "Happy ending." If anything goes wrong—but it can't—I'll telegraph, "Unhappy ending."'

'If you do, I shall be off to Callao.

'*On no condition*

*Is Extradition
Allowed in Callao*!'

said Merton.

'But if there is any uncertainty—and there *may* be,' said Miss Martin, 'I'll telegraph, "Will report."'

* * * * *

Merton passed a miserable week of suspense and perplexity of mind. Never had he been so imprudent; he felt sure of that, and it was the only thing of which he did feel sure. The newspapers contained bulletins of an epidemic of smallpox at Bulcester. How would that work into the plot? Then the high animal spirits and daring fancy of Miss Martin might carry her into undreamed-of adventures.

'But they won't let her have even a glass of champagne,' reflected Merton. 'One glass makes her reckless.'

It was with a trembling hand that Merton, about ten on the Monday morning, took the telegraphic envelope of Fate.

'I can't face it,' he said to Logan. 'Read the message to me.' Merton was unmanned!

Logan carelessly opened the envelope and read:

'*Happy ending, but awfully disappointed. Will call at one o'clock.*'

'Oh, thanks to all gracious Powers,' said Merton falling limply on to a sofa. 'Ring, Logan, and order a small whisky-and-soda.'

'I won't,' said Logan. 'Horrid bad habit. Would you like me to send out for smelling-salts? Be a man, Merton! Pull yourself together!'

'You don't know that awful girl,' said Merton, slowly recovering self- control. 'However, as she is disappointed though the ending is happy, her infernal plan must have been miscarried, whatever it was. It *must* be all right, though I sha'n't be quite happy till I see her. I am no coward, Logan' (and Merton was later to prove that he possessed coolness and audacity in no common measure), 'but it is the awful sense of responsibility. She is quite capable of getting us into the newspapers.'

'You funk being laughed at,' said Logan.

Merton lay on the sofa, smoking too many cigarettes, till, punctually at one o'clock, a peal at the bell announced the arrival of Miss Martin. She entered, radiant, smiling, and in her costume of innocence she looked like a sylph.

'It is all right—they are engaged, with Mr. Warren's full approval,' she exclaimed.

'Were we on the stage, I should embrace you!' exclaimed Merton rapturously.

'We are not on the stage,' replied Miss Martin demurely. 'And *I* have no occasion to congratulate myself. My plot did not come off; never had a look in. Do you want to be vaccinated? If so, shake hands,' and Miss Martin extended her own hands ungloved.

'I do not want to be vaccinated,' said Merton.

'Then don't shake hands,' said Miss Martin.

'What on earth do you mean?' asked Merton.

'Look there!' said the lady, lifting her hand to his eyes. Merton kissed it.

'Oh, *take care!*' shrieked Miss Martin. 'It would be awkward—on the lips. Do you see my ring?'

Merton and Logan examined her ring. It was a beautiful *cinque cento* jewel in white and blue enamel, with a high gold top containing a pointed ruby.

'It's very pretty,' said Merton—'quite of the best period. But what is the mystery?'

'It is a poison ring of the Borgias,' said Miss Martin. 'I borrowed it from Sir Josiah Wilkinson. If it scratched you' (here she exhibited the mechanism of the jewel), 'why, there you are!'

'Where? Poisoned?'

'No! Vaccinated!' said Miss Martin. 'It is full of the stuff they vaccinate you with, but it is quite safe as far as the old poison goes. Sir Josiah sterilised it, in case of accidents, before he put in the glycerinated lymph. My own idea! He was delighted. Shall I shake hands with the office-boy?—it might do him good—or would Kutuzoff give a paw?'

Kutuzoff was the Russian cat.

'By no means—not for worlds,' said Merton. 'Kutuzoff is a Conscientious Objector. But were you going to shake hands with Miss Truman with that horrible ring? Sacred emblems enamelled on it,' said Merton, gingerly examining the jewel.

'No; I was not going to do that,' replied Miss Martin. 'My idea was to acquire the confidence of the lover—the younger Mr. Warren—explain to him how the thing works, lend it to him, and then let him press his Jane's wrist with it in some shady arbour. Then his Jane would have been all that the heart of Mr. Warren *pere* could desire. But it did not come off.'

'Thank goodness!' ejaculated Merton. 'There might have been an awful row. I don't know what the offence would have been in the eye of the law. Vaccinating a Conscientious Objector, without consent, yet without violence,—what would the law say to *that*?'

'We might make it *hamesucken under trust* in Scotland,' said Logan, 'if it was done on the premises of the young lady's domicile.'

'We have not that elegant phrase in England,' said Merton. 'Perhaps it would have been a common assault; but, anyhow, it would have got into the newspapers. Never again be officer of mine, Miss Martin.'

'But how did all end happily?' asked Logan.

'Why, *you* may call it happily and so may the lovers, but *I* call it very disappointing,' said Miss Martin.

'Tell us all about it!' cried Logan.

'Well, I went down, simple as you see me.'

'*Simplex munditiis*!' said Merton.

'And was met at the station by young Mr. Warren. His father, with the wisdom of a Nonconformist serpent, had sent him alone to make my acquaintance and be fascinated. My things were put on a four-wheeler. I was all young enthusiasm in the manner of *The Young Girl*. He was a good-looking boy enough, though in a bowler hat, with turn-down collar. But he was gloomy. I was curious about the public buildings, ecstatic about the town hall, and a kind of Moeso-Gothic tabernacle (if it was not Moeso-Gothic in style I don't know what it was) where the Rev. Mr. Truman holds forth. But I could not waken him up, he seemed miserable. I soon found out the reason. The placards of the local newspapers shrieked in big type with

SPREAD OF SMALLPOX.
135 CASES.

When I saw that I took young Mr. Warren's hand.'

'Were you wearing the ring?' asked Merton.

'No; it was in my dressing-bag. I said, "Mr. Warren, I know what care clouds your brow. You are brooding over the fate of the young, the fair, the beloved—the unvaccinated. I know the story of your heart."

'"How the D— I mean, how do you know, Miss Martin, about my private affairs?"

'"A little bird has told me," I said (style of *The Young Girl*, you know). "I have friends in Bulcester who esteem you. No, I must not mention names, but I come, not too late, I hope, to bring you security. She shall be preserved from this awful scourge, and you shall be her preserver." He wanted to know how it was to be done, of course, and after taking his word of honour for secrecy, I told him that the remedy would lie in his own hands, showed him the ring, and taught him how to work it. Mr. Squeers,' went on Miss Martin, 'had never wopped a boy in a cab before, and I had never beheld a scene of passionate emotion before—in a four-wheeler. He called me his preserver, he said that I was an angel, he knelt at my feet, and, if we had been on the stage—as Mr. Merton said—'

'And were you on the stage?' asked Merton.

'That is neither here nor there. It was an instructive experience, and you little know the treasures of passion that may lie concealed in the heart of a young oilcloth manufacturer.'

'Happy young oilcloth manufacturer!' murmured Merton.

'They are both happy, but I did not manage my fortunate conclusion in my own way. When young Mr. Warren had moderated the transports of his gratitude we were in the suburbs of Bulcester, where the mill-owners live in houses of the most promiscuous architecture: Tudor, Jacobean, Queen Anne, Bedford Park Queen Anne, *chalets*, Chineseries, "all standing naked in the open air," for the trees have not grown up round them yet. Then we came to a gate without a lodge, the cabman got down and opened it, and we were in the visible presence of Mr. Warren's villa. The style is the Scottish Baronial; all pepper-pots, gables and crowsteps.

'"What a lovely old place!" I said to my companion. "Have you secret passages and sliding panels and dark turnpike stairs? What a house for conspiracies! There is a real turret window; can't you fancy it suddenly shot up and the king's face popped out, very red, and bellowing, 'Treason!'"

'At that moment, when my imagination was in full career, the turret window *was* shot up, and a face, very red, with red whiskers, was popped out.

"'That is my father," said young Mr. Warren; and we alighted, and a very small maidservant opened the portals of the baronial hall, while the cabman carried up my trunk, and Mr. Warren, senior, greeted me in the hall.

"'Welcome to Bulcester!" he said, with a florid air, and "hoped James and I had made friends on the way," and then he actually winked! He is a widower, and I was dying for tea, but there we sat, and when the little maid came in, it was to say that a gentleman wanted to see Mr. Warren in the study. So he went out, and then, James being the victim of gratitude, I took my courage in both hands and asked if I might have tea. James said that they usually had it after the lecture was over, which would not be till nine, and that some people had been asked to meet me. Then I knew that I was got among a strange, outlandish race who eat strange meats and keep High Teas, and my spirit fainted within me.

"'Oh, Mr. James!" I said, "if you love me have a cup of tea and some bread-and-butter sent up to my room, and tell the maid to show me the way to it."

'So he sent for her, and she showed me to the best spare room, with oleographs of Highland scenery on the walls, and coloured Landseer prints, and tartan curtains, and everything made of ormolu that can be made of ormolu. In about twenty minutes the girl returned with tea and poached eggs and toast, and jam and marmalade. So I dressed for the lecture, which was to begin at eight—just when people ought to be dining—and came down into the drawing-room. The elder Mr. Warren was sitting alone, reading the *Daily News*, and he rose with an air of happy solemnity and shook hands again.

"'You can let James alone now, Miss Martin," he said, and he winked again, rubbed his hands, and grinned all over his expansive face.

'"Let James alone!" I said.

'"Yes; don't go upsetting the lad—he's not used to young ladies like you. You leave James to himself. James will do very well. I have a little surprise for James."

'He certainly had a considerable surprise for me, but I merely asked if it was James's birthday, which it was not.

'Luckily James entered. All his gloom was gone, thanks to me, and he was remarkably smiling and particularly attentive to myself. Mr. Warren seemed perplexed.

'"James, have you heard any good news?" he asked. "You seem very gay all of a sudden."

'James caught my eye.

'"No, father," he said. "What news do you mean? Anything in business? A large order from Sarawak?"

'Mr. Warren was silent, but presently took me into a corner on the pretence of showing me some horrible *objet d'art*—a treacly bronze.

'"I say," he said, "you must have made great play in the cab coming from the station. James looks a new man. I never would have guessed him to be so fickle. But, mind you, no more of it! Let James be—he will do very well."

'How was James to do very well? Why were my fascinations not to be exercised, as per contract? I began to suspect the worst, and I was thinking of nothing else while we drove to the premises of the Bulcester Literary Society. Could Jane have drowned herself out of the way, or taken smallpox, which might ruin her charms? Well, I had not a large audience, on account of fear of infection, I suppose, and all the people present wore the red badge, like Mr. Warren, only he wore one on each arm. This somewhat amazed me, but as I had never spoken in public before I was rather in a flutter. However, I conquered my girlish shyness, and if the audience was not large it was enthusiastic. When I came to the peroration about wishing them all happy endings and real beginnings of true life, don't you know, the audience actually rose at me, and cheered like anything. Then someone proposed, "Three cheers for young Warren," and they gave them like mad; I did not know why, nor did he: he looked quite pale. Then his father, with tears in his voice, proposed a vote of thanks to me, and said that he and the brave hearts of old Bulcester, his old friends and brothers in arms, were once more united; and the people stormed the platform and shook his hand and slapped him on the back. At last we got out by a back way, where our cab was waiting. Young Mr. Warren was as puzzled as myself, and his father was greatly overcome and sobbing in a corner. We got into the house, where people kept arriving, and at last a fine old clerical-looking bird entered with a red badge on one arm and a very pretty girl in white on the other. She had a red badge too.

'Young Mr. Warren, who was near me when they came in, gave a queer sort of cry, and then *I* understood! The girl was his Jane, and she *had* been vaccinated, also her father, that afternoon, owing to the awful panic the old man got into after reading the evening papers about the smallpox. The gentleman whom Mr. Warren went to see in the study, just after my arrival, had brought him this gratifying intelligence, and he had sent the gentleman back to ask the Trumans to a High Tea of reconciliation. The people at the lecture had heard of this, and that was why they cheered so for young Warren, because his affair was as commonly known to all Bulcester as that of Romeo and Juliet at Verona. They are hearty people at Bulcester, and not without elements of old

English romance.

'Old Mr. Warren publicly embraced Jane Truman, and then brought her and presented her to me as James's bride. We both cried a little, I think, and then we all sat down to High Tea, and I am scarcely yet the woman I used to be. It was a height! And a weight! And a length! After tea Mr. Warren made a speech, and said that Bulcester had come back to him, and I was afraid that he would brag dreadfully, but he did not; he was too happy, I think. And then Mr. Truman made a speech and said that though they felt obliged to own that they had come to the conclusion that though Anti-vaccination was a holy thing, still (in the circumstances) vaccination was good enough. But they yet clung to principles for which Hampden died on the field, and Russell on the scaffold, and many of their own citizens in bed! There must be no Coercion. Everyone who liked must be allowed to have smallpox as much as he pleased. All other issues were unimportant except that of freedom!

'Here I rose—I was rather excited—and said that I hoped the reverend speaker was not deserting the sacred principle of compulsory temperance? Would the speaker allow people freedom to drink? All other issues were unimportant compared with that of freedom, *except* the interest of depriving a poor man of his beer. To catch smallpox was a Briton's birthright, but not to take a modest quencher. No freedom to drink! "Down with the drink!" I cried, and drained my tea-cup, and waved it, amidst ringing cheers. Mr. Truman admitted that there were exceptions—one exception, at least. Disease must be free to all, not alcohol nor Ritualism. He thanked his young friend the gifted lecturer for recalling him to his principles.

'The principles of the good old cause, the Puritan cause, were as pure as glycerinated lymph, and he proposed to found a

Liberal Vaccinationist League. They are great people for leagues at Bulcester, and they like the initials L. V. L. There was no drinking of toasts, for there was nothing to drink them in, and—do you know, Mr. Merton?—I think it must be nearly luncheon time.'

'Champagne appears to me to be indicated,' said Merton, who rang the bell and then summoned Miss Blossom from her typewriting.

'We have done nothing,' Merton said, 'but heaven only knows what we have escaped in the adventure of the Lady Novelist and the Vaccinationist.'

On taking counsel's opinion, Merton learned, with a shudder, that if young Warren had used the Borgia ring, and if Jane had resented it, he might have been indicted for a common assault, under 24 and 25 Victoria, cap. 100, sec. 24, for 'unlawfully and maliciously administering a noxious thing with intent to annoy.'

'I don't think she could have proved the intent to annoy,' said the learned counsel.

'You don't know a Bulcester jury as it was before the epidemic,' said Merton. 'And I might have been an accessory before the fact, and, anyhow, we should all have got into the newspapers.'

Miss Martin was the most admired of the bridesmaids at the Warren-Truman marriage.

X

ADVENTURE OF THE FAIR AMERICAN

I

The Prize of a Lady's Hand

'Yes, I guess that Pappa *was* reckoned considerable of a crank. A great educational reformer, and a progressive Democratic stalwart, *that* is the kind of hair-pin Pappa was! But it is awkward for me, some.'

These remarks, though of an obsolete and exaggerated transatlantic idiom, were murmured in the softest of tones, in the most English of silken accents, by the most beautiful of young ladies. She occupied the client's chair in Merton's office, and, as she sat there and smiled, Merton acknowledged to himself that he had never met a client so charming and so perplexing.

Miss McCabe had been educated, as Merton knew, at an aristocratic Irish convent in Paris, a sanctuary of old names and old creeds. This was the plan of her late father (spoken of by her as Pappa), an educational reformer of eccentric ideas, who, though of ancient (indeed royal) Irish descent, was of American birth. The young lady had thus acquired abroad, much against her will, that kind of English accent which some of her countrywomen reckon 'affected.' But her intense patriotism had induced her to study, in the works of American humourists, and to reproduce in her discourse, the flowers of speech of which a specimen has been presented. The national accent was beyond her, but at least she could be true to what she (erroneously) believed to be the national idiom.

'Your case is peculiar,' said Merton thoughtfully, 'and scarcely within our province. As a rule our clients are the parents, guardians, or children of persons entangled in undesirable engagements. But you, I understand, are dissatisfied with the matrimonial conditions imposed by the will of the late Mr. McCabe?'

'I want to take my own pick out of the crowd—' said Miss McCabe.

'I can readily understand,' said Merton, bowing, 'that the throng of wooers is enormous,' and he vaguely thought of Penelope.

'The scheme will be popular. It will hit our people right where they live,' said Miss McCabe, not appropriating the compliment. 'You see Pappa struck ile early, and struck it often. He was what our Howells calls a "multimillionaire," and I'm his only daughter. Pappa loved *me*, but he loved the people better. Guess Pappa was not mean, not worth a cent. He was a white man!'

Miss McCabe, with a glow of lovely enthusiasm, contemplated the unprecedented whiteness of the paternal character.

'"What the people want," Pappa used to say, "is education.

They want it short, and they want it striking." That was why he laid out five millions on his celebrated Museum of Freaks, with a staff of competent professors and lecturers. "The McCabe Museum of Natural Varieties, lectures and all, is open gratuitously to the citizens of our Republic, and to intelligent foreigners." That was how Pappa put it. *I* say that he dead-headed creation!'

'Truly Republican munificence,' said Merton, 'worthy of your great country.'

'Well, I should smile,' said Miss McCabe.

'But—excuse my insular ignorance—I do not exactly understand how a museum of freaks, admirably organised as no doubt it is, contributes to the cause of popular education.'

'You have museums even in London?' asked Miss McCabe.

Merton assented.

'Are they not educational?'

'The British Museum is mainly used by the children of the poor, as a place where they play a kind of subdued hide-and-seek,' said Merton.

'That's because they are not interested in tinned Egyptian corpses and broken Greek statuary ware,' answered the fair Republican. 'Now, Mr. Merton, did you ever see or hear of a *popular* museum, a museum that the People would give its cents to see?'

'I have heard of Mr. Barnum's museum,' said Merton.

'That's the idea: it is right there,' said Miss McCabe. 'But old man Barnum was not scientific. He saw what our people wanted, but he did not see, Pappa said, how to educate them through their natural instincts. Barnum's mermaid was not genuine business. It confused the popular mind, and fostered superstition—and got found out. The result was scepticism, both religious and scientific. Now, Pappa used to argue, the lives of our citizens are monotonous. They see yellow dogs, say, but each yellow dog has only one tail. They see men and women, but almost all of them have only one head: and even a hand with six fingers is not common. This is why the popular mind runs into grooves. This causes what they call "the dead level of democracy." Even our men of genius, Pappa allowed (for he was a very fair-minded man), do not go ahead of the European ticket, but rather the reverse. Your Tennyson has the inner tracks of our Longfellow: your Thackeray gives our Bertha Runkle his dust. The papers called Pappa unpatriotic, and a bad American. But he was *not*: he was a white man. When he saw his country's faults he put his finger on them, right there, and tried to cure them.'

'A noble policy,' murmured Merton.

Miss McCabe was really so pretty and unusual, that he did not care how long she was in coming to the point.

'Well, Pappa argued that there was more genius, or had been since the Declaration of Independence, even in England, than in the States. "And why?" he asked. "Why, because they have more *variety* in England. Things are not all on one level there—"'

'Our dogs have only one tail apiece,' said Merton, 'in spite of the proverb "*as proud as a dog with two tails*," and a plurality of heads is unusual even among British subjects.'

'Yes,' answered Miss McCabe, 'but you have varieties among

yourselves. You have a King and a Queen; and your peerage is rich in differentiated species. A Baronet is not a Marquis, nor is a Duke an Earl.'

'He may be both,' said Merton, but Miss McCabe continued to expose the parental philosophy.

'Now Pappa would not hear of aristocratic distinctions in our country. He was a Hail Columbia man, on the Democratic ticket. But *something* is wanted, he said, to get us out of grooves, and break the monotony. That something, said Pappa, Nature has mercifully provided in Freaks. The citizens feel this, unconsciously: that's why they spend their money at Barnum's. But Barnum was not scientific, and Barnum was not straight about his mermaid. So Pappa founded his Museum of Natural Varieties, all of them honest Injun. Here the lecturers show off the freaks, and explain how Nature works them, and how she can always see them and go one better. We have the biggest gold nugget and the weeniest cunning least gold nugget; the biggest diamond and the smallest diamond; the tallest man and the smallest man; the whitest negro and the yellowest red man in the world. We have the most eccentric beasts, and the queerest fishes, and everything is explained by lecturers of world-wide reputation, on the principles of evolution, as copyrighted by our Asa Gray and our Agassiz. *That* is what Pappa called popular education, and it hits our citizens right where they live.'

Miss McCabe paused, in a flush of filial and patriotic enthusiasm. Merton inwardly thought that among the queerest fishes the late Mr. McCabe must have been pre-eminent. But what he said was, 'The scheme is most original. Our educationists (to employ a term which they do not disdain), such as Mr. Herbert Spencer, Sir Joshua Fitch, and others, have I thought out nothing like this. Our capitalists never endow education on this more than imperial scale.'

'Guess they are scaly varmints!' interposed Miss McCabe.

Merton bowed his acquiescence in the sentiment.

'But,' he went on, 'I still do not quite understand how your own prospects in life are affected by Mr. McCabe's most original and, I hope, promising experiment?'

'Pappa loved me, but he loved his country better, and taught me to adore her, and be ready for any sacrifice.' Miss McCabe looked straight at Merton, like an Iphigenia blended with a Joan of Arc.

'I do sincerely trust that no sacrifice is necessary,' said Merton. 'The circumstances do not call for so—unexampled a victim.'

'I am to be Lady Principal of the museum when I come to the age of twenty- five: that is, in six years,' said Miss McCabe proudly. 'You don't call *that* a sacrifice?'

Merton wanted to say that the most magnificent of natural varieties would only be in its proper place. But the *man of business* and the manager of a great and beneficent association overcame the mere amateur of beauty, and he only said that the position of Lady Principal was worthy of the ambition of a patriot, and a friend of the species.

'Well, I reckon! But a clause in Pappa's will is awkward for me, some. It is about my marriage,' said Miss McCabe bravely.

Merton assumed an air of grave interest.

'Pappa left it in his will that I was to marry the man (under the age of five-and-thirty, and of unimpeachable character and education) who should discover, and add to the museum, the most original and unheard-of natural variety, whether found in the Old or the New World.'

Merton could scarcely credit the report of his ears.

'Would you oblige me by repeating that statement?' he said, and Miss McCabe repeated it in identical terms, obviously quoting textually from the will.

'Now I understand your unhappy position,' said Merton, thoroughly agreeing with the transatlantic critics who had pronounced the late Mr. McCabe 'considerable of a crank.' 'But this is far too serious a matter for me—for our Association. I am no legist, but I am convinced that, at least British, and I doubt not American, law would promptly annul a testatory clause so utterly unreasonable and unprecedented.'

'Unreasonable!' exclaimed Miss McCabe, rising to her feet with eyes of flame, 'I am my father's daughter, and his wish is my law, whatever the laws that men make may say.'

Her affectation of slang had fallen off; she was absolutely natural now, and entirely in earnest.

Merton rose also.

'One moment,' he said. 'It would be impertinence in me to express my admiration of you—of what you say. As the question is not a legal one (in such I am no fit adviser) I shall think myself honoured if you will permit me to be of any service in the circumstances. They are less unprecedented than I hastily supposed. History records many examples of fathers, even of royal rank, who have attached similar conditions to the disposal of their daughters' hands.'

Merton was thinking of the kings in the treatises of Monsieur Charles Perrault, Madame d'Aulnoy, and other historians of Fairyland; of monarchs who give their daughters to the bold adventurers that bring the smallest dog, or the singing rose, or the horse magical.

'What you really want, I think,' he went on, as Miss McCabe resumed her seat, 'is to have your choice, as you said, among the competitors?'

'Yes,' replied the fair American, 'that is only natural.'

'But then,' said Merton, 'much depends on who decides as to the merits of the competitors. With whom does the decision rest?'

'With the people.'

'With the people?'

'Yes, with the popular vote, as expressed through the newspaper that my father founded—*The Yellow Flag*. The public is to see the exhibits, the new varieties of nature, and the majority of votes is to carry the day. "Trust the people!" that was Pappa's word.'

'Then anyone who chooses, of the age, character, and education stipulated under the clause in the will, may go and bring in whatever variety of nature he pleases and take his chance?'

'That is it all the time,' said the client. 'There is a trust, and the trustees, friends of Pappa's, decide on the qualifications of the young men who enter for the competition. If the trustees are satisfied they allot money for expenses out of the exploration fund, so that nobody may be stopped because he is poor.'

'There will be an enormous throng of competitors in these conditions—and with such a prize,' Merton could not help adding.

'I reckon the trustees are middling particular. They'll weed them out.'

'Is there any restriction on the nationality of the competitors?' asked Merton, on whom an idea was dawning.

'Only members of the English speaking races need apply,' said Miss McCabe. 'Pappa took no stock in Spaniards or Turks.'

'The voters will be prejudiced in favour of their own fellow citizens?' asked Merton. 'That is only natural.'

'Trust the people,' said Miss McCabe. 'The whole thing is to be kept as dark as a blind coloured person hunting in a dark cellar for a black cat that is not there.'

'A truly Miltonic illustration,' said Merton.

'The advertisement for competitors will be carefully worded, so as to attract only young men of science. The young men are not to be told about *me*: the prize is in dollars, "with other advantages to be later specified." The varieties found are to be conveyed to a port abroad, not yet named, and shipped for New York in a steamer belonging to the McCabe Trust.'

'Then am I to understand that the conditions affecting your marriage are still an entire secret?'

'That is so,' said Miss McCabe, 'and I guess from what the

marchioness told me, your reference, that you can keep a secret.'

'To keep secrets is the very essential of my vocation,' said Merton.

But *this* secret, as will be seen, he did not absolutely keep.

'The arrangements,' he added, 'are most judicious.'

'Guess Pappa was 'cute,' said Miss McCabe, relapsing into her adopted mannerisms.

'I think I now understand the case in all its bearings,' Merton went on. 'I shall give it my serious consideration. Perhaps I had better say no more at present, but think over the matter. You remain in town for the season?'

'Guess we've staked out a claim in Berkeley Square,' said Miss McCabe, 'an agreeable location.' She mentioned the number of the house.

'Then we are likely to meet now and then,' said Merton, 'and I trust that I may be permitted to wait on you occasionally.'

Miss McCabe graciously assented; her chaperon, Lady Rathcoffey, was summoned by her from the inner chamber and the society of Miss Blossom, the typewriter; the pair drove away, and Merton was left to his own reflections.

'I do not know what can be done for her,' he thought, 'except to see that there is at least one eligible man, a gentleman, among the crowd of competitors, and that he is a likely man to win the beautiful prize. And that man is Bude, by Jove, if he wants to win it.'

The Earl of Bude, whose name at once occurred to Merton, was a remarkable personage. The world knew him as rich, handsome, happy, and a mighty hunter of big game. They knew not the mysterious grief that for years had gnawed at his heart. Why did not Bude marry? No woman could say. The world, moreover, knew not, but Merton did, that Lord Bude was the mysterious Mr. Jones Harvey, who contributed the most original papers to the Proceedings of the Geographical and Zoological Societies, and who had conferred many strange beasts on the Gardens of the latter learned institution. The erudite papers were read, the eccentric animals were conferred, in the name of Mr. Jones Harvey. They came from outlandish addresses in the ends of the earth, but, in the flesh, Jones Harvey had been seen by no man, and his secret had been confided to Merton only, to Logan, and two other school friends. He did good to science by stealth, and blushed at the idea of being a F.R.S. There was no show of science about Bude, and nothing exotic, except the singular circumstance that, however he happened to be dressed, he always wore a ring, or pin, or sleeve links set with very ugly and muddy looking pearls. From these ornaments Lord Bude was inseparable; to chaff about presents from dusky princesses on undiscovered shores he was impervious. Even Merton did not know the cause of his attachment to these ungainly jewels, or the dark memory of mysterious loss with which they were associated.

Merton's first care was to visit the divine Althaea, Mrs. Brown-Smith, and other ladies of his acquaintance. Their cards were deposited at the claim staked out by Miss McCabe in Berkeley Square, and that young lady soon 'went everywhere,' and publicly confessed that she 'was having a real lovely time.' By a little diplomacy Lord Bude was brought acquainted with Miss McCabe. She consented to overlook his possession of a coronet; titles were, to this heroine, not marvels (as to some of her countrywomen and ours), but rather matters of indifference, scarcely even suggesting hostile prejudice. The observers in society, mothers and maids, and the chroniclers of fashion, soon perceived that there was at least a marked *camaraderie* between *the elegant aristocrat*, hitherto indifferent to woman, untouched, as was deemed, by love, and the lovely Child of Freedom. Miss McCabe sat by him while he drove his coach; on the roof of his drag at Lord's; and of his houseboat at Henley, where she fainted when the crew of Johns Hopkins University, U. S., was defeated by a length by Balliol (where Lord Bude had been the favourite pupil of the great Master). Merton remarked these tokens of friendship with approval. If Bude could be induced to enter for the great competition, and if he proved successful, there seemed no reason to suppose that Miss McCabe would be dissatisfied with the People's choice.

Towards the end of the season, and in Bude's smoking-room, about five in the July morning after a ball at Eglintoun House, Merton opened his approaches. He began, cautiously, from talk of moors and forests; he touched on lochs, he mentioned the Highland traditions of water bulls (which haunt these meres); he spoke of the *Beathach mor Loch Odha*, a legendary animal of immeasurable length. The *Beathach* has twelve feet; he has often been heard crashing through the ice in the nights of winter. These tales the narrator has gleaned from the lips of the Celtic peasantry of Letter Awe.

'I daresay he does break the ice,' said Bude. 'In the matter of cryptic survivals of extinct species I can believe a good deal.'

'The sea serpent?' asked Merton.

'Seen him thrice,' said Bude.

'Then why did not Jones Harvey weigh in with a letter to *Nature*?'

'Jones Harvey has a scientific reputation to look after, and knows he would be laughed at. That's the kind of hair-pin *he* is,' said Bude, quoting Miss McCabe. 'By Jove, Merton, that girl—' and he paused.

'Yes, she is pretty,' said Merton.

'Pretty! I have seen the women of the round world—before I went to—well, never mind where, I used to think the Poles the most magnificent, but *she*—'

'Whips creation,' said Merton. 'But I,' he went on, 'am rather more interested in these other extraordinary animals. Do you seriously believe, with your experience, that some extinct species are—not extinct?'

'To be sure I do. The world is wide. But they are very shy. I once stalked a Bunyip, in Central Australia, in a lagoon. The natives said he was there: I watched for a week, squatting in the reeds, and in the grey of the seventh dawn I saw him.'

'Did you shoot?'

'No, I observed him through a field glass first.'

'What is the beggar like?'

'Much like some of the Highland water cattle, as described, but it is his ears they take for horns. Australia has no indigenous horned animal. He is, I should say, about nine feet long, marsupial (he rose breast high), and web-footed. I saw that when he dived. Other white men have seen him—Buckley, the convict, for one, when he lived among the blacks.'

'Buckley was not an accurate observer.'

'Jones Harvey is.'

'Any other queer beasts?'

'Of course, plenty. You have heard of the Mylodon, the gigantic Sloth? His bones, skin, and hair were lately found in a cave in Patagonia, with a lot of his fodder. You can see them at the British Museum in South Kensington. Primitive Patagonian man used the female of the species as a milch-cow. He was a genial friendly kind of brute, accessible to charm of manner and chopped hay. They fed him on that, in a domesticated state.'

'But he is extinct. Hesketh Pritchard went to look for a live Mylodon, and did not find him.'

'Did not know where to look,' said Bude.

'But you do?' asked Merton.

'Yes, I think so.'

'Then why don't you bring one over to the Zoo?'

'I may some day.'

'Are there any more survivors of extinct species?'

'Merton, is this an interview? Are you doing Mr. Jones Harvey at home for a picture paper?'

'No, I've dropped the Press,' said Merton, 'I ask in a spirit of scientific curiosity.'

Andrew Lang

'Well, there is the Dinornis, the Moa of New Zealand. A bird as big as the Roc in the "Arabian Nights."'

'Have you seen *him*?'

'No, but I have seen *her*, the hen bird. She was sitting on eggs. No man knows her nest but myself, and old Te-iki-pa, the chief medicine-man, or Tohunga, of the Maori King. The Moa's eyrie is in the King's country. It is a difficult country, and a dangerous business, if the cock Moa chances to come home.'

'Bude, is this worthy of an old friend, this *blague*?'

'Do you doubt my word?'

'If you give me your word I must believe—that you dreamed it.'

Then a strange thing happened.

Bude walked to a small case of instruments that stood on a table in the smoking-room. He unlocked it, took out a lancet, brought a Rhodian bowl from a shelf, and bared his arm.

'Do you want proof?'

'Proof that you saw a hen Moa sitting?' asked Merton in amazement.

'Not exactly, but proof that Te-iki-pa knew a thing or two, quite as out of the way as the habitat of the Moa.'

'What do you want me to do?'

'Bare your arm, and hold it over the bowl.'

The room was full of the yellow dusky light of an early summer morning in London. Outside the heavy carts were rolling by: in full civilisation the scene was strange.

'The Blood Covenant?' asked Merton.

Bude nodded.

Merton turned up his cuff, Bude let a little blood drop into the bowl, then performed the same operation on his own arm.

'This is all rot,' he said, 'but without this I cannot show you, by virtue of my oath to Te-iki-pa, what I mean to show you. Now repeat after me what I am going to say.'

He spoke a string of words, among which Merton, as he repeated them, could only recognise *mana* and *atua*. The vowel sounds were as in Italian.

'Now these words you must never report to any one, without my permission.'

'Not likely,' said Merton, 'I only remember two of them, and these I knew before.'

'All right,' said Bude.

He then veiled his face in a piece of silk that lay on a sofa, and rapidly, in a low voice, chanted a kind of hymn in a tongue unknown to Merton. All this he did with a bored air, as if he thought the performance a superfluous mummery.

'Now what shall I show you? Something simple. Look at the bookcase, and think of any book you may want to consult.'

Merton thought of the volume in M. of the *Encyclopaedia Britannica*. The volume slowly slid from the shelf, glided through the air to Merton, and gently subsided on the table near him, open at the word *Moa*.

Merton walked across to the bookcase, took all the volumes from the shelf, and carefully examined the backs and sides for springs and mechanical advantages. There were none.

'Not half bad!' he said, when he had completed his investigation.

'You are satisfied that Te-iki-pa knew something? If you had seen what I have seen, if you had seen the three days dead—' and Bude shivered slightly.

'I have seen enough. Do you know how it is done?'

'No.'

'Well, a miracle is not what you call logical proof, but I believe that you did see the Moa, and a still more extraordinary bird, Te-iki-pa.'

'Yes, they talk of strange beasts, but "nothing is stranger than man." Did you ever hear of the Berbalangs of Cagayan Sulu?'

'Never in my life,' said Merton.

'Heaven preserve me from *them*,' said Bude, and he gently stroked the strange muddy pearls in the sleeve-links on his loose shirt-cuff. 'Angels and ministers of grace defend us,' he exclaimed, crossing himself (he was of the old faith), and he fell silent.

It was a moment of emotion. Six silvery strokes were sounded from a little clock on the chimney-piece. The hour of confidences had struck.

'Bude, you are serious about Miss McCabe?' asked Merton.

'I mean to put it to the touch at Goodwood.'

'No use!' said Merton.

Bude changed colour.

'Are *you*?'

'No,' interrupted Merton. 'But she is not free.'

'There is somebody in America? Nobody here, I think.'

'It is hardly that,' said Merton. 'Can you listen to rather a long story? I'll cut it as much as possible. You must remember that I am practically breaking my word of honour in telling you this. My honour is in your hands.'

'Fire away,' said Bude, pouring a bottle of Apollinaris water into a long tumbler, and drinking deep.

Merton told the tale of Miss McCabe's extraordinary involvement, and of the wild conditions on which her hand was to be won. 'And as to her heart, I think,' he added, 'if you pull off the prize—

 If my heart by signs can tell, Lordling, I have marked her daily, And I think she loves thee well.'

'Thank you for that, old cock,' replied the peer, shaking Merton's hand. He had recovered from his emotion.

'I'm on,' he added, after a moment's silence, 'but I shall enter as Jones Harvey.'

'His name and his celebrated papers will impress the trustees,' said Merton. 'Now what variety of nature shall you go for? Wild *men* count. Shall you fetch a Berbalang of what do you call it?'

Bude shuddered. 'Not much,' he said. 'I think I shall fetch a Moa.'

'But no steamer could hold that gigantic denizen of the forests.'

'You leave that to Jones Harvey. Jones is 'cute, some,' he said, reminiscent of the adored one, and he fell into a lover's reverie.

He was aroused by Merton's departure: he finished the Apollinaris water, took a bath, and went to bed.

II

The Adventure of the Muddy Pearls

The Earl of Bude had meant to lay his heart, coronet, and other possessions, real and personal, before the tiny feet of the fair American at Goodwood. But when he learned from Merton the involvements of this heiress and paragon, that her hand depended on the choice of the people, that the choice of the people was to settle on the adventurer who brought to New York the rarest of nature's varieties, the earl honourably held his peace. Yet he and the object of his love were constantly meeting, on the yachts and in the country houses of their friends, the aristocracy, and, finally, at shooting lodges in the Highlands. Their position, as the Latin Delectus says concerning the passion of love in general, was 'a strange thing, and full of anxious fears.' Bude could not declare himself, and Miss McCabe, not knowing that he knew her situation, was constantly wondering why he did not speak. Between fear of letting her secret show itself in a glance or a blush and hope of listening to the words which she desired to hear, even though she could not answer them as her heart prompted, she was unhappy. Bude could not resist the temptation to be with her—indeed he argued to himself that, as her suitor and an adventurer about to risk himself in her cause, he had a right to be near her. Meanwhile Merton was the confidant of both of the perplexed lovers; at least Miss

McCabe (who, of course, told him nothing about Bude) kept him apprised as to the conduct of her trustees.

They had acted with honourable caution and circumspection. Their advertisements guardedly appealed to men of daring and of scientific distinction under the age of thirty-five. A professorship might have been in view for all that the world could see, if the world read the advertisements. Perhaps it was something connected with the manufacture of original explosives, for daring is not usually required in the learned. The testimonials and printed works of applicants were jealously scrutinised. At personal interviews with competitors similar caution was observed. During three weeks in August the papers announced that Lord Bude was visiting the States; arrangements about a yachting match in the future were his pretence. He returned, he came to Scotland, and it was in a woodland path beside the Lochy that his resolution failed, and that he spoke to Miss McCabe. They were walking home together from the river in the melancholy and beautiful close of a Highland day in September. Behind them the gillies, at a respectful distance, were carrying the rods and the fish. The wet woods were fragrant, the voice of the stream was deepening, strange lights came and went on moor and hills and the distant loch. It was then that Bude opened his heart. He first candidly explained that his heart, he had supposed, was dead—buried on a distant and a deadly shore.

'I reckon there's a lost Lenore most times,' Miss McCabe had replied to this confession.

But, though never to be forgotten, the memory of the lost one, Bude averred, was now merged in the light of a living love; his heart was no longer tenanted only by a shadow.

The heart of Miss McCabe stood still for a moment, her

cheek paled, but the gallant girl was true to herself, to her father's wish, to her native land, to the flag. She understood her adorer.

'Guess *I*'m bespoke,' said Miss McCabe abruptly.

'You are another's! Oh, despair!' exclaimed the impassioned earl.

'Yes, I reckon I'm the Bride of Seven, like the girl in the poem.'

'The Bride of Seven?' said Bude.

'One out of *that* crowd will call me his,' said Miss McCabe, handing to her adorer the list, which she had received by mail a day or two earlier, of the accepted competitors. He glanced over the names.

1. Dr. Hiram P. Dodge, of the Smithsonian Institute.

2. Alfred Jenkins, F.R.S., All Souls College, Oxford.

3. Dr. James Rustler, Columbia University.

4. Howard Fry, M.A., Ph.D., Trinity College, Cambridge.

5. Professor Potter, F.R.S., University of St. Andrews.

6. Professor Wilkinson, University of Harvard.

7. Jones Harvey, F.G.S., London, England.

'In Heaven's name,' asked the earl, 'what means this mystification? Miss McCabe, Melissa, do not trifle with me. Is this part of the great American Joke? You are playing it pretty low down on me, Melissa!' he ended, the phrase being one of those with which she had made him familiar.

She laughed hysterically: 'It's honest Injun,' she said, and in the briefest terms she told him (what he knew very well) the conditions on which her future depended.

'They are a respectable crowd, I don't deny it,' she went on, 'but, oh, how dull! That Mr. Jenkins, I saw him at your Commemoration. He gave us luncheon, and showed us dry old bones of beasts and savage notions at the Museum. I *druther* have been on the creek,' by which name she intended the classical river Isis.

'Dr. Hiram P. Dodge is one of our rising scientists, a boss of the Smithsonian Institute. Well, Washington is a finer location than Oxford! Dr. Rustler is a crank; he thinks he can find a tall talk mummy that speaks an unknown tongue.'

'A Toltec mummy? Ah,' said Bude, 'I know where to find one of *them*.'

'Find it then, Alured!' exclaimed Miss McCabe, blushing scarlet and turning aside. 'But you are not on the list. You are an idler, and not scientific, not worth a red cent. There, I've given myself away!' She wept.

They were alone, beneath the walls of a crumbling fortalice of Lochiel. The new risen moon saw Bude embrace her and dry her tears. A nameless blissful hope awakened in the fair American; help there *must* be, she thought, with these strong arms around her.

She rapidly disposed of the remaining names: of Howard Fry, who had a red beard; of Professor Potter of St. Andrews, whose accent was Caledonian; of Wilkinson, an ardent but unalluring scientist. 'As for Jones Harvey,' she said, 'I've canvassed everywhere, and I can't find anybody that ever saw him. I am more afraid of him than of all the other galoots; I don't know why.'

'He is reckoned very learned,' said Bude, 'and has not been thought ill-looking.'

'Do tell!' said Miss McCabe.

'Oh, Melissa, can you even *dream* of another in an hour like this?'

'Did you ever see Jones Harvey?'

'Yes, I have met him.'

'Do you know him well?'

'No man knows him better.'

'Can't you get him to stand out, and, Alured, can't you—fetch along that old tall talk mummy? He would hit our people, being American himself.'

'It is impossible. Jones Harvey will never stand out,' and Bude smiled.

By the telepathy of the affections Miss McCabe was slowly informed, especially as Bude's smile widened almost unbecomingly, while he gazed into the deeps of her golden eyes.

'Alured,' she exclaimed, '*that's* why you went to the States. *You*—are—Jones Harvey!'

'Secret for secret,' whispered the earl. 'We have both given ourselves away. Unknown to the world I *am* Jones Harvey; to live for you: to love you: to dare; if need be, to die for you.'

'Well, you surprise me!' said Miss McCabe.

* * * * *

The narrator is unwilling to dilate on the delights of a privileged affection. In this love affair neither of the lovers could feel absolutely certain that their affection *was* privileged. The fair American had her own secret scheme if her hopes were blighted. She *could* not then obey the paternal will: she would retire into the life religious, and, as Sister Anna, would strive to forget the sorrows of Melissa McCabe. Bude had his own hours of gloom.

'It is a six-to-one chance,' he said to Merton when they met.

'Better than that, I think,' said Merton. 'First, you know exactly what you are entered for. Do the others? When you saw the trustees in the States, did they tell you about the prize?'

'Not they. They spoke of a pecuniary reward which would be eminently satisfactory, and of the opportunity for research and distinction, and all expenses found. I said that I preferred to pay my own way, which surprised and pleased them a good deal.'

'Well, then, knowing the facts, and the lady, you have a far stronger motive than the other six.'

'That's true,' said Bude.

'Again, though the others are good men (not that I like Jenkins of All Souls), none of them has your experience and knowledge. Jones Harvey's testimonials would carry it if it were a question of election to a professorship.'

'You flatter me,' answered Bude.

'Lastly, did the trustees ask you if you were a married man?'

'No, by Jove, they didn't.'

'Well, nothing about the competitors being unmarried men occurs in the clause of McCabe's last will and testament. He took it for granted, the prize being what it is, that only bachelors were eligible. But he forgot to say so, in so many words, and the trustees did not go beyond the deed. Now, Dodge is married; Fry of Trinity is a married don; Rustler (I happen to know) is an engaged man, who can't afford to marry a charming girl in Detroit, Michigan; and Professor Potter has buried one wife, and wedded another. If Rustler is loyal to his plighted word, you have nobody against you but Wilkinson and old Jenkins of All Souls—a tough customer, I admit, though what a Stinks man like him has to do at All Souls I don't know.'

'I say, this is hard on the other sportsmen! What ought I to do? Should I tell them?'

'You can't: you have no official knowledge of their existence. You only know through Miss McCabe. You have just to sit tight.'

'It seems beastly unsportsmanlike,' said Bude.

'Wills are often most carelessly drafted,' answered Merton, 'and the usual consequences follow.'

'It is not cricket,' said Bude, and really he seemed much more depressed than elated by the reduction of the odds against him from 6 to 1 to 2 to 1.

This is the magnificent type of character produced by our British system of athletic sports, though it is not to be doubted that the spirit of Science, in the American gentlemen, would have been equally productive of the sense of fair play.

* * * * * *

A year, by the terms of McCabe's will, was allotted to the quest. Candidates were to keep the trustees informed as to their whereabouts. Six weeks before the end of the period the competitors would be instructed as to the port of rendezvous, where an ocean liner, chartered by the trustees, was to await them. Bude, as Jones Harvey, had obtained leave to sail his own steam yacht of 800 tons.

The earl's preparations were simple. He carried his usual stock of scientific implements, his usual armament, including two Maxim guns, and a package of considerable size and weight, which was stored in the hold. As to the preparations of the others he knew nothing, but Miss McCabe became aware that Rustler had not left the American continent. Concerning Jenkins, and the probable aim of his enterprise, the object of his quest, she gleaned information from a junior Fellow of All Souls, who was her slave, was indiscreet, and did not know how deeply concerned she was in the expeditions. But she never whispered a word of what she knew to her lover, not even in the hour of parting.

It was in an unnamed creek of the New Zealand coast, six weeks before the end of the appointed year, that Bude received a telegram in cipher from the trustees. Bearded, and in blue spectacles, clad rudely as a mariner, Bude was to all, except Logan, who had accompanied him, plain Jones Harvey. None could have recognised in his rugged aspect the elegant aristocrat of Mayfair.

Bude took the message from the hands of the Maori bearer. As he deciphered it his fingers trembled with eagerness. 'Oh, Heaven! Here is the Hand of Destiny!' he exclaimed, when he had read the message; and with pallid face he dropped into a deck-chair.

'No bad news?' asked Logan with anxiety.

'The port of rendezvous,' said Bude, much agitated. 'Come down to my cabin.'

Entering the sumptuous cabin, Bude opened the locked door of a state-room, and uttered some words in an unknown tongue. A tall and very ancient Maori, tatooed with the native 'Moka' on every inch of his body, emerged. The snows of some eighty winters covered his broad breast and majestic head. His eyes were full of the secrets of primitive races. For clothing he wore two navy revolvers stuck in a waist-cloth.

'Te-iki-pa,' said Bude, in the Maori language, 'watch by the door, we must have no listeners, and your ears are keen as those of the youngest Rangatira' (warrior).

The august savage nodded, and, lying down on the floor, applied his ear to the chink at its foot.

'The port of tryst,' whispered Bude to Logan, as they seated themselves at the remotest extremity of the cabin, 'is in Cagayan Sulu.'

'And where may that be?' asked Logan, lighting a cigarette.

'It is a small volcanic island, the most southerly of the Philippines.'

'American territory now,' said Logan. 'But what about it? If it was anybody but you, Bude, I should say he was in a funk.'

'I *am* in a funk,' answered Bude simply.

'Why?'

'I have been there before and left—a blood-feud.'

'What of it? We have one here, with the Maori King, about you know what. Have we not the Maxims, and any quantity of Lee-Metfords? Besides, you need not go ashore at Cagayan Sulu.'

'But they can come aboard. Bullets won't stop *them*.'

'Stop whom? The natives?'

'The Berbalangs: you might as well try to stop mosquitoes with Maxims.'

'Who are the Berbalangs then?'

Bude paced the cabin in haggard anxiety. 'Least said, soonest mended,' he muttered.

'Well, I don't want your confidence,' said Logan, hurt.

'My dear fellow,' said Bude affectionately, 'you are likely to know soon enough. In the meantime, please accept this.'

He opened a strong box, which appeared to contain jewellery, and offered Logan a ring. Between two diamonds of the finest water it contained a bizarre muddy coloured pearl. 'Never let that leave your finger,' said Bude. 'Your life may hang on it.'

'It is a pretty talisman,' said Logan, placing the jewel on the little finger of his right hand. 'A token of some friendly chief, I suppose, at Cagayan—what do you call it?'

'Let us put it at that,' answered Bude; 'I must take other precautions.'

It seemed to Logan that these consisted in making similar presents to the officers and crew, all of whom were Englishmen. Te-iki-pa displaced his nose-ring and inserted his pearl in the orifice previously occupied by that ornament. A little chain of the pearls was hung on the padlock of the huge packing-case, which was the special care of Te-iki-pa.

'Luckily I had the yacht's painting altered before leaving England,' said Bude. 'I'll sail her under Spanish colours, and perhaps they won't spot her. Any way, with the pearls—lucky I bought a lot—we ought to be safe enough. But if any one of the competitors has gone for specimens of the Berbalangs, I fear, I sadly fear, the consequences.' His face clouded; he fell into a reverie.

Logan made no reply, but puffed rings of cigarette smoke into the still blue air. There was method in Bude's apparent madness, but Logan suspected that there was madness in his method.

A certain coolness had not ceased to exist between the friends when, after their long voyage, they sighted the volcanic craters of the lonely isle of Cagayan Sulu and beheld the Stars and Stripes waving from the masthead of the *George Washington* (Captain Noah P. Funkal).

Andrew Lang

Logan landed, and noted the harmless but well-armed half-Mahometan natives of the village. He saw the other competitors, whose 'exhibits,' as Miss McCabe called them, were securely stored in the *George Washington*—strange spoils of far-off mysterious forests, and unplumbed waters of the remotest isles. Occasionally a barbaric yap, or a weird yell or hoot, was wafted on the air at feeding time. Jenkins of All Souls (whom he knew a little) Logan did not meet on the beach; he, like Bude, tarried aboard ship. The other adventurers were civil but remote, and there was a jealous air of suspicion on every face save that of Professor Potter. He, during the day of waiting on the island, played golf with Logan over links which he had hastily improvised. Beyond admitting, as they played, that *his* treasure was in a tank, 'and as well as could be expected, poor brute, but awful noisy,' Professor Potter offered no information.

'Our find is quiet enough,' said Logan.

'Does he give you trouble about food?' asked Mr. Potter.

'Takes nothing,' said Logan, adding, as he holed out, 'that makes me dormy two.'

From the rest of the competitors not even this amount of information could be extracted, and as for Captain Noah Funkal, he was taciturn, authoritative, and, Logan thought, not in a very good temper.

The *George Washington* and the *Pendragon* (so Jones Harvey had christened the yacht which under Bude's colours sailed as *The Sabrina*) weighed anchor simultaneously. If possible they were not to lose sight of each other, and they corresponded by signals and through the megalophone.

The hours of daylight on the first day of the return voyage

passed peacefully at deck-cricket, as far as Logan, Bude, and such of the officers and men as could be spared were concerned. At last night came 'at one stride,' and the vast ocean plain was only illuminated by the pale claritude that falls from the stars. Logan and Bude (they had not dressed for dinner, but wore yachting suits) were smoking on deck, when, quite suddenly, a loud, almost musical, roar or hum was heard from the direction of the distant island.

'What's that?' asked Logan, leaping up and looking towards Cagayan Sulu.

'The Berbalangs,' said Bude coolly. 'You are wearing the ring I gave you?'

'Yes, always do,' said Logan, looking at his hand.

'All the men have their pearls; I saw to that,' said Bude.

'Why, the noise is dwindling,' said Logan. 'That is odd; it seemed to be coming this way.'

'So it is,' said Bude; 'the nearer they approach the less you hear them. When they have come on board you won't hear them at all.'

Logan stared, but asked no more questions.

The musical boom as it approached had died to a whisper, and then had fallen into perfect silence. At the very moment when the mysterious sound ceased, a swarm of things like red fire-flies, a host of floating specks of ruby light, invaded the deck in a cluster. The red points then scattered, approached each man on board, and paused when within a yard of his head or breast. Then they vanished. A queer kind of chill ran down Logan's spine; then the faint whispered

Andrew Lang

musical moan tingled in each man's ears, and the sounds as they departed eastwards gathered volume and force till, in a moment, there fell perfect stillness.

Stillness, broken only by a sudden and mysterious chorus of animal cries from the *George Washington*. A kind of wail, high, shrieking, strenuous, ending in a noise as of air escaping from a pipe; a torrent of barks such as no known beast could utter, subsiding into moans that chilled the blood; a guttural scream, broken by heavy sounds as if of water lapping on a rock at uncertain intervals; a human cry, human words, with unfamiliar vowel sounds, soon slipping into quiet—these were among the horrors that assailed the ears of the voyagers in the *Pendragon*. Such a discord of laments has not tingled to the indifferent stars since the ice-wave swept into their last retreats, and crushed among the rocks that bear their fossil forms, the fauna of the preglacial period, the Ichthyosaurus, the Brontosaurus, the Guyas Cutis (or Ring-tailed Roarer), the Mastodon, and the Mammoth.

'What a row in the menagerie!' said Logan.

He was not answered.

Bude had fallen into a deck-chair, his face buried in his hands, his arms rocking convulsively.

'I say, old cock, pull yourself together,' said Logan, and rushing down the companion stairs, he reappeared with a bottle of champagne. To extract the cork (how familiar, how reassuring, sounded the *cloop*!), and to pour the foaming beverage into two long tumblers, was, to the active Logan, the work of a moment. Shaking Bude, he offered him the beaker; the earl drained it at a draught. He shuddered, but rose to his feet.

'Not a man alive on that doomed vessel,' he was saying, when anew the still air was rent by the raucous notes of a megalophone:

'Is *your* exhibit all right?'

'Fit as a fiddle,' answered Logan through a similar instrument.

'Our exhibits are gone bust,' answered Captain Noah Funkal. 'Our professors are in fits. Our darkeys are all dead. Can your skipper come aboard?'

'Just launching a boat,' cried Logan.

Bude gave the necessary orders. His captain stepped up to him and saluted.

'Do you know what these red fire-flies were that come aboard, sir?' he asked.

'Fire-flies? Oh, *musae volitantes sonorae*, a common phenomenon in these latitudes,' answered Bude.

Logan rejoiced to see that the earl was himself again.

'The other gentlemen's scientific beasts don't seem to like them, sir?'

'So Captain Funkal seems to imply,' said Bude, and, taking the ropes, with Logan beside him, while the *Pendragon* lay to, he steered the boat towards the *George Washington*.

The captain welcomed them on deck in a scene of unusual character. He himself had a revolver in one hand, and a belaying pin in the other; he had been quelling, by the tranquillising methods of Captain Kettle, a mutiny caused by the terror of the crew. The sailors had attempted to leap overboard in the alarm caused by the invasion of the Berbalangs.

'You will excuse my friend and myself for not being in evening dress, during a visit at this hour,' said Bude in the silkiest of tones.

'Glad to see you shipshape, gentlemen,' answered the American mariner. 'My dudes of professors were prancing round in Tuxedos and Prince Alberts when the darned fire-flies came aboard.'

Bude bowed. Study of Miss McCabe had taught him that Tuxedos and Prince Alberts mean evening dress and frock-coats.

'Did *your* men have fits?' asked the captain.

'My captain, Captain Hardy, made a scientific inquiry about the—insects,' said Bude. 'The crew showed no emotion.'

'I guess our fire-bugs were more on business than yours,' said Captain Funkal; 'they've wrecked the exhibits, and killed the darkeys with fright: except two, and *they* were exhibits themselves. Will you honour me by stepping into my cabin, gentlemen. I am glad to see sane white men to-night.'

Bude and Logan followed him through a scene of melancholy interest. Beside the mast, within a shattered palisade, lay huddled the vast corpse of the Mylodon of Patagonia, couchant amidst his fodder of chopped hay. The expression of the huge animal was placid and urbane in death. He was the victim of the ceaseless curiosity of science. Two of the five-horned antelope giraffes of Central

Africa lay in a confused heap of horns and hoofs. Beside an immense tank couched a figure in evening dress, swearing in a subdued tone. Logan recognised Professor Potter. He gently laid his hand on the Professor's shoulder. The Scottish savant looked up:

'It is a dommed mismanaged affair,' he said. 'I could have brought the poor beast safe enough from the Clyde to New York, but the Americans made me harl him round by yon island of camstairy deevils,' and he shook his fist in the direction of Cagayan Sulu.

'What had you got?' asked Logan.

'The *Beathach na Loch na bheiste*,' said Potter. 'I drained the Loch to get him. Fortunately,' he added, 'it was at the expense of the Trust.'

After a few words of commonplace but heartfelt condolence, Logan descended the companion, and followed Bude and Captain Funkal into the cabin of that officer. The captain placed refreshments on the table.

'Now, gentlemen,' he said, 'you have seen the least riled of my professors, and you can guess what the rest are like. Professor Rustler is weeping in his cabin over a shrivelled old mummy. "Never will he speak again," says he, and I am bound to say that I *hev* heard the critter discourse once. The mummy let some awful yells out of him when the fire-bugs came aboard.'

'Yes, we heard a human cry,' said Bude.

'I had thought the talk was managed with a concealed gramophone,' said the captain, 'but it wasn't. The Bunyip from Central Australia has gone to his long home. That was

Professor Wilkinson's pet. There is nothing left alive out of the lot but the natives that Professor Jenkins of England brought in irons from Cagayan Sulu. I reckon them two niggers are somehow at the bottom of the whole ruction.'

'Indeed, and why?' asked Bude.

'Why, sir—I am addressing Professor Jones Harvey?'

Bude bowed. 'Harvey, captain, but not professor—simple amateur seaman and explorer.'

'Sir, your hand,' said the captain. 'Your friend is not a professor?'

'Not I,' said Logan, smiling.

The captain solemnly shook hands. 'Gentlemen, you have sand,' he said, a supreme tribute of respect. 'Well, about these two natives. I never liked taking them aboard. They are, in consequence of the triumph of our arms, American subjects, natives of the conquered Philippines. I am no lawyer, and they may be citizens, they may have votes. They are entitled, anyway, to the protection of the Flag, and I would have entered them as steerage passengers. But that Professor Jenkins (and the other professors agreed) would have it that they came under the head of scientific exhibits. And they did allow that the critters were highly dangerous. I guess they were right.'

'Why, what could they do?'

'Well, gentlemen, I heard stories on shore that I took no stock in. I am not a superstitious man, but they allowed that these darkeys are not of a common tribe, but what the papers call "highly developed mediums." And I guess they are at the bottom of the stramash.'

'Captain Funkal, may I be frank with you?' asked Bude.

'I am hearing you,' said the captain.

'Then, to put it shortly, I have been at Cagayan Sulu before, on an exploring cruise. That was in 1897. I never wanted to go back to it. Logan, did I not regret the choice of that port when the news reached us in New Zealand?'

Logan nodded. 'You funked it,' he said.

'When I was at Cagayan Sulu in 1897 I heard from the natives of a singular tribe in the centre of the island. This tribe is the Berbalangs.'

'That's what Professor Jenkins called them,' said the captain.

'The Berbalangs are subject to neither of the chiefs in the island. No native will approach their village. They are cannibals. The story is that they can throw themselves into a kind of trance. They then project a something or other— spirit, astral body, influence of some kind—which flies forth, making a loud noise when distant.'

'That's what we heard,' said the captain.

'But is silent when they are close at hand.'

'Silent they were,' said the captain.

'They then appear as points of red flame.'

'That's so,' interrupted the captain.

Andrew Lang

'And cause death to man and beast, apparently by terror. I have seen,' said Bude, shuddering, 'the face of a dead native of high respectability, into whose house, before my own eyes, these points of flame had entered. I had to force the door, it was strongly barred within. I never mentioned the fact before, knowing that I could not expect belief.'

'Well, sir, I believe you. You are a white man.'

Bude bowed, and went on. 'The circumstances, though not generally known, have been published, captain, by a gentleman of reputation, Mr. Edward Forbes Skertchley, of Hong Kong. His paper indeed, in the *Journal* of a learned association, the Asiatic Society of Bengal, {232}induced me, most unfortunately, to visit Cagayan Sulu, when it was still nominally in the possession of the Spaniards. My experience was similar to that of Mr. Skertchley, but, for personal reasons, was much more awful and distressing. One of the most beautiful of the island girls, a person of most amiable and winning character, not, alas! of my own faith'—Bude's voice broke—'was one of the victims of the Berbalangs. . . . I loved her.'

He paused, and covered his face with his hands. The others respected and shared his emotion. The captain, like all sailors, sympathetic, dashed away a tear.

'One thing I ought to add,' said Bude, recovering himself, 'I am no more superstitious than you are, Captain Funkal, and doubtless science will find a simple, satisfactory, and normal explanation of the facts, the existence of which we are both compelled to admit. I have heard of no well authenticated instance in which the force, whatever it is, has been fatal to Europeans. The superstitious natives, much as they dread the Berbalangs, believe that they will not attack a person who wears a cocoa- nut pearl. Why this should be so, if so it is, I cannot guess. But, as it is always well to be on the safe side, I provided myself five years ago with a collection of these objects, and when I heard that we were ordered to Cagayan Sulu I distributed them among my crew. My friend, you may observe, wears one of the pearls. I have several about my person.' He disengaged a pin from his necktie, a muddy pearl set with burning rubies. 'Perhaps, Captain Funkal, you will honour me by accepting this specimen, and wearing it while we are in these latitudes? If it does no good, it can do no harm. We, at least, have not been molested, though we witnessed the phenomena.'

'Sir,' said the captain, 'I appreciate your kindness, and I value your gift as a memorial of one of the most singular experiences in a seafaring life. I drink your health and your friend's. Mr. Logan, to *you*.' The captain pledged his guests.

'And now, gentlemen, what am I to do?'

'That, captain, is for your own consideration.'

'I'll carpet that lubber, Jenkins,' said the captain, and leaving the cabin, he returned with the Fellow of All Souls. His shirt front was ruffled, his white neckcloth awry, his pallid countenance betrayed a sensitive second-rate mind, not at unity with itself. He nodded sullenly to Logan: Bude he did not know.

'Professor Jenkins, Mr. Jones Harvey,' said the captain. 'Sit down, sir. Take a drink; you seem to need one.' Jenkins drained the tumbler, and sat with downcast eyes, his finger drumming nervously on the table.

'Professor Jenkins, sir, I reckon you are the cause of the unparalleled disaster to this exploring expedition. Why did you bring these two natives of our territory on board, you well and duly knowing that the end would not justify the proceedings?' A furtive glance from Jenkins lighted on the diamonds that sparkled in Logan's ring. He caught Logan's hand.

'Traitor!' he cried. 'What will not scientific jealousy dare, that meanest of the passions!'

'What the devil do you mean?' said Logan angrily, wrenching his hand away.

'You leave Mr. Logan alone, sir,' said the captain. 'I have two minds to put you in irons, Mr. Professor Jenkins. If you please, explain yourself.'

'I denounce this man and his companion,' said Jenkins, noticing a pearl ring on Bude's finger; 'I denounce them of conspiracy, mean conspiracy, against this expedition, and against the American flag.'

'As how?' inquired the captain, lighting a cigar with irritating calmness.

'They wear these pearls, in which I had trusted for absolute security against the Berbalangs.'

'Well, I wear one too,' said the captain, pointing to the pin in his necktie. 'Are you going to tell me that *I* am a traitor to the flag, sir? I warn you Professor, to be careful.'

'What am I to think?' asked Jenkins.

'It is rather more important what you *say*,' replied the captain. 'What is this fine conspiracy?'

'I had read in England about the Berbalangs.'

'Probably in Mr. Skertchley's curious paper in the Journal of the Asiatic Society of Bengal?' asked Bude with suavity.

Jenkins merely stared at him.

'I deemed that specimens of these American subjects, dowered with their strange and baneful gift, were well worthy of the study of American savants; and I knew that the pearls were a certain prophylactic.'

'What's that?' asked the captain.

'A kind of Universal Pain-Killer,' said Jenkins.

'Well, you surprise me,' said the captain, 'a man of your education. Pain- Killer!' and he expectorated dexterously.

'I mean that the pearls keep off the Berbalangs,' said Jenkins.

'Then why didn't you lay in a stock of the pearls?' asked the captain.

'Because these conspirators had been before me. These men, or their agents, had bought up, just before our arrival, every pearl in the island. They had wormed out my secret, knew the object of my adventure, knew how to ruin us all, and I denounce them.'

'A corner in pearls. Well, it was darned 'cute,' said the captain impartially. 'Now, Mr. Jones Harvey, and Mr. Logan, sir, what have *you* to say?'

'Did Mr. Jenkins—I think you said that this gentleman's name is Jenkins?—see the agent engaged in making this corner in pearls, or learn his name?' asked Bude.

'He was an Irish American, one McCarthy,' answered Jenkins sullenly.

'I am unacquainted with the gentleman,' said Bude, 'and I never employed any one for any such purpose. My visit to Cagayan Sulu was some years ago, just after that of Mr. Skertchley. Captain Funkal, I have already acquainted you with the facts, and you were kind enough to say that you accepted my statement.'

'I did, sir, and I do,' answered the captain. 'As for *you*,' he went on, 'Mr. Professor Jenkins, when you found that your game was dangerous, indeed likely to be ruinous, to this scientific expedition, and to the crew of the *George Washington*—damn you, sir—you should have dropped it. I don't know that I ever swore at a passenger before, and I beg your pardon, you two English gentlemen, for so far forgetting myself. I don't know, and these gentlemen don't know, who made the corner, but I don't think our citizens want either you or your exhibits. The whole population of the States, sir, not to mention the live stock, cannot afford to go about wearing cocoa-nut pearls, a precaution which would be necessary if I landed these venomous Berbalangs of yours on our shores: man and wife too, likely to have a family of young Berbalangs. Snakes are not a patch on these darkeys, and our coloured population, at least, would be busted up.'

The captain paused, perhaps attracted by the chance of thus solving the negro problem.

'So, I'll tell you what it is, gentlemen; and, Professor Jenkins, I'll turn back and land these two native exhibits, and I'll put *you* on shore, Professor Jenkins, at Cagayan Sulu. Perhaps before a steamer touches there—which is not once in a blue moon—you'll have had time to write an exhaustive monograph on the Berbalangs, their manners and customs.'

Jenkins (who knew what awaited him) threw himself on the floor at the feet of Captain Funkal. Horrified by the abject distress of one who, after all, was their countryman, Bude and Logan induced the captain to seclude Jenkins in his cabin. They then, by their combined entreaties, prevailed on the officer to land the Berbalangs on their own island, indeed, but to drop Jenkins later on civilised shores. Dawn saw the *George Washington* and the *Pendragon* in the port of Cagayan Sulu, where the fetters of the two natives, ill looking people enough, were knocked off, and they themselves deposited on the quay, where, not being popular, they were received by a hostile demonstration. The two vessels then resumed their eastward course. The taxidermic appliances without which Jones Harvey never sailed, and the services of his staff of taxidermists, were placed at the disposal of his brother savants. By this means a stuffed Mylodon, a stuffed Beathach, stuffed five-horned antelopes and a stuffed Bunyip, with a common gorilla and the Toltec mummy, now forever silent, were passed through the New York Custom House, and consigned to the McCabe Museum of Natural Varieties.

The immense case that contained the discovery of Jones Harvey was also carefully conveyed to an apartment prepared for it in the same repository. The competitors sought their hotels, Te-iki-pa marching beside Logan and Jones Harvey. But, by special arrangement, either Jones Harvey or his Maori ally always slept beside their mysterious case, which they watched with passionate attention. Two or three days were spent in setting up the stuffed exhibits. Then the trustees, through *The Yellow Flag* (the paper founded by the late Mr. McCabe), announced to the startled citizens the nature of the competition. On successive days the vast theatre of the McCabe Museum would be open, and each competitor, in turn, would display to the public his contribution, and lecture on his adventures and on the variety of nature which he had secured.

While the death of the animals was deplored, nothing was said, for obvious reasons, about the causes of the catastrophe.

The general excitement was intense. Interviewers scoured the city, and flocked, to little purpose, around the officials of the McCabe Museum. Special trains were run from all quarters. The hotels were thronged. 'America,' it was announced, 'had taken hold of science, and was just going to make science hum.'

On the first day of the exhibition, Dr. Hiram Dodge displayed the stuffed Mylodon. The agitation was unprecedented. America had bred, in ancient days, and an American citizen had discovered, the monstrous yet amiable animal whence prehistoric Patagonia drew her milk supplies and cheese stuffs. Mr. Dodge's adventures, he modestly said, could only be adequately narrated by Mr. Rider Haggard. Unluckily the Mylodon had not survived the conditions of the voyage, the change of climates. The applause was thunderous. Mr. Dodge gracefully expressed his obligations to his fair and friendly rival, Mr. Jones Harvey, who had loaned his taxidermic appliances. It did not appear to the public that the Mylodon could be excelled in interest. The Toltec mummy, as he could no longer talk, was flat on a falling market, nor was Mr. Rustler's narrative of its conversational powers accepted by the scepticism of the populace, though it was corroborated by Captain Funkal, Professor Dodge, and Professor Wilkinson, who swore affidavits before a notary, within the hearing of the multitude. The Beathach, exhibited by Professor Potter, was reckoned of high anatomical interest by scientific characters, but it was not of American habitat, and left the people relatively cold. On the other hand, all the Macleans and Macdonnells of Canada and Nova Scotia wept tears of joy at the corroboration of their tribal legends, and the popularity of Professor Potter rivalled even that of Mr. Ian Maclaren. He was at once engaged by Major Pond for a series of lectures. The adventures of Howard Fry, in the taking of his gorilla, were reckoned interesting, as were those of the captor of the Bunyip, but both animals were now undeniably dead. The people could not feed them with waffles and hominy cakes in the gardens of the institute. The savants wrangled on the anatomical differences and resemblances of the Bunyip and the Beathach; still the critters were, to the general mind, only stuffed specimens, though unique. The African five-horned brutes (though in quieter times they would have scored a triumph) did not now appeal to the heart of the people.

At last came the day when, in the huge crowded amphi-theatre, with Te-iki- pa by his side, Jones Harvey addressed the congregation. First he exhibited a skeleton of a dinornis, a bird of about twenty-five feet in height.

'Now,' he went on, 'thanks to the assistance of a Maori gentleman, my friend the Tohunga Te-iki-pa'—(cheers, Te-iki bows his acknowledgments)—'I propose to exhibit to you *this*.'

With a touch on the mechanism he unrolled the valves of a gigantic incubator. Within, recumbent on cotton wool, the almost frenzied spectators perceived two monstrous eggs, like those of the Roc of Arabian fable. Te-iki-pa now chanted a brief psalm in his own language. One of the eggs rolled gently in its place; then the other. A faint crackling noise was heard, first from one, then from the other egg. From each emerged the featherless head of a fowl—the species hitherto unknown to the American continent. The necks pushed forth, then the shoulders, then both shells rolled away in fragments, and the spectators gazed on two fledgling Moas. Te-iki-pa, on inspection, pronounced them to be cock and hen, and in healthy condition. The breed, he said, could doubtless be acclimatised.

The professors of the museum, by Jones Harvey's request, then closely examined the chickens. There could be no doubt of it, they unanimously asserted: these specimens were living deinornithe (which for scientific men, is not a bad shot at the dual of deinornis). The American continent was now endowed, through the enterprise of Mr. Jones Harvey, not only with living specimens, but with a probable breed of a species hitherto thought extinct.

The cheering was led by Captain Funkal, who waved the Stars and Stripes and the Union Jack. Words cannot do justice to the scene. Women fainted, strong men wept, enemies embraced each other. For details we must refer to the files of *The Yellow Flag*. A *plebiscite* to select the winner of the McCabe Prize was organised by that Journal. The Moas (bred and exhibited by Mr. Jones Harvey) simply romped in, by 1,732,901 votes, the Mylodon being a bad second, thanks to the Irish vote.

Bude telegraphed 'Victory,' and Miss McCabe by cable answered 'Bully for us.'

The secret of these lovers was well kept. None who watches the fascinating Countess of Bude as she moves through the gilded saloons of Mayfair guesses that her hand was once the prize of success in a scientific exploration. The identity of Jones Harvey remains a puzzle to the learned. For the rest, a letter in which Jenkins told the story of the Berbalangs was rejected by the Editor of *Nature*, and has not yet passed even the Literary Committee of the Society for Psychical

Research. The classical authority on the Berbalangs is still the paper by Mr. Skertchley in the *Journal* of the Asiatic Society of Bengal. {242}The scientific gentlemen who witnessed the onslaught of the Berbalangs have convinced themselves (except Jenkins) that nothing of the sort occurred in their experience. The evidence of Captain Funkal is rejected as 'marine.'

Te-iki-pa decided to remain in New York as custodian of the Moas. He occasionally obliges by exhibiting a few feats of native conjuring, when his performances are attended by the *elite* of the city. He knows that his countrymen hold him in feud, but he is aware that they fear even more than they hate the ex-medicine man of his Maori Majesty.

The generosity of Bude and his Countess heaped rewards on Merton, who vainly protested that his services had not been professional.

The frequent appearance of new American novelists, whose works sell 250,000 copies in their first month, demonstrate that Mr. McCabe's scheme for raising the level of genius has been as satisfactory as it was original. Genius is riz.

But who 'cornered' the muddy pearls in Cagayan Sulu?

That secret is only known to Lady Bude, her confessor, and the Irish-American agent whom she employed. For she, as we saw, had got at the nature of poor Jenkins's project and had acquainted herself with the wonderful properties of the pearls, which she cornered.

As a patriot, she consoles herself for the loss of the other exhibits to her country, by the reflection that Berbalangs would have been the most mischievous of pauper immigrants. But of all this Bude knows nothing.

XI

ADVENTURE OF THE MISERLY MARQUIS

I

The Marquis consults Gray and Graham

Few men were, and perhaps no marquis was so unpopular as the Marquis of Restalrig, Logan's maternal Scotch cousin, widely removed. He was the last of his family, in the direct line, and on his death almost all his vast wealth would go to nobody knew where. To be sure Logan himself would succeed to the title of Fastcastle, which descends to heirs general, but nothing worth having went with the title. Logan had only the most distant memory of seeing the marquis when he himself was a little boy, and the marquis gave him two sixpences. His relationship to his opulent though remote kinsman had been of no service to him in the struggle for social existence. It carried no 'expectations,' and did not afford the most shadowy basis for a post obit. There was no entail, the marquis could do as he liked with his own.

'The Jews *may* have been credulous in the time of Horace,' Logan said, 'but now they insist on the most drastic evidence of prospective wealth. No, they won't lend me a shekel.'

Events were to prove that other financial operators were better informed than the chosen people, though to be sure their belief was displayed in a manner at once grotesque and painfully embarrassing.

Why the marquis was generally disliked we might explain, historically, if we were acquainted with the tale of his infancy, early youth, and adolescence. Perhaps he had been betrayed in his affections, and was 'taking it out' of mankind in general. But this notion implies that the marquis once had some affections, a point not hitherto substantiated by any evidence. Perhaps heredity was to blame, some unhappy blend of parentage. An ancestor at an unknown period may have bequeathed to the marquis the elements of his unalluring character. But the only ancestor of marked temperament was the festive Logan of Restalrig, who conspired over his cups to kidnap a king, laid out his plot on the lines of an Italian novel, and died without being detected. This heroic ancestor admitted that he hated 'arguments derived from religion,' and, so far, the Marquis of Restalrig was quite with him, if the arguments bore on giving to the poor, or, indeed, to any one.

In fact the marquis was that unpopular character, a miser. Your miser may be looked up to, in a way, as an ideal votary of Mammon, but he is never loved. On his vast possessions, mainly in coal-fields, he was even more detested than the ordinary run of capitalists. The cottages and farmhouses on his estates were dilapidated and insanitary beyond what is endurable. Of his many mansions, some were kept in decent repair, because he drew many shillings from tourists admitted to view them. But his favourite abode was almost as ruinous as his cottages, and an artist in search of a model for the domestic interior of the Master of Ravenswood might have found what he wanted at Kirkburn, the usual lair of this avaricious nobleman. It was a keep of the sixteenth century, and looked as if it had never been papered or painted since Queen Mary's time. But it was near the collieries; and within its blackened walls, and among its bleak fields and grimy trees, Lord Restalrig chose to live alone, with an old man and an old woman for his attendants. The woman had been his nurse; it was whispered in the district that she was also his illegal-aunt, or perhaps even, so to speak, his illegal stepmother. At all events, she endured more than anybody but a Scotch woman who had been his nurse in childhood would have tolerated. To keep her in his service saved him the cost of a pension, which even the marquis, people thought, could hardly refuse to allow her. The other old servitor was her husband, and entirely under her domination. Both might be reckoned staunch, in the old fashion, 'to the name,' which Logan only bore by accident, his grandmother having wedded a kinless Logan who had no demonstrable connection with the house of Restalrig. Any mortal but the marquis would probably have brought Logan up as his heir, for the churlish peer had no nearer connection. But the marquis did more than sympathise with the Roman emperor who quoted 'after me the Last Day.' The emperor only meant that, after his time, he did not care how soon earth and fire were mingled. The marquis, on the other hand, gave the impression that, he once out of the way, he ardently desired the destruction of the whole human race. He was not known ever to have consciously benefited man or woman. He screwed out what he might from everybody in his power, and made no returns which the law did not exact; even these, as far as the income tax went, he kept at the lowest figure possible.

Such was the distinguished personage whose card was handed to Merton one morning at the office. There had been no previous exchange of letters, according to the rules of the Society, and yet Merton could not suppose that the marquis wished to see him on any but business matters. 'He wants to put a spoke in somebody's wheel,' thought Merton, 'but whose?'

He hastily scrawled a note for Logan, who, as usual, was late, put it in an envelope, and sealed it. He wrote: '*On no account come in. Explanation later*! Then he gave the note to the office boy, impressed on him the necessity of placing it in Logan's hands when he arrived, and told the boy to admit the visitor.

The marquis entered, clad in rusty black not unlike a Scotch peasant's best raiment as worn at funerals. He held a dripping umbrella; his boots were muddy, his trousers had their frayed ends turned up. He wore a hard, cruel red face, with keen grey eyes beneath penthouses where age had touched the original tawny red with snow. Merton, bowing, took the umbrella and placed it in a stand.

'You'll not have any snuff?' asked the marquis.

Trevor had placed a few enamelled snuff-boxes of the eighteenth century among the other costly *bibelots* in the rooms, and, by an unusual chance, one of them actually did contain what the marquis wanted. Merton opened it and handed it to the peer, who, after trying a pinch on his nostrils, poured a quantity into his hand and thence into a little black mull made of horn, which he took from his breast pocket. 'It's good,' he said. 'Better than I get at Kirkburn. You'll know who I am?' His accent was nearly as broad as that of one of his own hinds, and he sometimes used Scottish words, to Merton's perplexity.

'Every one has heard of the Marquis of Restalrig,' said Merton.

'Ay, and little to his good, I'll be bound?'

'I do not listen to gossip,' said Merton. 'I presume, though you have not addressed me by letter, that your visit is not unconnected with business?'

'No, no, no letters! I never was wasteful in postage stamps. But as I was in London, to see the doctor, for the Edinburgh ones can make nothing of the case—a kind of dwawming—I looked in at auld Nicky Maxwell's. She gave me a good character of you, and she is one to lippen to. And you make no charge for a first interview.'

Merton vaguely conjectured that to 'lippen' implied some sort of caress; however, he only said that he was obliged to Miss Maxwell for her kind estimate of his firm.

'Gray and Graham, good Scots names. You'll not be one of the Grahams of Netherby, though?'

'The name of the firm is merely conventional, a trading title,' said Merton; 'if you want to know my name, there it is,' and he handed his card to the marquis, who stared at it, and (apparently from motiveless acquisitiveness) put it into his pocket.

'I don't like an alias,' he said. 'But it seems you are to lippen to.'

From the context Merton now understood that the marquis probably wished to signify that he was to be trusted. So he bowed, and expressed a hope that he was 'all that could be desired in the lippening way.'

'You're laughing at my Doric?' asked the nobleman. 'Well, in the only important way, it's not at my *expense*. Ha! Ha!' He shook a lumbering laugh out of himself.

Merton smiled—and was bored.

'I'm come about stopping a marriage,' said the marquis, at last arriving at business.

'My experience is at your service,' said Merton.

'Well,' went on the marquis, 'ours is an old name.'

Merton remarked that, in the course of historical study, he had made himself acquainted with the achievements of the house.

'Auld warld tales! But I wish I could tell where the treasure is that wily auld Logan quarrelled over with the wizard Laird of Merchistoun. Logan would not implement the contract—half profits. But my wits are wool gathering.'

He began to wander round the room, looking at the mezzotints. He stopped in front of one portrait, and said 'My Aunt!' Merton took this for an exclamation of astonishment, but later found that the lady (after Lawrence) really had been the great aunt of the marquis.

Merton conceived that the wits of his visitor were worse than 'wool gathering,' that he had 'softening of the brain.' But circumstances presently indicated that Lord Restalrig was actually suffering from a much less common disorder—softening of the heart.

He returned to his seat, and helped himself to snuff out of the enamelled gold box, on which Merton deemed it politic to keep a watchful eye.

'Man, I'm sweir' (reluctant) 'to come to the point,' said Lord Restalrig.

Merton erroneously understood him to mean that he was under oath or vow to come to the point, and showed a face of attention.

'I'm not the man I was. The doctors don't understand my case—they take awful fees—but I see they think ill of it. And that sets a body thinking. Have you a taste of brandy in the house?'

As the visitor's weather-beaten ruddiness had changed to a ghastly ashen hue, rather bordering on the azure, Merton set forth the liqueur case, and drew a bottle of soda water.

'No water,' said the peer; 'it's just ma twal' ours, an auld Scotch fashion,' and he took without winking an orthodox dram of brandy. Then he looked at the silver tops of the flasks.

'A good coat!' he said. 'Yours?'

Merton nodded.

'Ye quarter the Douglas Heart. A good coat. Dod, I'll speak plain. The name, Mr. Merton, when ye come to the end o' the furrow, the name is all ye have left. We brought nothing into the world but the name, we take out nothing else. A sore dispensation. I'm not the man I was, not this two years. I must dispone, I know it well. Now the name, that I thought that I cared not an empty whistle for, is worn to a rag, but I cannot leave it in the mire. There's just one that bears it, one Logan by name, and true Logan by the mother's blood. The mother's mother, my cousin, was a bonny lass.'

He paused; his enfeebled memory was wandering, no doubt, in scenes more vivid to him than those of yesterday.

Merton was now attentive indeed. The miserly marquis had become, to him, something other than a curious survival of times past. There was a chance for Logan, his friend, the last of the name, but Logan was firmly affianced to Miss Markham, of the cloak department at Madame Claudine's. And the marquis, as he said, 'had come about stopping a marriage,' and Merton was to help him in stopping it, in disentangling Logan!

The old man aroused himself. 'I have never seen the lad but once, when he was a bairn. But I've kept eyes on him. He *has* nothing, and since I came to London I hear that he has gone gyte, I mean—ye'll not understand me—he is plighted to a long-legged shop-lass, the daughter of a ne'er-do-well Australian land-louper, a doctor. This must not be. Now I'll speak plain to you, plainer than to Tod and Brock, my doers—ye call them lawyers. *They* did not make my will.'

Merton prevented himself, by an effort, from gasping. He kept a countenance of cold attention. But the marquis was coming to the point.

'I have left all to the name, lands and rents, and mines, and money. But, unless the lad marries in his own rank, I'll change my will. It's in the hidie hole at Kirkburn, that Logan built to keep King Jamie in, when he caught him. But the fool Ruthvens marred that job, and got their kail through the reek. I'm wandering.' He helped himself to another dram, and went on, 'Ye see what I want, ye must stop that marriage.'

'But,' said Merton, 'as you are so kindly disposed towards your kinsman, this Mr. Logan, may I ask whether it would not be wise to address him yourself, as the head of his house? He may, surely he will, listen to your objections.'

'Ye do not know the Logans.'

Merton concealed his smile.

'Camstairy deevils! It's in the blood. Never once has he asked me for a pound, never noticed me by word or letter. Faith, I wish all the world had been as considerate to auld Restalrig! For me to say a word, let be to make an offer, would just tie him faster to the lass. "Tyne troth, tyne a'," that is the old bye-word.'

Merton recognised his friend in this description, but he merely shook a sympathetic head. 'Very unusual,' he remarked. 'You really have no hope by this method?'

'None at all, or I would not be here on this daft ploy. There's no fool like an auld fool, and, faith, I hardly know the man I was. But they cannot dispute the will. I drew doctors to witness that I was of sound and disponing mind, and I've since been thrice to kirk and market. Lord, how they stared to see auld Restalrig in his pew, that had not smelt appleringie these forty years.'

Merton noted these words, which he thought curious and obscure. 'Your case interests me deeply,' he said, 'and shall receive my very best attention. You perceive, of course, that it is a difficult case, Mr. Logan's character and tenacity being what you describe. I must make careful inquiries, and shall inform you of progress. You wish to see this engagement ended?'

'And the lad on with a lass of his rank,' said the marquis.

'Probably that will follow quickly on the close of his present affection. It usually does in our experience,' said Merton, adding, 'Am I to write to you at your London address?'

'No, sir; these London hotels would ruin the cunzie' (the Mint).

Merton wondered whether the Cunzie was the title of some wealthy Scotch peer.

'And I'm off for Kirkburn by the night express. Here's wishing luck,' and the old sinner finished the brandy.

'May I call a cab for you—it still rains?'

'No, no, I'll travel,' by which the economical peer meant that he would walk.

He then shook Merton by the hand, and hobbled downstairs attended by his adviser.

'Did Mr. Logan call?' Merton asked the office boy when the marquis had trotted off.

'Yes, sir; he said you would find him at the club.'

'Call a hansom,' said Merton, 'and put up the notice, "out."' He drove to the club, where he found Logan ordering luncheon.

'Hullo, shall we lunch together?' Logan asked.

'Not yet: I want to speak to you.'

'Nothing gone wrong? Why did you shut me out of the office?'

'Where can we talk without being disturbed?'

'Try the smoking-room on the top storey,' said Logan, 'Nobody will have climbed so high so early.'

They made the ascent, and found the room vacant: the

windows looked out over swirling smoke and trees tossing in a wind of early spring.

'Quiet enough,' said Logan, taking an arm-chair. 'Now out with it! You make me quite nervous.'

'A client has come with what looks a promising piece of business. We are to disentangle—'

'A royal duke?'

'No. *You*!'

'A practical joke,' said Logan. 'Somebody pulling your leg, as people say, a most idiotic way of speaking. What sort of client was he, or she? We'll be even with them.'

'The client's card is here,' said Merton, and he handed to Logan that of the Marquis of Restalrig.

'You never saw him before; are you sure it was the man?' asked Logan, staggered in his scepticism.

'A very good imitation. Dressed like a farmer at a funeral. Talked like all the kailyards. Snuffed, and asked for brandy, and went and came, walking, in this weather.'

'By Jove, it is my venerated cousin. And he had heard about me and Miss—'

'He was quite well informed.'

Logan looked very grave. He rose and stared out of the window into the mist. Then he came back, and stood beside Merton's chair. He spoke in a low voice:

'This can only mean one thing.'

'Only that one thing,' said Merton, dropping his own voice.

'What did you say to him?'

'I told him that his best plan, as the head of the house, was to approach you himself.'

'And he said?'

'That it was of no use, and that I do not know the Logans.'

'But you do?'

'I think so.'

'You think right. No, not for all his lands and mines I won't.'

'Not for the name?'

'Not for the kingdoms of the earth,' said Logan.

'It is a great refusal.'

'I have really no temptation to accept,' said Logan. 'I am not built that way. So what next? If the old boy could only see her—'

'I doubt if that would do any good, though, of course, if I were you I should think so. He goes north to-night. You can't take the lady to Kirkburn. And you can't write to him.'

'Of course not,' said Logan; 'of course it would be all up if he knew that I know.'

'There is this to be said—it is not a very pleasant view to take—he can't live long. He came to see some London specialist—it is his heart, I think—'

'*His* heart!

   How Fortune aristophanises
   And how severe the fun of Fate!'

quoted Logan.

'The odd thing is,' said Merton, 'that I do believe he has a heart. I rather like him. At all events, I think, from what I saw, that a sudden start might set him off at any moment, or an unusual exertion. And he may go off before I tell him that I can do nothing with you—'

'Oh, hang that,' said Logan, 'you make me feel like a beastly assassin!'

'I only want you to understand how the land lies.' Merton dropped his voice again, 'He has made a will leaving you everything.'

'Poor old cock! Look here, I believe I had better write, and say that I'm awfully touched and obliged, but that I can't come into his views, or break my word, and then, you know, he can just make another will. It would be a swindle to let him die, and come into his property, and then go dead against his wishes.'

'But it would be all right to give me away, I suppose, and let him understand that I had violated professional confidence?'

'Only with a member of the firm. That is no violation.'

'But then I should have told him that you *were* a member of the firm.'

'I'm afraid you should.'

'Logan, you have the ideas of a schoolboy. I *had* to be certain as to how you would take it, though, of course, I had a very good guess. And as to what you say about the chances of his dying and leaving everything where he would not have left it if he had been sure you would act against his wishes—I believe you are wrong. What he really cares about is "the name." His ghost will put up with your disobedience if the name keeps its old place. Do you see?'

'Perhaps you are right,' said Logan.

'Anyhow, there is no such pressing hurry. One *may* bring him round with time. A curious old survival! I did not understand all that he said. There was something about having been thrice at kirk and market since he made his will; and something about not having smelled appleringie for forty years. What is appleringie?'

Logan laughed.

'It is a sacred Presbyterian herb. The people keep it in their Bibles and it perfumes the churches. But look here—'

He was interrupted by the entrance of a page, who handed to him a letter. Logan read it and laughed. 'I knew it; they are sharp!' he said, and handed the letter to Merton. It was from a famous, or infamous, money- lender, offering princely accommodation on terms which Mr. Logan would find easy and reasonable.

'They have nosed the appleringie, you see,' he said.

'But I don't see,' said Merton.

'Why the hounds have heard that the old nobleman has been thrice to kirk lately. And as he had not been there for forty years, they have guessed that he has been making his will. Scots law has, or used to have, something in it about going thrice to kirk and market after making a will—disponing they call it—as a proof of bodily and mental soundness. So they have spotted the marquis's pious motives for kirk-going, and guessed that I am his heir. I say—' Logan began to laugh wildly.

'What do you say?' asked Merton, but Logan went on hooting.

'I say,' he repeated, 'it must never be known that the old lord came to consult us,' and here he was again convulsed.

'Of course not,' said Merton. 'But where is the joke?'

'Why, don't you see—oh, it is too good—he has taken every kind of precaution to establish his sanity when he made his will.'

'He told me that he had got expert evidence,' said Merton.

'And then he comes and consults US!' said Logan, with a crow of laughter. 'If any fellow wants to break the will on the score of insanity, and knows, knows he came to us, a jury, when they find he consulted us, will jolly well upset the cart.' Merton was hurt.

'Logan,' he said, 'it is you who ought to be in an asylum, an Asylum for Incurable Children. Don't you see that he made the will long *before* he took the very natural and proper step of consulting Messrs. Gray and Graham?'

'Let us pray that, if there is a suit, it won't come before a Scotch jury,' said Logan. 'Anyhow, nobody knows that he came except you and me.'

'And the office boy,' said Merton.

'Oh, we'll square the office boy,' said Logan. 'Let's lunch!'

They lunched, and Logan, as was natural, though Merton urged him to abstain, hung about the doors of Madame Claudine's emporium at the hour when the young ladies returned to their homes. He walked home with Miss Markham. He told her about his chances, and his views, and no doubt she did not think him a person of schoolboy ideas, but a Bayard.

Two days passed, and in the afternoon of the third a telegram arrived for Logan from Kirkburn.

'Come at once, Marquis very ill. Dr. Douglas, Kirkburn.'

There was no express train North till 8.45 in the evening. Merton dined with Logan at King's Cross, and saw him off. He would reach his cousin's house at about six in the morning if the train kept time.

About nine o'clock on the morning following Logan's arrival at Kirkburn Merton was awakened: the servant handed to him a telegram.

'Come instantly. Highly important. Logan, Kirkburn.'

Merton dressed himself more rapidly than he had ever done, and caught the train leaving King's Cross at 10 a.m.

II

The Emu's Feathers

The landscape through which Merton passed on his northward way to Kirkburn, whither Logan had summoned him, was blank with snow. The snow was not more than a couple of inches deep where it had not drifted, and, as frost had set in, it was not likely to deepen. There was no fear of being snowed up.

Merton naturally passed a good deal of his time in wondering what had occurred at Kirkburn, and why Logan needed his presence. 'The poor old gentleman has passed away suddenly, I suppose,' he reflected, 'and Logan may think that I know where he has deposited his will. It is in some place that the marquis called "the hidie hole," and that, from his vagrant remarks, appears to be a secret chamber, as his ancestor meant to keep James VI. there. I wish he had cut the throat of that prince, a bad fellow. But, of course, I don't know where the chamber is: probably some of the people about the place know, or the lawyer who made the will.'

However freely Merton's consciousness might play round the problem, he could get no nearer to its solution. At Berwick he had to leave the express, and take a local train. In the station, not a nice station, he was accosted by a stranger, who asked if he was Mr. Merton? The stranger, a wholesome, red-faced, black-haired man, on being answered in the affirmative, introduced himself as Dr. Douglas, of Kirkburn. 'You telegraphed to my friend Logan the news of the marquis's illness,' said Merton. 'I fear you have no better news to give me.'

Dr. Douglas shook his head.

A curious little crowd was watching the pair from a short distance. There was an air of solemnity about the people, which was not wholly due to the chill grey late afternoon, and the melancholy sea.

'We have an hour to wait, Mr. Merton, before the local train starts, and afterwards there is a bit of a drive. It is cold, we would be as well in the inn as here.'

The doctor beat his gloved hands together to restore the circulation.

Merton saw that the doctor wished to be with him in private, and the two walked down into the town, where they got a comfortable room, the doctor ordering boiling water and the other elements of what he called 'a cheerer.' When the cups which cheer had been brought, and the men were alone, the doctor said:

'It is as you suppose, Mr. Merton, but worse.'

'Great heaven, no accident has happened to Logan?' asked Merton.

'No, sir, and he would have met you himself at Berwick, but he is engaged in making inquiries and taking precautions at Kirkburn.'

'You do not mean that there is any reason to suspect foul play? The marquis, I know, was in bad health. You do not suspect—murder?'

'No, sir, but—the marquis is gone.'

'I *know* he is gone, your telegram and what I observed of his health led me to fear the worst.'

'But his body is gone—vanished.'

'You suppose that it has been stolen (you know the American and other cases of the same kind) for the purpose of extracting money from the heir?'

'That is the obvious view, whoever the heir may be. So far, no will has been found,' the doctor added some sugar to his cheerer, and some whisky to correct the sugar. 'The neighbourhood is very much excited. Mr. Logan has tele-graphed to London for detectives.'

Merton reflected in silence.

'The obvious view is not always the correct one,' he said. 'The marquis was, at least I thought that he was, a very eccentric person.'

'No doubt about *that*,' said the doctor.

'Very well. He had reasons, such reasons as might occur to a mind like his, for wanting to test the character and conduct of Mr. Logan, his only living kinsman. What I am going to say will seem absurd to you, but—the marquis spoke to me of his malady as a kind of "dwawming," I did not know what he meant, at the time, but yesterday I consulted the glossary of a Scotch novel: to *dwawm*, I think, is to lose consciousness?'

The doctor nodded.

'Now you have read,' said Merton, 'the case published by Dr. Cheyne, of a gentleman, Colonel Townsend, who could voluntarily produce a state of "dwawm" which was not then to be distinguished from death?'

'I have read it in the notes to Aytoun's *Scottish Cavaliers*,' said the doctor.

'Now, then, suppose that the marquis, waking out of such a state, whether voluntarily induced (which is very improbable) or not, thought fit to withdraw himself, for the purpose of secretly watching, from some retreat, the behaviour of his heir, if he has made Mr. Logan his heir? Is that hypothesis absolutely out of keeping with his curious character?'

'No. It's crazy enough, if you will excuse me, but, for these last few weeks, at any rate, I would have swithered about signing a fresh certificate to the marquis's sanity.'

'You did, perhaps, sign one when he made his will, as he told me?'

'I, and Dr. Gourlay, and Professor Grant,' the doctor named two celebrated Edinburgh specialists. 'But just of late I would not be so certain.'

'Then my theory need not necessarily be wrong?'

'It can't but be wrong. First, I saw the man dead.'

'Absolute tests of death are hardly to be procured, of course you know that better than I do,' said Merton.

'Yes, but I am positive, or as positive as one can be, in the circumstances. However, that is not what I stand on. *There was a witness who saw the marquis go.*'

'Go—how did he go?'

'He disappeared.'

'The body disappeared?'

'It did, but you had better hear the witness's own account; I don't think a second-hand story will convince you, especially as you have a theory.'

'Was the witness a man or a woman?'

'A woman,' said the doctor.

'Oh!' said Merton.

'I know what you mean,' said the doctor. 'You think, it suits your theory, that the marquis came to himself and—'

'And squared the female watcher,' interrupted Merton; 'she would assist him in his crazy stratagem.'

'Mr. Merton, you've read ower many novels,' said the doctor, lapsing into the vernacular. 'Well, your notion is not unthinkable, nor pheesically impossible. She's a queer one, Jean Bower, that waked the corpse, sure enough. However, you'll soon be on the spot, and can examine the case for yourself. Mr. Logan has no idea but that the body was stolen for purposes of blackmail.' He looked at his watch. 'We must be going to catch the train, if she's anything like punctual.'

The pair walked in silence to the station, were again watched curiously by the public (who appeared to treat the station as a club), and after three-quarters of an hour of slow motion and stoppages, arrived at their destination, Drem.

The doctor's own man with a dog-cart was in waiting.

'The marquis had neither machine nor horse,' the doctor explained.

Through the bleak late twilight they were driven, past two or three squalid mining villages, along a road where the ruts showed black as coal through the freezing snow. Out of one village, the lights twinkling in the windows, they turned up a steep road, which, after a couple of hundred yards, brought them to the old stone gate posts, surmounted by heraldic animals.

'The late marquis sold the worked-iron gates to a dealer,' said the doctor.

At the avenue gates, so steep was the ascent, both men got out and walked.

'You see the pits come up close to the house,' said the doctor, as they reached the crest. He pointed to some tall chimneys on the eastern slope, which sank quite gradually to the neighbouring German Ocean, but ended in an abrupt rocky cliff.

'Is that a fishing village in the cleft of the cliffs? I think I see a red roof,' said Merton.

'Ay, that's Strutherwick, a fishing village,' replied the doctor.

'A very easy place, on your theory, for an escape with the body by boat,' said Merton.

'Ay, that is just it,' acquiesced the doctor.

'But,' asked Merton, as they reached the level, and saw the old keep black in front of them, 'what is that rope stretched about the lawn for? It seems to go all round the house, and there are watchers.' Dark figures with lanterns were visible at intervals, as Merton peered into the gathering gloom. The watchers paced to and fro like sentinels.

The door of the house opened, and a man's figure stood out against the lamp light within.

'Is that you, Merton?' came Logan's voice from the doorway.

Merton answered; and the doctor remarked, 'Mr. Logan will tell you what the rope's for.'

The friends shook hands; the doctor, having deposited Merton's baggage, pleaded an engagement, and said 'Good-bye,' among the thanks of Logan. An old man, a kind of silent Caleb Balderstone, carried Merton's light luggage up a black turnpike stair.

'I've put you in the turret; it is the least dilapidated room,' said Logan. 'Now, come in here.'

He led the way into a hall on the ground-floor. A great fire in the ancient hearth, with its heavy heraldically carved stone chimney-piece, lit up the desolation of the chamber.

'Sit down and warm yourself,' said Logan, pushing forward a ponderous oaken chair, with a high back and short arms.

'I know a good deal,' said Merton, his curiosity hurrying him to the point; 'but first, Logan, what is the rope on the stakes driven in round the house for?'

'That was my first precaution,' said Logan. 'I heard of the—of what has happened—about four in the morning, and I instantly knocked in the stakes—hard work with the frozen ground—and drew the rope along, to isolate the snow about the house. When I had done that, I searched the snow for footmarks.'

'When had the snow begun to fall?'

'About midnight. I turned out then to look at the night before going to bed.'

'And there was nothing wrong then?'

'He lay on his bed in the laird's chamber. I had just left it. I left him with the watcher of the dead. There was a plate of salt on his breast. The housekeeper, Mrs. Bower, keeps up the old ways. Candles were burning all round the bed. A fearful waste he would have thought it, poor old man. The devils! If I could get on their track!' said Logan, clenching his fist.

'You have found no tracks, then?'

'None. When I examined the snow there was not a footmark on the roads to the back door or the front—not a footmark on the whole area.'

'Then the removal of the body from the bedroom was done from within. Probably the body is still in the house.'

'Certainly it has been taken out by no known exit, if it *has* been taken out, as I believe. I at once arranged relays of sentinels—men from the coal-pits. But the body is gone; I am certain of it. A fishing-boat went out from the village, Struitherwick, before the dawn. It came into the little harbour after midnight—some night-wandering lover saw it enter—and it must have sailed again before dawn.'

'Did you examine the snow near the harbour?'

'I could not be everywhere at once, and I was single-handed; but I sent down the old serving-man, John Bower. He is stupid enough, but I gave him a note to any fisherman he might meet. Of course these people are not detectives.'

'And was there any result?'

'Yes; an odd one. But it confirms the obvious theory of body-snatching. Of course, fishers are early risers, and they went trampling about confusedly. But they did find curious tracks. We have isolated some of them, and even managed to carry off a couple. We dug round them, and lifted them. A neighbouring laird, Mr. Maitland, lent his ice-house for storing these, and I had one laid down on the north side of this house to show you, if the frost held. No ice-house or refrigerator *here*, of course.'

'Let me see it now.'

Logan took a lighted candle—the night was frosty, without a wind—and led Merton out under the black, ivy-clad walls. Merton threw his greatcoat on the snow and knelt on it, peering at the object. He saw a large flat clod of snow and earth. On its surface was the faint impress of a long oval, longer than the human foot; feathery marks running in both directions from the centre could be descried. Looking closer, Merton detected here and there a tiny feather and a flock or two of down adhering to the frozen mass.

'May I remove some of these feathery things?' Merton asked.

'Certainly. But why?'

'We can't carry the clod indoors, it would melt; and it *may* melt if the weather changes; and by bad luck there may be no feathers or down adhering to the other clods—those in the laird's ice-house.'

'You think you have a clue?'

'I think,' said Merton, 'that these are emu's feathers; but, whether they are or not, they look like a clue. Still, I *think* they are emu's feathers.'

'Why? The emu is not an indigenous bird.'

As he spoke, an idea—several ideas—flashed on Merton. He wished that he had held his peace. He put the little shreds into his pocket-book, rose, and donned his greatcoat. 'How cold it is!' he said. 'Logan, would you mind very much if I said no more just now about the feathers? I really have a notion—which may be a good one, or may be a silly one—and, absurd as it appears, you will seriously oblige me by letting me keep my own counsel.'

'It is damned awkward,' said Logan testily.

'Ah, old boy, but remember that "damned awkward" is a damned awkward expression.'

'You are right,' said Logan heartily; 'but I rose very early, I'm very tired, I'm rather savage. Let's go in and dine.'

'All right,' said Merton.

'I don't think,' said Logan, as they were entering the house, 'that I need keep these miners on sentry go any longer. The bird—the body, I mean—has flown. Whoever the fellows were that made these tracks, and however they got into and out of the house, they have carried the body away. I'll pay the watchers and dismiss them.'

'All right,' said Merton. 'I won't dress. I must return to town by the night train. No time to be lost.'

'No train to be caught,' said Logan, 'unless you drive or walk to Berwick from here—which you can't. You can't walk to Dunbar, to catch the 10.20, and I have nothing that you can drive.'

'Can I send a telegram to town?'

'It is four miles to the nearest telegraph station, but I dare say one of the sentinels would walk there for a consideration.'

'No use,' said Merton. 'I should need to wire in a cipher, when I come to think of it, and cipher I have none. I must go as early as I can to- morrow. Let us consult Bradshaw.'

They entered the house. Merton had a Bradshaw in his dressing-bag. They found that he could catch a train at 10.49 A.M., and be in London about 9 P.M.

'How are you to get to the station?' asked Logan. 'I'll tell you how,' he went on. 'I'll send a note to the inn at the place, and order a trap to be here at ten. That will give you lots of time. It is about four miles.'

'Thank you,' said Merton; 'I see no better way.' And while Logan went to pay and dismiss the sentries and send a messenger, a grandson of the old butler with the note to the innkeeper, Merton toiled up the narrow turnpike stair to the turret chamber. A fire had been burning all day, and in firelight almost any room looks tolerable. There was a small four-poster bed, with slender columns, a black old wardrobe, and a couple of chairs, one of the queer antiquated little dressing-tables, with many drawers, and boxes, and a tiny basin, and there was a perfectly new tub, which Logan had probably managed to obtain in the course of the day. Merton's evening clothes were neatly laid out, the shutters were closed, curtains there were none; in fact, he had been in much worse quarters.

As he dressed he mused. 'Cursed spite,' thought he, 'that ever I was born to be an amateur detective! And cursed be my confounded thirst for general information! Why did I ever know what *Kurdaitcha* and *Interlinia* mean? If I turn out to be right, oh, shade of Sherlock Holmes, what a pretty kettle of fish there will be! Suppose I drop the whole affair! But I've been ass enough to let Logan know that I have an idea. Well, we shall see how matters shape themselves. Sufficient for the day is the evil thereof.'

Merton descended the turnpike stair, holding on to the rope provided for that purpose in old Scotch houses. He found Logan standing by the fire in the hall. They were waited on by the old man, Bower. By tacit consent they spoke, while he was present, of anything but the subject that occupied their minds. They had quite an edible dinner—cock-a-leekie, brandered haddocks, and a pair of roasted fowls, with a mysterious sweet which was called a 'Hattit Kit.'

'It is an historical dish in this house,' said Logan. 'A favourite with our ancestor, the conspirator.'

The wine was old and good, having been laid down before the time of the late marquis.

'In the circumstances, Logan,' said Merton, when the old

serving man was gone, 'you have done me very well.'

'Thanks to Mrs. Bower, our butler's wife,' said Logan. 'She is a truly remarkable woman. She and her husband, they are cousins, are members of an ancient family, our hereditary retainers. One of them, Laird Bower, was our old conspirator's go-between in the plot to kidnap the king, of which you have heard so much. Though he was an aged and ignorant man, he kept the secret so well that our ancestor was never even suspected, till his letters came to light after his death, and after Laird Bower's death too, luckily for both of them. So you see we can depend on it that this pair of domestics, and their family, were not concerned in this new abomination; so far, the robbery was not from within.'

'I am glad to hear that,' said Merton. 'I had invented a theory, too stupid to repeat, and entirely demolished by the footmarks in the snow, a theory which hypothetically implicated your old housekeeper. To be sure it did not throw any doubt on her loyalty to the house, quite the reverse.'

'What was your theory?'

'Oh, too silly for words; that the marquis had been only in a trance, had come to himself when alone with the old lady, who, the doctor said, was watching in the room, and had stolen away, to see how you would conduct yourself. Childish hypothesis! The obvious one, body-snatching, is correct. This is very good port.'

'If things had been as you thought possible, Jean Bower was not the woman to balk the marquis,' said Logan. 'But you must see her and hear her tell her own story.'

'Gladly,' said Merton, 'but first tell me yours.'

'When I arrived I found the poor old gentleman unconscious. Dr. Douglas was in attendance. About noon he pronounced life extinct. Mrs. Bower watched, or "waked" the corpse. I left her with it about midnight, as I told you; about four in the morning she aroused me with the news that the body had vanished. What I did after that you know. Now you had better hear the story from herself.'

Logan rang a handbell, there were no other bells in the keep, and asked the old serving-man, when he came, to send in Mrs. Bower.

She entered, a very aged woman, dressed in deep mourning. She was tall, her hair of an absolutely pure white, her aquiline face was drawn, her cheeks hollow, her mouth almost toothless. She made a deep courtesy, repeating it when Logan introduced 'my friend, Mr. Merton.'

'Mrs. Bower,' Logan said, 'Mr. Merton is my oldest friend, and the marquis saw him in London, and consulted him on private business a few days ago. He wishes to hear you tell what you saw the night before last.'

'Maybe, as the gentleman is English, he'll hardly understand me, my lord. I have a landward tongue,' said Mrs. Bower.

'I can interpret if Mr. Merton is puzzled, Mrs. Bower, but I think he will understand better if we go to the laird's chamber.'

Logan took two lighted candles, handing two to Merton, and the old woman led them upstairs to a room which occupied the whole front of the ancient 'peel,' or square tower, round which the rest of the house was built. The room was nearly bare of furniture, except for an old chair or two, a bureau, and a great old bed of state, facing the narrow deep window, and standing on a kind of dais, or platform of three steps. The heavy old green curtains were drawn all round it. Mrs. Bower opened them at the front and sides. At the back against the wall the curtains, embroidered with the arms of Restalrig, remained closed.

'I sat here all the night,' said Mrs. Bower, 'watching the corp that my hands had streikit. The candles were burning a' about him, the saut lay on his breast, only aefold o' linen covered him. My back was to the window, my face to his feet. I was crooning the auld dirgie; if it does nae guid, it does nae harm.' She recited in a monotone:

'When thou frae here away art past—
Every nicht and all—
To Whinny-muir thou comest at last,
And Christ receive thy saul.

'If ever thou gavest hosen and shoon—
Every nicht and all—
Sit thee down and put them on,
And Christ receive thy saul

'Alas, he never gave nane, puir man,' said the woman with a sob.

At this moment the door of the chamber slowly opened. The woman turned and gazed at it, frowning, her lips wide apart.

Logan went to the door, looked into the passage, closed the door and locked it; the key had to be turned twice, in the old fashion, and worked with a creaking jar.

'I had crooned thae last words,

And Christ receive thy saul,

when the door opened, as ye saw it did the now. It is weel kenned that a corp canna lie still in a room with the door hafflins open. I rose to lock it, the catch is crazy. I was backing to the door, with my face to the feet o' the corp. I saw them move backwards, slow they moved, and my heart stood still in my breist. Then I saw'—here she stepped to the head of the bed and drew apart the curtains, which opened in the middle—'I saw the curtain was open, and naething but blackness ahint it. Ye see, my Lord, ahint the bed-heid is the entrance o' the auld secret passage. The stanes hae lang syne fallen in, and closed it, but my Lord never would have the hole wa'ed up. "There's nae draught, Jean, or nane to mention, and I never was wastefu' in needless repairs," he aye said. Weel, when I looked that way, his face, down to the chafts, was within the blackness, and aye draw, drawing further ben. Then, I shame to say it, a sair dwawm cam ower me, I gae a bit chokit cry, and I kenned nae mair till I cam to mysel, a' the candles were out, and the chamber was mirk and lown. I heard the skirl o' a passing train, and I crap to the bed, and the skirl kind o' reminded me o' living folk, and I felt a' ower the bed wi' my hands. There was nae corp. Ye ken that the Enemy has power, when a corp lies in a room, and the door is hafflins closed. Whiles they sit up, and grin and yammer. I hae kenned that. Weel, how long I had lain in the dwawm I canna say. The train that skirled maun hae been a coal train that rins by about half-past three in the morning. There was a styme o' licht that streeled in at the open door, frae a candle your lordship set on a table in the lobby; the auld lord would hae nae lichts in the house after the ten hours. Sae I got to the door, and grippit to the candle, and flew off to your lordship's room, and the rest ye ken.'

'Thank you, very much, Mrs. Bower,' said Logan. 'You quite understand, Merton, don't you?'

'I thoroughly understand your story, Mrs. Bower,' said Merton.

'We need not keep you any longer, Mrs. Bower,' said Logan. 'Nobody need sit up for us; you must be terribly fatigued.'

'You wunna forget to rake out the ha' fire, my lord?' said the old lady, 'I wush your Lordship a sound sleep, and you, sir,' so she curtsied and went, Logan unlocking the door.

'And I was in London this morning!' said Merton, drawing a long breath.

'You're over Tweed, now, old man,' answered Logan, with patriotic satisfaction.

'Don't go yet,' said Merton. 'You examined the carpet of the room; no traces there of these odd muffled foot-coverings you found in the snow?'

'Not a trace of any kind. The salt was spilt, some of it lay on the floor. The plate was not broken.'

'If they came in, it would be barefoot,' said Merton.

'Of course the police left traces of official boots,' said Logan. 'Where are they now—the policemen, I mean?'

'Two are to sleep in the kitchen.'

'They found out nothing?'

'Of course not.'

'Let me look at the hole in the wall.' Merton climbed on to the bed and entered the hole. It was about six feet long by four wide. Stones had fallen in, at the back, and had closed the passage in a rough way, indeed what extent of the floor of the passage existed was huddled with stones. Merton examined the sides of the passage, which were mere rubble.

'Have you looked at the floor beneath those fallen stones?' Merton asked.

'No, by Jove, I never thought of that,' said Logan.

'How could they have been stirred without the old woman hearing the noise?'

'How do you know they were there before the marquis's death?' asked Merton, adding, 'this hole was not swept and dusted regularly. Either the entrance is beneath me, or—"the Enemy had power"—as Mrs. Bower says.'

'You must be right,' said Logan. 'I'll have the stones removed to-morrow. The thing is clear. The passage leads to somewhere outside of the house. There's an abandoned coal mine hard by, on the east. Nothing can be simpler.'

'When once you see it,' said Merton.

'Come and have a whisky and soda,' said Logan.

III

A Romance of Bradshaw

Merton slept very well in the turret room. He was aroused early by noises which he interpreted as caused by the arrival of the London detectives. But he only turned round, like the sluggard, and slumbered till Logan aroused him at eight o'clock. He descended about a quarter to nine, breakfast was at nine, and he found Logan looking much disturbed.

'They don't waste time,' said Logan, handing to Merton a letter in an opened envelope. Logan's hand trembled.

'Typewritten address, London postmark,' said Merton. 'To Robert Logan, Esq., at Kirkburn Keep, Drem, Scotland.'

Merton read the letter aloud; there was no date of place, but there were the words:

'March 6, 2.45 P.M.
'SIR,—Perhaps I ought to say my Lord—'

'What a fool the fellow is,' said Merton.

'Why?'

'Shows he is an educated man.'

'You may obtain news as to the mortal remains of your kinsman, the late Marquis of Restalrig, and as to his Will, by walking in the Burlington Arcade on March 11, between the hours of three and half-past three p.m. You must be attired in full mourning costume, carrying a glove in your left hand, and a black cane, with a silver top, in your right. A lady will drop her purse beside you. You will accost her.'

Here the letter, which was typewritten, ended.

'You won't?' said Merton. 'Never meet a black-mailer halfway.'

'I wouldn't,' said Logan. 'But look here!'

He gave Merton another letter, in outward respect exactly similar to the first, except that the figure 2 was typewritten in the left corner. The letter ran thus:

'March 6, 4.25 p.m.

'SIR,—I regret to have to trouble you with a second communication, but my former letter was posted before a change occurred in the circumstances. You will be pleased to hear that I have no longer the affliction of speaking of your noble kinsman as "*the late* Marquis of Restalrig."'

'Oh my prophetic soul!' said Merton, 'I guessed at first that he was not dead after all! Only catalepsy.' He went on reading: 'His Lordship recovered consciousness in circumstances which I shall not pain you by describing. He is now doing as well as can be expected, and may have several years of useful life before him. I need not point out to you that the conditions of the negotiation are now greatly altered. On the one hand, my partners and myself may seem to occupy the position of players who work a double ruff at whist. We are open to the marquis's offers for release, and to yours for his eternal absence from the scene of life and enjoyment. But it is by no means impossible that you may have scruples about outbidding your kinsman, especially as, if you did, you would, by the very fact, become subject to perpetual "blackmailing" at our hands. I speak plainly, as one man of the world to another. It is also a drawback to our position that you could attain your ends without blame or scandal (your ends being, of course, if the law so determines, immediate succession to the property of the marquis), by merely pushing us, with the aid of the police, to a fatal extreme. We are, therefore reluctantly obliged to conclude that we cannot put the marquis's life up to auction between you and him, as my partners, in the first flush of triumph, had conceived. But any movement on your side against us will be met in such a way that the consequences, both to yourself and your kinsman, will prove to the last degree prejudicial. For the rest, the arrangements specified in my earlier note of this instant (dated 2.45 P. M.) remain in force.'

Merton returned the letter to Logan. Their faces were almost equally blank.

'Let me think!' said Merton. He turned, and walked to the window. Logan re-read the letters and waited. Presently Merton came back to the fireside. 'You see, after all, this resolves itself into the ordinary dilemma of brigandage. We do not want to pay ransom, enormous ransom probably, if we can rescue the marquis, and destroy the gang. But the marquis himself—'

'Oh, *he* would never offer terms that they would accept,' said

Logan, with conviction. 'But I would stick at no ransom, of course.'

'But suppose that I see a way of defeating the scoundrels, would you let me risk it?'

'If you neither imperil yourself nor him too much.'

'Never mind me, I like it. And, as for him, they will be very loth to destroy their winning card.'

'You'll be cautious?'

'Naturally, but, as this place and the stations are sure to be watched, as the trains are slow, local, and inconvenient, and as, thanks to the economy of the marquis, you have no horses, it will be horribly difficult for me to leave the house and get to London and to work without their spotting me. It is absolutely essential to my scheme that I should not be known to be in town, and that I should be supposed to be here. I'll think it out. In the meantime we must do what we can to throw dust in the eyes of the enemy. Wire an identical advertisement to all the London papers; I'll write it.'

Merton went to a table on which lay some writing materials, and wrote:—

'BURLINGTON ARCADE. SILVER-TOPPED EBONY STICK. Any offer made by the other party will be doubled on receipt of that consignment uninjured. Will meet the lady. Traps shall be kept here till after the date you mention. CHURCH BROOK.'

'Now,' said Merton, 'he will see that Church Brook is Kirkburn, and that you will be liberal. And he will understand that the detectives are not to return to London.

You did not show them the letters?'

'Of course not till you saw them, and I won't.'

'And, if nothing can be done before the eleventh, why you must promenade in the Burlington Arcade.'

'You see one weak point in your offers, don't you?'

'Which?'

'Why, suppose they do release the marquis, how am I to get the money to pay double his offer? He won't stump up and recoup me.'

Merton laughed. 'We must risk it,' he said. 'And, in the changed circumstances, the tin might be raised on a post-obit. But *he* won't bid high; you may double safely enough.'

On considering these ideas Logan looked relieved. 'Now,' he asked, 'about your plan; is it following the emu's feather?'

Merton nodded. 'But I must do it alone. The detectives must stay here. Now if I leave, dressed as I am, by the 10.49, I'll be tracked all the way. Is there anybody in the country whom you can absolutely trust?'

'Yes, there's Bower, the gardener, the son of these two feudal survivals, and there is *his* son.'

'What is young Bower?'

'A miner in the collieries; the mine is near the house.'

'Is he about my size? Have you seen him?'

'I saw him last night; he was one of the watchers.'

'Is he near my size?'

'A trifle broader, otherwise near enough.'

'What luck!' said Merton, adding, 'well, I can't start by the 10.49. I'm ill. I'm in bed. Order my breakfast in bed, send Mrs. Bower, and come up with her yourself.'

Merton rushed up the turnpike stair; in two minutes he was undressed, and between the sheets. There he lay, reading Bradshaw, pages 670, 671.

Presently there was a knock at the door, and Logan entered, followed by Mrs. Bower with the breakfast tray.

Merton addressed her at once.

'Mrs. Bower, we know that we can trust you absolutely.'

'To the death, sir—me and mine.'

'Well, I am not ill, but people must think I am ill. Is your grandson on the night shift or the day shift?'

'Laird is on the day shift, sir.'

'When does he leave his work?'

'About six, sir.'

'That is good. As soon as he appears—'

'I'll wait for him at the pit's mouth, sir.'

'Thank you. You will take him to his house; he lives with your son?'

'Yes, sir, with his father.'

'Make him change his working clothes—but he need not wash his face much—and bring him here. Mr. Logan, I mean Lord Fastcastle, will want him. Now, Mrs. Bower—you see I trust you absolutely—what he is wanted for is *this*. I shall dress in your grandson's clothes, I shall blacken my hands and face slightly, and I must get to Drem. Have I time to reach the station by ten minutes past seven?'

'By fast walking, sir.'

'Mr. Logan and your grandson—your grandson in my clothes—will walk later to your son's house, as they find a chance, unobserved, say about eleven at night. They will stay there for some time. Then they will be joined by some of the police, who will accompany Mr. Logan home again. Your grandson will go to his work as usual in the morning. That is all. You quite understand? You have nothing to do but to bring your grandson here, dressed as I said, as soon as he leaves his work. Oh, wait a moment! Is your grandson a teetotaller?'

'He's like the other lads, sir.'

'All the better. Does he smoke?'

'Yes, sir.'

'Then pray bring me a pipe of his and some of his tobacco. And, ah yes, does he possess such a thing as an old greatcoat?'

'His auld ane's sair worn, sir.'

'Never mind, he had better walk up in it. He has a better one?'

'Yes, sir.'

'I think that is all,' said Merton. 'You understand, Mrs. Bower, that I am going away dressed as your grandson, while your grandson, dressed as myself, returns to his house to-night, and to work to-morrow. But it is not to be known that I *have* gone away. I am to be supposed ill in bed here for a day or two. You will bring my meals into the room at the usual hours, and Logan—of course you can trust Dr. Douglas?'

'I do.'

'Then he had better be summoned to my sick bed here to-morrow. I may be so ill that he will have to call twice. That will keep up the belief that I am here.'

'Good idea,' said Logan, as the old woman left the room. 'What had I better do now?'

'Oh, send your telegrams—the advertisements—to the London papers. They can go by the trap you ordered for me, that I am too ill to go in. Then you will have to interview the detectives, take them into the laird's chamber, and, if they start my theory about the secret entrance being under the fallen stones, let them work away at removing them. If they don't start it, put them up to it; anything to keep them employed and prevent them from asking questions in the villages.'

'But, Merton, I understand your leaving in disguise; still,

why go first to Edinburgh?'

'The trains from your station to town do not fit. You can look.' And Merton threw Bradshaw to Logan, who caught it neatly.

When he had satisfied himself, Logan said, 'The shops will be closed in Edinburgh, it will be after eight when you arrive. How will you manage about getting into decent clothes?'

'I have my idea; but, as soon as you can get rid of the detectives, come back here; I want you to coach me in broad Scots words and pronunciation. I shall concoct imaginary dialogues. I say, this is great fun.'

'Dod, man, aw 'm the lad that'll lairn ye the pronoonciation,' said Logan, and he was going.

'Wait,' said Merton, 'sign me a paper giving me leave to treat about the ransom. And promise that, if I don't reappear by the eleventh, you won't negotiate at all.'

'Not likely I will,' said Logan.

Merton lay in bed inventing imaginary dialogues to be rendered into Scots as occasion served. Presently Logan brought him a little book named *Mansie Waugh*.

'That is our lingo here,' he said; and Merton studied the work carefully, marking some phrases with a pencil.

In about an hour Logan reported that the detectives were at work in the secret passage. The lesson in the Scots of the Lothians began, accompanied by sounds of muffled laughter. Not for two or three centuries can the turret chamber at

Kirkburn have heard so much merriment.

The afternoon passed in this course of instruction. Merton was a fairly good mimic, and Logan felt at last that he could not readily be detected for an Englishman. Six o'clock had scarcely struck when Mrs. Bower's grandson was ushered into the bedroom. The exchange of clothes took place, Merton dressing as the young Bower undressed. The detectives, who had found nothing, were being entertained by Mrs. Bower at dinner.

'I know how the trap in the secret passage is worked,' said Merton, 'but you keep them hunting for it.'

Had the worthy detectives been within earshot the yells of laughter echoing in the turret as the men dressed must have suggested strange theories to their imaginations.

'Larks!' said Merton, as he blackened his face with coal dust.

Dismissing young Bower, who was told to wait in the hall, Merton made his final arrangements. 'You will communicate with me under cover to Trevor,' he said. He took a curious mediaeval ring that he always wore from his ringer, and tied it to a piece of string, which he hung round his neck, tucking all under his shirt. Then he arranged his thick comforter so as to hide the back of his head and neck (he had bitten his nails and blackened them with coal).

'Logan, I only want a bottle of whisky, the cork drawn and loose in the bottle, and a few dirty Scotch one pound notes; and, oh! has Mrs. Bower a pack of cards?'

Having been supplied with these properties, and said farewell to Logan, Merton stole downstairs, walked round the house, entered the kitchen by the back door, and said to

Mrs. Bower, 'Grannie, I maun be ganging.'

'My grandson, gentlemen,' said Mrs. Bower to the detectives. Then to her grandson, she remarked, 'Hae, there's a jeely piece for you'; and Merton, munching a round of bread covered with jam, walked down the steep avenue. He knew the house he was to enter, the gardener's lodge, and also that he was to approach it by the back way, and go in at the back door. The inmates expected him and understood the scheme; presently he went out by the door into the village street, still munching at his round of bread.

To such lads and lassies as hailed him in the waning light he replied gruffly, explaining that he had 'a sair hoast,' that is, a bad cough, from which he had observed that young Bower was suffering. He was soon outside of the village, and walking at top speed towards the station. Several times he paused, in shadowy corners of the hedges, and listened. There was no sound of pursuing feet. He was not being followed, but, of course, he might be dogged at the station. The enemy would have their spies there: if they had them in the village his disguise had deceived them. He ran, whenever no passer-by was in sight; through the villages he walked, whistling 'Wull ye no come back again!' He reached the station with three minutes to spare, took a third-class ticket, and went on to the platform. Several people were waiting, among them four or five rough-looking miners, probably spies. He strolled towards the end of the platform, and when the train entered, leaped into a third-class carriage which was nearly full. Turning at the door, he saw the rough customers making for the same carriage. 'Come on,' cried Merton, with a slight touch of intoxication in his voice; 'come on billies, a' freens here!' and he cast a glance of affection behind him at the other occupants of the carriage. The roughs pressed in.

'I won't have it,' cried a testy old gentleman, who was

economically travelling by third-class, 'there are only three seats vacant. The rest of the train is nearly empty. Hi, guard! station-master, hi!'

'A' *freens* here,' repeated Merton stolidly, taking his whisky bottle from his greatcoat pocket. Two of the roughs had entered, but the guard persuaded the other two that they must bestow themselves elsewhere. The old gentleman glared at Merton, who was standing up, the cork of the bottle between his teeth, as the train began to move. He staggered and fell back into his seat.

'We are na fou, we're no *that* fou,'

Merton chanted, directing his speech to the old gentleman,

'But just a wee drap in oor 'ee!'

'The curse of Scotland,' muttered the old gentleman, whether with reference to alcohol or to Robert Burns, is uncertain.

'The Curse o' Scotland,' said Merton, 'that's the nine o' diamonds. I hae the cairts on me, maybe ye'd take a hand, sir, at Beggar ma Neebour, or Catch the Ten? Ye needna be feared, a can pay gin I lose.' He dragged out his cards, and a handful of silver.

The rough customers between whom Merton was sitting began to laugh hoarsely. The old gentleman frowned.

'I shall change my carriage at the next station,' he said, 'and I shall report you for gambling.'

'A' freens!' said Merton, as if horrified by the austere reception of his cordial advances. 'Wha's gaumlin'? We mauna play, billies, till he's gane. An unco pernicketty auld carl, thon ane,' he remarked, *sotto voce*. 'But there's naething in the Company's by-laws again refraishments,' Merton added. He uncorked his bottle, made a pretence of sucking at it, and passed it to his neighbours, the rough customers. They imbibed with freedom.

The carriage was very dark, the lamp 'moved like a moon in a wane,' as Merton might have quoted in happier circumstances. The rough customers glared at him, but his cap had a peak, and he wore his comforter high.

'Man, ye're the kind o' lad I like,' said one of the rough customers.

'A' freens!' said Merton, again applying himself to the bottle, and passing it. 'Ony ither gentleman tak' a sook?' asked Merton, including all the passengers in his hospitable glance. 'Nane o' ye dry?

   'Oh! fill yer ain glass,
   And let the jug pass,
   Hoo d'ye ken but yer neighbour's dry?'

Merton carolled.

'Thon's no a Scotch lilt,' remarked one of the roughs.

'A ken it's Irish,' said Merton. 'But, billie, the whusky's Scotch!'

The train slowed and the old gentleman got out. From the platform he stormed at Merton.

'Ye're no an awakened character, ma freend,' answered Merton. 'Gude nicht to ye! Gie ma love to the gude wife and the weans!'

The train pursued her course.

'Aw 'm saying, billie, aw 'm saying,' remarked one of the roughs, thrusting his dirty beard into Merton's face.

'Weel, *be* saying,' said Merton.

'You're no Lairdie Bower, ye ken, ye haena the neb o' him.'

'And wha the deil said a *was* Lairdie Bower? Aw 'm a Lanerick man. Lairdie's at hame wi' a sair hoast,' answered Merton.

'But ye're wearing Lairdie Bower's auld big coat.'

'And what for no? Lairdie has anither coat, a brawer yin, and he lent me the auld yin because the nichts is cauld, and I hae a hoast ma'sel! Div *ye* ken Lairdie Bower? I've been wi' his auld faither and the lasses half the day, but speakin's awfu' dry work.'

Here Merton repeated the bottle trick, and showed symptoms of going to sleep, his head rolling on to the shoulder of the rough.

'Haud up, man!' said the rough, withdrawing the support.

'A' freens here,' remarked Merton, drawing a dirty clay pipe from his pocket. 'Hae ye a spunk?'

The rough provided him with a match, and he killed some time, while Preston Pans was passed, in filling and lighting his pipe.

'Ye're a Lanerick man?' asked the inquiring rough.

Andrew Lang

'Ay, a Hamilton frae Moss End. But I'm taking the play. Ma auld tittie has dee'd and left me some siller,' Merton dragged a handful of dirty notes out of his trousers pocket. 'I've been to see the auld Bowers, but Lairdie was on the shift.'

'And ye're ganging to Embro?'

'When we cam' into Embro Toon
We were a seemly sicht to see; Ma luve was in the—

I dinna mind what ma luve was in—

'And I ma'sel in cramoisie,'

sang Merton, who had the greatest fear of being asked local questions about Moss End and Motherwell. 'I dinna ken what cramoisie is, ma'sel',' he added. 'Hae a drink!'

'Man, ye're a bonny singer,' said the rough, who, hitherto, had taken no hand in the conversation.

'Ma faither was a precentor,' said Merton, and so, in fact, Mr. Merton *pere* had, for a short time, been—of Salisbury Cathedral.

They were approaching Portobello, where Merton rushed to the window, thrust half of his body out and indulged in the raucous and meaningless yells of the festive artisan. Thus he tided over a rather prolonged wait, but, when the train moved on, the inquiring rough returned to the charge. He was suspicious, and also was drunk, and obstinate with all the brainless obstinacy of intoxication.

'Aw 'm sayin',' he remarked to Merton, 'you're no Lairdie Bower.'

'Hear till the man! Aw 'm Tammy Hamilton, o' Moss End in Lanerick. Aw 'm ganging to see ma Jean.

'For day or night
Ma fancy's flight
Is ever wi' ma Jean—
Ma bonny, bonny, flat-footed Jean,'

sang Merton, gliding from the strains of Robert Burns into those of Mr. Boothby. 'Jean's a Lanerick wumman,' he added, 'she's in service in the Pleasance. Aw 'm ganging to my Jo. Ye'll a' hae Jos, billies?'

'Aw 'm sayin',' the intoxicated rough persisted, 'ye're no a Lanerick man. Ye're the English gentleman birkie that cam' to Kirkburn yestreen. Or else ye're ane o' the polis' (police).

'*Me* ane o' the polis! Aw 'm askin' the company, *div* a look like a polisman? *Div* a look like an English birkie, or ane o' the gentry?'

The other passengers, decent people, thus appealed to, murmured negatives, and shook their heads. Merton certainly did not resemble a policeman, an Englishman, or a gentleman.

'Ye see naebody lippens to ye,' Merton went on. 'Man, if we were na a' freens, a wad gie ye a jaud atween yer twa een! But ye've been drinking. Tak anither sook!'

The rough did not reject the conciliatory offer.

'The whiskey's low,' said Merton, holding up the bottle to the light, 'but there's mair at Embro' station.'

They were now drawing up at the station. Merton floundered

out, threw his arms round the necks of each of the roughs, yelled to their companions in the next carriage to follow, and staggered into the third- class refreshment room. Here he leaned against the counter and feebly ogled the attendant nymph.

'Ma lonny bassie, a mean ma bonny lassie,' he said, 'gie's five gills, five o' the Auld Kirk' (whisky).

'Hoots man!' he heard one of the roughs remark to another. 'This falla's no the English birkie. English he canna be.'

'But aiblins he's ane o' oor ain polis,' said the man of suspicions.

'Nane o' oor polis has the gumption; and him as fou as a fiddler.'

Merton, waving his glass, swallowed its contents at three gulps. He then fell on the floor, scrambled to his feet, tumbled out, and dashed his own whisky bottle through the window of the refreshment room.

'Me ane o' the polis!' he yelled, and was staggering towards the exit, when he was collared by two policemen, attracted by the noise. He embraced one of them, murmuring 'ma bonny Jean!' and then doubled up, his head lolling on his shoulder. His legs and arms jerked convulsively, and he had at last to be carried off, in the manner known as 'The Frog's March,' by four members of the force. The roughs followed, like chief mourners, Merton thought, at the head of the attendant crowd.

'There's an end o' your clash about the English gentleman,' Merton heard the quieter of his late companions observe to the obstinate inquirer. 'But he's a bonny singer. And noo, wull ye tell me hoo we're to win back to Drem the nicht?'

'Dod, we'll make a nicht o't,' said the other, as Merton was carried into the police-station.

He permitted himself to be lifted into one of the cells, and then remarked, in the most silvery tones:

'Very many thanks, my good men. I need not give you any more trouble, except by asking you, if possible, to get me some hot water and soap, and to invite the inspector to favour me with his company.'

The men nearly dropped Merton, but, finding his feet, he stood up and smiled blandly.

'Pray make no apologies,' he said. 'It is rather I who ought to apologise.'

'He's no drucken, and he's no Scotch,' remarked one of the policemen.

'But he'll pass the nicht here, and maybe apologise to the Baillie in the morning,' said another.

'Oh, pardon me, you mistake me,' said Merton. 'This is not a stupid practical joke.'

'It's no a very gude ane,' said the policeman.

Merton took out a handful of gold. 'I wish to pay for the broken window at once,' he said. 'It was a necessary part of the *mise en scene*, of the stage effect, you know. To call your attention.'

'Ye'll settle wi' the Baillie in the morning,' said the policeman.

Things were looking untoward.

'Look here,' said Merton, 'I quite understand your point of view, it does credit to your intelligence. You take me for an English tourist, behaving as I have done by way of a joke, or for a bet?'

'That's it, sir,' said the spokesman.

'Well, it does look like that. But which of you is the senior officer here?'

'Me, sir,' said the last speaker.

'Very well, if you can be so kind as to call the officer in charge of the station, or even one of senior standing—the higher the better—I can satisfy him as to my identity, and as to my reasons for behaving as I have done. I assure you that it is a matter of the very gravest importance. If the inspector, when he has seen me, permits, I have no objections to you, or to all of you hearing what I have to say. But you will understand that this is a matter for his own discretion. If I were merely playing the fool, you must see that I have nothing to gain by giving additional annoyance and offence.'

'Very well, sir, I will bring the officer in charge,' said the policeman.

'Just tell him about my arrest and so on,' said Merton.

In a few minutes he returned with his superior.

'Well, my man, what's a' this aboot?' said that officer sternly.

'If you can give me an interview, alone, for five minutes, I shall enlighten you,' said Merton.

The officer was a huge and stalwart man. He threw his eye over Merton. 'Wait in the yaird,' he said to his minions, who retreated rather reluctantly. 'Weel, speak up,' said the officer.

'It is the body snatching case at Kirkburn,' said Merton.

'Do ye mean that ye're an English detective?'

'No, merely a friend of Mr. Logan's who left Kirkburn this evening. I have business to do for him in London in connection with the case—business that nobody can do but myself—and the house was watched. I escaped in the disguise which you see me wearing, and had to throw off a gang of ruffians that accompanied me in the train by pretending to be drunk. I could only shake them off and destroy the suspicions which they expressed by getting arrested.'

'It's a queer story,' said the policeman.

'It *is* a queer story, but, speaking without knowledge, I think your best plan is to summon the chief of your detective department, I need his assistance. And I can prove my identity to him—to *you*, if you like, but you know best what is official etiquette.'

'I'll telephone for him, sir.'

'You are very obliging. All this is confidential, you know. Expense is no object to Mr. Logan, and he will not be ungrateful if strict secrecy is preserved. But, of all things, I want a wash.'

'All right, sir,' said the policeman, and in a few minutes Merton's head, hands, and neck, were restored to their pristine propriety.

'No more kailyard talk for me,' he thought, with satisfaction.

The head of the detective department arrived in no long time. He was in evening dress. Merton rose and bowed.

'What's your story, sir?' the chief asked; 'it has brought me from a dinner party at my own house.'

'I deeply regret it,' said Merton, 'though, for my purpose, it is the merest providence.'

'What do you mean, sir?'

'Your subordinate has doubtless told you all that I told him?'

The chief nodded.

'Do you—I mean as an official—believe me?'

'I would be glad of proof of your personal identity.'

'That is easily given. You may know Mr. Lumley, the Professor of Toxicology in the University here?'

'I have met him often on matters of our business.'

'He is an old college friend of mine, and can remove any doubts you may entertain. His wife is a tall woman luckily,' added Merton to himself, much to the chief's bewilderment.

'Mr. Lumley's word would quite satisfy me,' said the chief.

'Very well, pray lend me your attention. This affair—'

'The body snatching at Kirkburn?' asked the chief.

'Exactly,' said Merton. 'This affair is very well organised. Your house is probably being observed. Now what I propose is *this*. I can go nowhere dressed as I am. You will, if you please, first send a constable, in uniform, to your house with orders to wait till you return. Next, I shall dress, by your permission, in any spare uniform you may have here and in that costume I shall leave this office and accompany you to your house in a closed cab. You will enter it, bring out a hat and cloak, come into the cab, and I shall put them on, leaving my policeman's helmet in the cab, which will wait. Then, minutes later, the constable will come out, take the cab, and drive to any police office you please. Once within your house, I shall exchange my uniform for any old evening suit you may be able to lend me, and, when your guests have departed, you and I will drive together to Professor Lumley's, where he will identify me. After that, my course is perfectly clear, and I need give you no further trouble.'

'It is too complicated, sir,' said the chief, smiling. 'I don't know your name?'

'Merton,' said our hero, 'and yours?'

'Macnab. I can lend you a plain suit of morning clothes from here, and we don't want the stratagem of the constable. You don't even need the extra trouble of putting on evening dress in my house.'

'How very fortunate,' said Merton, and in a quarter of an hour he was attired as a simple citizen, and was driving to the house of Mr. Macnab. Here he was merely introduced to the guests—it was a men's party—as a gentleman from England on business. The guests had too much tact to tarry long, and by eleven o'clock the chief and Merton were ringing at the door bell of Professor Lumley. The servant knew both of them, and ushered them into the professor's study. He was reading examination papers. Mrs. Lumley had not returned from a party. Lumley greeted Merton warmly.

'I am passing through Edinburgh, and thought I might find you at home,' Merton said.

'Mr. Macnab,' said Lumley, shaking hands with the chief, 'you have not taken my friend into custody?'

'No, professor; Mr. Merton will tell you that he is released, and I'll be going home.'

'You won't stop and smoke?'

'No, I should be *de trop*,' answered the chief; 'good night, professor; good night, Mr. Merton.'

'But the broken window?'

'Oh, we'll settle that, and let you have the bill.'

Merton gave his club address, and the chief shook hands and departed.

'Now, what *have* you been doing, Merton?' asked Lumley.

Merton briefly explained the whole set of circumstances, and added, 'Now, Lumley, you are my sole hope. You can give me a bed to-night?'

'With all the pleasure in the world.'

'And lend me a set of Mrs. Lumley's raiment and a lady's portmanteau?'

'Are you quite mad?'

'No, but I must get to London undiscovered, and, for certain reasons, with which I need not trouble you, that is absolutely the only possible way. You remember, at Oxford, I made up fairly well for female parts.'

'Is there absolutely no other way?'

'None, I have tried every conceivable plan, mentally. Mourning is best, and a veil.'

At this moment Mrs. Lumley's cab was heard, returning from her party.

'Run down and break it to Mrs. Lumley,' said Merton. 'Luckily we have often acted together.'

'Luckily you are a favourite of hers,' said Lumley.

In ten minutes the pair entered the study. Mrs. Lumley, a tall lady, as Merton had said, came in, laughing and blushing.

'I shall drive with you myself to the train. My maid must be in the secret,' she said.

'She is an old acquaintance of mine,' said Merton. 'But I think you had better not come with me to the station. Nobody is likely to see me, leaving your house about nine, with my veil down. But, if any one *does* see me, he must take me for you.'

'Oh, it is I who am running up to town incognita?'

'For a day or two—you will lend me a portmanteau to give local colour?'

'With pleasure,' said Mrs. Lumley.

'And Lumley will telegraph to Trevor to meet you at King's Cross, with his brougham, at 6.15 P. M.?'

This also was agreed to, and so ended this romance of Bradshaw.

IV

Greek meets Greek

At about twenty-five minutes to seven, on March 7, the express entered King's Cross. A lady of fashionable appearance, with her veil down, gazed anxiously out of the window of a reserved carriage. She presently detected the person for whom she was looking, and waved her parasol. Trevor, lifting his hat, approached; the lady had withdrawn into the carriage, and he entered.

'Mum's the word!' said the lady.

'Why, it's—hang it all, it's Merton!'

'Your sister is staying with you?' asked Merton eagerly.

'Yes; but what on earth—'

'I'll tell you in the brougham. But you take a weight off my bosom! I am going to stay with you for a day or two; and now my reputation (or Mrs. Lumley's) is safe. Your servants never saw Mrs. Lumley?'

'Never,' said Trevor.

'All right! My portmanteau has her initials, S. M. L., and a crimson ticket; send a porter for it. Now take me to the brougham.'

Trevor offered his arm and carried the dressing-bag; the lady was led to his carriage. The portmanteau was recovered, and they drove away.

'Give me a cigarette,' said Merton, 'and I'll tell you all about it.'

He told Trevor all about it—except about the emu's feathers.

'But a male disguise would have done as well,' said Trevor

'Not a bit. It would not have suited what I have to do in town. I cannot tell you why. The affair is complex. I have to settle it, if I can, so that neither Logan nor any one else—except the body-snatcher and polite letter-writer—shall ever know how I managed it.'

Trevor had to be content with this reply. He took Merton, when they arrived, into the smoking-room, rang for tea, and 'squared his sister,' as he said, in the drawing-room. The pair were dining out, and after a solitary dinner, Merton (in a tea-gown) occupied himself with literary composition. He put his work in a large envelope, sealed it, marked it with a St. Andrew's cross, and, when Trevor returned, asked him to put it in his safe. 'Two days after to-morrow, if I do not appear, you must open the envelope and read the contents,' he said.

After luncheon on the following day—a wet day—Miss Trevor and Merton (who was still arrayed as Mrs. Lumley) went out shopping. Miss Trevor then drove off to pay a visit (Merton could not let her know his next move), and he himself, his veil down, took a four-wheeled cab, and drove to

Madame Claudine's. He made one or two purchases, and then asked for the head of the establishment, an Irish lady. To her he confided that he had to break a piece of distressing family news to Miss Markham, of the cloak department; that young lady was summoned; Madame Claudine, with a face of sympathy, ushered them into her private room, and went off to see a customer. Miss Markham was pale and trembling; Merton himself felt agitated.

'Is it about my father, or—' the girl asked.

'Pray be calm,' said Merton. 'Sit down. Both are well.'

The girl started. 'Your voice—' she said.

'Exactly,' said Merton; 'you know me.' And taking off his glove, he showed a curious mediaeval ring, familiar to his friends. 'I could get at you in no other way than this,' he said, 'and it was absolutely necessary to see you.'

'What is it? I know it is about my father,' said the girl.

'He has done us a great service,' said Merton soothingly. He had guessed what the 'distressing circumstances' were in which the marquis had been restored to life. Perhaps the reader guesses? A discreet person, who has secretly to take charge of a corpse of pecuniary value, adopts certain measures (discovered by the genius of ancient Egypt), for its preservation. These measures, doubtless, had revived the marquis, who thus owed his life to his kidnapper.

'He has, I think, done us a great service,' Merton repeated; and the girl's colour returned to her beautiful face, that had been of marble.

'Yet there are untoward circumstances,' Merton admitted. 'I

wish to ask you two or three questions. I must give you my word of honour that I have no intention of injuring your father. The reverse; I am really acting in his interests. Now, first, he has practised in Australia. May I ask if he was interested in the Aborigines?'

'Yes, very much,' said the girl, entirely puzzled. 'But,' she added, 'he was never in the Labour trade.'

'Blackbird catching?' said Merton. 'No. But he had, perhaps, a collection of native arms and implements?'

'Yes; a very fine one.'

'Among them were, perhaps, some curious native shoes, made of emu's feathers—they are called *Interlinia* or, by white men, *Kurdaitcha* shoes?'

'I don't remember the name,' said Miss Markham, 'but he had quite a number of them. The natives wear them to conceal their tracks when they go on a revenge party.'

Merton's guess was now a certainty. The marquis had spoken of Miss Markham's father as a 'landlouping' Australian doctor. The footmarks of the feathered shoes in the snow at Kirkburn proved that an article which only an Australian (or an anthropologist) was likely to know of had been used by the body-snatchers.

Merton reflected. Should he ask the girl whether she had told her father what, on the night of the marquis's appearance at the office, Logan had told her? He decided that this was superfluous; of course she had told her father, and the doctor had taken his measures (and the body of the marquis) accordingly. To ask a question would only be to enlighten the girl.

'That is very interesting,' said Merton. 'Now, I won't pretend that I disguised myself in this way merely to ask you about Australian curiosities. The truth is that, in your father's interests, I must have an interview with him.'

'You don't mean to do him any harm?' asked the girl anxiously.

'I have given you my word of honour. As things stand, I do not conceal from you that I am the only person who can save him from a situation which might be disagreeable, and that is what I want to do.'

'He will be quite safe if he sees you?' asked the girl, wringing her hands.

'That is the only way in which he can be safe, I am afraid.'

'You would not use a girl against her own father?'

'I would sooner die where I sit,' said Merton earnestly. 'Surely you can trust a friend of Mr. Logan's—who, by the bye, is very well.'

'Oh, oh,' cried the girl, 'I read that story of the stolen corpse in the papers. I understand!'

'It was almost inevitable that you should understand,' said Merton.

'But then,' said the girl, 'what did you mean by saying that my father has done you a great service. You are deceiving me. I have said too much. This is base!' Miss Markham rose, her eyes and cheeks burning.

'What I told you is the absolute and entire truth,' said Merton, nearly as red as she was.

'Then,' exclaimed Miss Markham, 'this is baser yet! You must mean that by doing what you think he has done my father has somehow enabled Robert—Mr. Logan—to come into the marquis's property. Perhaps the marquis left no will, or the will—is gone! And do you believe that Mr. Logan will thank you for acting in this way?' She stood erect, her hand resting on the back of a chair, indignant and defiant.

'In the first place, I have a written power from Mr. Logan to act as I think best. Next, I have not even informed myself as to how the law of Scotland stands in regard to the estate of a man who dies leaving no will. Lastly, Miss Markham, I am extremely hampered by the fact that Mr. Logan has not the remotest suspicion of what I suspected—and now know—to be the truth as to the disappearance of his cousin's body. I successfully concealed my idea from Mr. Logan, so as to avoid giving pain to him and you. I did my best to conceal it from you, though I never expected to succeed. And now, if you wish to know how your father has conferred a benefit on Mr. Logan, I must tell you, though I would rather be silent. Mr. Logan is aware of the benefit, but will never, if you can trust yourself, suspect his benefactor.'

'I can never, never see him again,' the girl sobbed.

'Time is flying,' said Merton, who was familiar, in works of fiction, with the situation indicated by the girl. 'Can you trust me, or not?' he asked, 'My single object is secrecy and your father's safety. I owe that to my friend, to you, and even, as it happens, to your father. Can you enable me, dressed as I am, to have an interview with him?'

'You will not hurt him? You will not give him up? You will not bring the police on him?'

'I am acting as I do precisely for the purpose of keeping the police off him. They have discovered nothing.'

The girl gave a sigh of relief.

'Your father's only danger would lie in my—failure to return from my interview with him. Against *that* I cannot safeguard him; it is fair to tell you so. But my success in persuading him to adopt a certain course would be equally satisfactory to Mr. Logan and to himself.'

'Mr. Logan knows nothing?'

'Absolutely nothing. I alone, and now you, know anything.'

The girl walked up and down in agony.

'Nobody will ever know if I do not tell you how to find him,' she said.

'Unhappily that is not the case. I only ask *you*, so that it may not be necessary to take other steps, tardy, but certain, and highly undesirable.'

'You will not go to him armed?'

'I give you my word of honour,' said Merton. 'I have risked myself unarmed already.'

The girl paused with fixed eyes that saw nothing. Merton watched her. Then she took her resolve.

'I do not know where he is living. I know that on Wednesdays, that is, the day after to-morrow, he is to be found at Dr. Fogarty's, a private asylum, a house with a garden, in Water Lane, Hammersmith.'

It was the lane in which stood the Home for Destitute and Decayed Cats, whither Logan had once abducted Rangoon, the Siamese puss.

'Thank you,' said Merton simply. 'And I am to ask for?'

'Ask first for Dr. Fogarty. You will tell him that you wish to see the *Ertwa Oknurcha*.'

'Ah, Australian for "The Big Man,"' said Merton.

'I don't know what it means,' said Miss Markham. 'Dr. Fogarty will then ask, "Have you the *churinga*?"'

The girl drew out a slim gold chain which hung round her neck and under her dress. At the end of it was a dark piece of wood, shaped much like a large cigar, and decorated with incised concentric circles, stained red.

'Take that and show it to Dr. Fogarty,' said Miss Markham, detaching the object from the chain.

Merton returned it to her. 'I know where to get a similar *churinga*,' he said. 'Keep your own. Its absence, if asked for, might lead to awkward questions.'

'Thank you, I can trust you,' said Miss Markham, adding, 'You will address my father as Dr. Melville.'

'Again thanks, and good-bye,' said Merton. He bowed and withdrew.

'She is a good deal upset, poor girl,' Merton remarked to Madame Claudine, who, on going to comfort Miss Markham with tea, found her weeping. Merton took another cab, and drove to Trevor's house.

After dinner (at which there were no guests), and in the smoking-room, Trevor asked whether he had made any progress.

'Everything succeeded to a wish,' said Merton. 'You remember Water Lane?'

'Where Logan carried the Siamese cat in my cab,' said Trevor, grinning at the reminiscence. 'Rather! I reconnoitred the place with Logan.'

'Well, on the day after to-morrow I have business there.'

'Not at the Cats' Home?'

'No, but perhaps you might reconnoitre again. Do you remember a house with high walls and spikes on them?'

'I do,' said Trevor; 'but how do you know? You never were there. You disapproved of Logan's method in the case of the cat.'

'I never was there; I only made a guess, because the house I am interested in is a private asylum.'

'Well, you guessed right. What then?'

'You might reconnoitre the ground to-morrow—the exits, there are sure to be some towards waste land or market gardens.'

'Jolly!' said Trevor. 'I'll make up as a wanderer from Suffolk, looking for a friend in the slums; semi-bargee kind of costume.'

'That would do,' said Merton. 'But you had better go in the

early morning.'

'A nuisance. Why?'

'Because, later, you will have to get a gang of fellows to be about the house the day after, when I pay my visit.'

'Fellows of our own sort, or the police?'

'Neither. I thought of fellows of our own sort. They would talk and guess.'

'Better get some of Ned Mahony's gang?' asked Trevor.

Mr. Mahony was an ex-pugilist, and a distinguished instructor in the art of self-defence. He also was captain of a gang of 'chuckers out.'

'Yes,' said Merton, 'that is my idea. *They* will guess, too; but when they know the place is a private lunatic asylum their hypothesis is obvious.'

'They'll think that a patient is to be rescued?'

'That will be their idea. And the old trick is a good trick. Cart of coals blocked in the gateway, or with another cart—the bigger the better—in the lane. The men will dress accordingly. Others will have stolen to the back and sides of the house; you will, in short, stop the earths after I enter. Your brougham, after setting me down, will wait in Hammersmith Road, or whatever the road outside is.'

'I may come?' asked Trevor.

'In command, as a coal carter.'

'Hooray!' said Trevor, 'and I'll tell you what, I won't reconnoitre as a bargee, but as a servant out of livery sent to look for a cat at the Home. And I'll mistake the asylum for the Home for Cats, and try to scout a little inside the gates.'

'Capital,' said Merton. 'Then, later, I want you to go to a curiosity shop near the Museum' (he mentioned the street), 'and look into the window. You'll see a little brown piece of wood like *this*.' Merton sketched rapidly the piece of wood which Miss Markham wore under her dress. 'The man has several. Buy one about the size of a big cigar for me, and buy one or two other trifles first.'

'The man knows me,' said Trevor, 'I have bought things from him.'

'Very good, but don't buy it when any other customer is in the shop. And, by the way, take Mrs. Lumley's portmanteau—the lock needs mending—to Jones's in Sloane Street to be repaired. One thing more, I should like to add a few lines to that manuscript I gave you to keep in your safe.'

Trevor brought the sealed envelope. Merton added a paragraph and resealed it. Trevor locked it up again.

On the following day Trevor started early, did his scouting in Water Lane, and settled with Mr. Mahony about his gang of muscular young prize- fighters. He also brought the native Australian curiosity, and sent Mrs. Lumley's portmanteau to have the lock repaired.

Merton determined to call at Dr. Fogarty's asylum at four in the afternoon. The gang, under Trevor, was to arrive half an hour later, and to surround and enter the premises if Merton did not emerge within half an hour.

At four o'clock exactly Trevor's brougham was at the gates of the asylum. The footman rang the bell, a porter opened a wicket, and admitted a lady of fashionable aspect, who asked for Dr. Fogarty. She was ushered into his study, her card ('Louise, 13—Street') was taken by the servant, and Dr. Fogarty appeared. He was a fair, undecided looking man, with blue wandering eyes, and long untidy, reddish whiskers. He bowed and looked uncomfortable, as well he might.

'I have called to see the *Ertwa Oknurcha*, Dr. Fogarty,' said Merton.

'Oh Lord,' said Dr. Fogarty, and murmured, 'Another of his lady friends!' adding, 'I must ask, Miss, have you the *churinga?*'

Merton produced, out of his muff, the Australian specimen which Trevor had bought.

The doctor inspected it. 'I shall take it to the *Ertwa Oknurcha*,' he said, and shambled out. Presently he returned. 'He will see you, Miss.'

Merton found the redoubtable Dr. Markham, an elderly man, clean shaven, prompt-looking, with very keen dark eyes, sitting at a writing table, with a few instruments of his profession lying about. The table stood on an oblong space of uncarpeted and polished flooring of some extent. Dr. Fogarty withdrew, the other doctor motioned Merton to a chair on the opposite side of the table. This chair was also on the uncarpeted space, and Merton observed four small brass plates in the parquet. Arranging his draperies, and laying aside his muff, Merton sat down, slightly shifting the position of the chair.

'Perhaps, Dr. Melville,' he said, 'it will be more reassuring to you if I at once hold my hands up,' and he sat there and smiled, holding up his neatly gloved hands.

The doctor stared, and *his* hand stole towards an instrument like an unusually long stethoscope, which lay on his table.

Merton sat there 'hands up,' still smiling. 'Ah, the blow-tube?' he said. 'Very good and quiet! Do you use *urali*? Infinitely better, at close quarters, than the noisy old revolver.'

'I see I have to do with a cool hand, sir,' said the doctor.

'Ah,' said Merton. 'Then let us talk as between man and man.' He tilted his chair backwards, and crossed his legs. 'By the way, as I have no Aaron and Hur to help me to hold up my hands, may I drop them? The attitude, though reassuring, is fatiguing.'

'If you won't mind first allowing me to remove your muff,' said the doctor. It lay on the table in front of Merton.

'By all means, no gun in my muff,' said Merton. 'In fact I think the whole pistol business is overdone, and second rate.'

'I presume that I have the honour to speak to Mr. Merton?' asked the doctor. 'You slipped through the cordon?'

'Yes, I was the intoxicated miner,' said Merton. 'No doubt you have received a report from your agents?'

'Stupid fellows,' said the doctor.

'You are not flattering to me, but let us come to business. How much?'

'I need hardly ask,' said the doctor, 'it would be an insult to your intelligence, whether you have taken the usual precautions?'

Merton, whose chair was tilted, threw himself violently backwards, upsetting his chair, and then scrambled nimbly to his feet. Between him and the table yawned a square black hole of unknown depth.

'Hardly fair, Dr. Melville,' said he, picking up the chair, and placing it on the carpet, 'besides, I *have* taken the ordinary precautions. The house is surrounded—Ned Mahony's lambs—the usual statement is in the safe of a friend. We must really come to the point. Time is flying,' and he looked at his watch. 'I can give you twenty minutes.'

'Have you anything in the way of terms to propose?' asked the doctor, filling his pipe.

'Well, first, absolute secrecy. I alone know the state of the case.'

'Has Mr. Logan no guess?'

'Not the faintest suspicion. The detectives, when I left Kirkburn, had not even found the trap door, you understand. You hit on its discovery through knowing the priest's hole at Oxburgh Hall, I suppose?'

The doctor nodded.

'You can guarantee absolute secrecy?' he asked.

'Naturally, the knowledge is confined to me, you, and your partners. I want the secrecy in Mr. Logan's interests, and you know why.'

'Well,' said the doctor, 'that is point one. So far I am with you.'

'Then, to enter on odious details,' said Merton, 'had you thought of any terms?'

'The old man was stiff,' said the doctor, 'and your side only offered to double him in your advertisement, you know.'

'That was merely a way of speaking,' said Merton. 'What did the marquis propose?'

'Well, as his offer is not a basis of negotiation?'

'Certainly not,' said Merton.

'Five hundred he offered, out of which we were to pay his fare back to Scotland.'

Both men laughed.

'But you have your own ideas?' said Merton.

'I had thought of 15,000*l.* and leaving England. He is a multimillionaire, the marquis.'

'It is rather a pull,' said Merton. 'Now speaking as a professional man, and on honour, how *is* his lordship?' Merton asked.

'Speaking as a professional man, he *may* live a year; he cannot live eighteen months, I stake my reputation on that.'

Merton mused.

'I'll tell you what we can do,' he said. 'We can guarantee the interest, at a fancy rate, say five per cent, during the marquis's life, which you reckon as good for a year and a half, at most. The lump sum we can pay on his decease.'

The doctor mused in his turn.

'I don't like it. He may alter his will, and then—where do I come in?'

'Of course that is an objection,' said Merton. 'But where do you come in if you refuse? Logan, I can assure you (I have read up the Scots law since I came to town), is the heir if the marquis dies intestate. Suppose that I do not leave this house in a few minutes, Logan won't bargain with you; we settled *that*; and really you will have taken a great deal of trouble to your own considerable risk. You see the usual document, my statement, is lodged with a friend.'

'There is certainly a good deal in what you say,' remarked the doctor.

'Then, to take a more cheerful view,' said Merton, 'I have medical authority for stating that any will made now, or later, by the marquis, would probably be upset, on the ground of mental unsoundness, you know. So Logan would succeed, in spite of a later will.'

The doctor smiled. 'That point I grant. Well, one must chance something. I accept your proposals. You will give me a written agreement, signed by Mr. Logan, for the arrangement.'

'Yes, I have power to act.'

'Then, Mr. Merton, why in the world did you not let your friend walk in Burlington Arcade, and see the lady? He would have been met with the same terms, and could have proposed the same modifications.'

'Well, Dr. Melville, first, I was afraid that he might accidentally discover the real state of the case, as I surmised that it existed—that might have led to family inconveniences, you know.'

'Yes,' the doctor admitted, 'I have felt that. My poor daughter, a good girl, sir! It wrung my heartstrings, I assure you.'

'I have the warmest sympathy with you,' said Merton, going on. 'Well, in the second place, I was not sure that I could trust Mr. Logan, who has rather a warm temper, to conduct the negotiations. Thirdly, I fear I must confess that I did what I have done—well, "for human pleasure."'

'Ah, you are young,' said the doctor, sighing.

'Now,' said Merton, 'shall I sign a promise? We can call Dr. Fogarty up to witness it. By the bye, what about "value received"? Shall we say that we purchase your ethnological collection?'

The doctor grinned, and assented, the deed was written, signed, and witnessed by Dr. Fogarty, who hastily retreated.

'Now about restoring the marquis,' said Merton. 'He's here, of course; it was easy enough to get him into an asylum. Might I suggest a gag, if by chance you have such a thing about you? To be removed, of course, when once I get him into the house of a friend. And the usual bandage over his eyes: he must never know where he has been.'

'You think of everything, Mr. Merton,' said the doctor. 'But, how are you to account for the marquis's reappearance alive?'

he asked.

'Oh *that*—easily! My first theory, which I fortunately mentioned to his medical attendant, Dr. Douglas, in the train, before I reached Kirkburn, was that he had recovered from catalepsy, and had secretly absconded, for the purpose of watching Mr. Logan's conduct. We shall make him believe that this is the fact, and the old woman who watched him—'

'Plucky old woman,' said the doctor.

'Will swear to anything that he chooses to say.'

'Well, that is your affair,' said the doctor.

'Now,' said Merton, 'give me a receipt for 750*l.*; we shall tell the marquis that we had to spring 250*l.* on his original offer.'

The doctor wrote out, stamped, and signed the receipt. 'Perhaps I had better walk in front of you down stairs?' he asked Merton.

'Perhaps it really would be more hospitable,' Merton acquiesced.

Merton was ushered again into Dr. Fogarty's room on the ground floor. Presently the other doctor reappeared, leading a bent and much muffled up figure, who preserved total silence—for excellent reasons. The doctor handed to Merton a sealed envelope, obviously the marquis's will. Merton looked closely into the face of the old marquis, whose eyes, dropping senile tears, showed no sign of recognition.

Dr. Fogarty next adjusted a silken bandage, over a wad of cotton wool, which he placed on the eyes of the prisoner.

Merton then took farewell of Dr. Melville (*alias* Markham); he and Dr. Fogarty supported the tottering steps of Lord Restalrig, and they led him to the gate.

'Tell the porter to call my brougham,' said Merton to Dr. Fogarty.

The brougham was called and came to the gate, evading a coal-cart which was about to enter the lane. Merton aided the marquis to enter, and said 'Home.' A few rough fellows, who were loitering in the lane, looked curiously on. In half an hour the marquis, his gag and the bandage round his eyes removed, was sitting in Trevor's smoking-room, attended to by Miss Trevor.

It is probably needless to describe the simple and obvious process (rather like that of the Man, the Goose, and the Fox) by which Mrs. Lumley, with her portmanteau, left Trevor's house that evening to pay another visit, while Merton himself arrived, in evening dress, to dinner at a quarter past eight. He had telegraphed to Logan: 'Entirely successful. Come up by the 11.30 to-night, and bring Mrs. Bower.'

The marquis did not appear at dinner. He was in bed, and, thanks to a sleeping potion, slumbered soundly. He awoke about nine in the morning to find Mrs. Bower by his bedside.

'Eh, marquis, finely we have jinked them,' said Mrs. Bower; and she went on to recount the ingenious measures by which the marquis, recovering from his 'dwawm,' had secretly withdrawn himself.

'I mind nothing of it, Jeanie, my woman,' said the marquis. 'I thought I wakened with some deevil running a knife into me; he might have gone further, and I might have fared worse. He asked for money, but, faith, we niffered long and came to no bargain. And a woman brought me away. Who was the woman?'

'Oh, dreams,' said Mrs. Bower. 'Ye had another sair fit o' the dwawming, and we brought you here to see the London doctors. Hoo could ony mortal speerit ye away, let be it was the fairies, and me watching you a' the time! A fine gliff ye gie'd me when ye sat up and askit for sma' yill' (small beer).

'I mind nothing of it,' replied the marquis. However, Mrs. Bower stuck to her guns, and the marquis was, or appeared to be, resigned to accept her explanation. He dozed throughout the day, but next day he asked for Merton. Their interview was satisfactory; Merton begged leave to introduce Logan, and the marquis, quite broken down, received his kinsman with tears, and said nothing about his marriage.

'I'm a dying man,' he remarked finally, 'but I'll live long enough to chouse the taxes.'

His sole idea was to hand over (in the old Scottish fashion) the main part of his property to Logan, *inter vivos*, and then to live long enough to evade the death-duties. Merton and Logan knew well enough the unsoundness of any such proceedings, especially considering the mental debility of the old gentleman. However, the papers were made out. The marquis retired to one of his English seats, after which event his reappearance was made known to the world. In his English home Logan sedulously nursed him. A more generous diet than he had ever known before did wonders for the marquis, though he peevishly remonstrated against every bottle of wine that was uncorked. He did live for the span which he deemed necessary for his patriotic purpose, and peacefully expired, his last words being 'Nae grand funeral.'

Public curiosity, of course, was keenly excited about the

mysterious reappearance of the marquis in life. But the interviewers could extract nothing from Mrs. Bower, and Logan declined to be interviewed. To paragraphists the mystery of the marquis was 'a two months' feast,' like the case of Elizabeth Canning, long ago.

Logan inherited under the marquis's original will, and, of course, the Exchequer benefitted in the way which Lord Restalrig had tried to frustrate.

Miss Markham (whose father is now the distinguished head of the ethnological department in an American museum) did not persist in her determination never to see Logan again. The beautiful Lady Fastcastle never allows her photograph to appear in the illustrated weekly papers. Logan, or rather Fastcastle, does not unto this day, know the secret of the Emu's feathers, though, later, he sorely tried the secretiveness of Merton, as shall be shown in the following narrative.

XII

ADVENTURE OF THE CANADIAN HEIRESS

I

At Castle Skrae

'How vain a thing is wealth,' said Merton. 'How little it can give of what we really desire, while of all that is lost and longed for it can restore nothing—except churches—and to do *that* ought to be made a capital offence.'

'Why do you contemplate life as a whole, Mr. Merton? Why are you so moral? If you think it is amusing you are very much mistaken! Isn't the scenery, isn't the weather, beautiful enough for you? *I* could gaze for ever at the "unquiet bright Atlantic plain," the rocky isles, those cliffs of basalt on either hand, while I listened to the crystal stream that slips into the sea, and waves the yellow fringes of the seaweed. Don't be melancholy, or I go back to the castle. Try another line!'

'Ah, I doubt that I shall never wet one here,' said Merton.

'As to the crystal stream, what business has it to be crystal? That is just what I complain of. Salmon and sea-trout are waiting out there in the bay and they can't come up! Not a drop of rain to call rain for the last three weeks. That is what I meant by moralising about wealth. You can buy half a county, if you have the money; you can take half a dozen rivers, but all the millions of our host cannot purchase us a spate, and without a spate you might as well break the law by fishing in the Round Pond as in the river.'

'Luckily for me Alured does not much care for fishing,' said Lady Bude, who was Merton's companion. The Countess had abandoned, much to her lord's regret, the coloured and figurative language of her maiden days, the American slang. Now (as may have been observed) her style was of that polished character which can only be heard to perfection in circles socially elevated and intellectually cultured—'in that Garden of the Souls'—to quote Tennyson.

The spot where Merton and Lady Bude were seated was beautiful indeed. They reclined on the short sea grass above a shore where long tresses of saffron-hued seaweed clothed the boulders, and the bright sea pinks blossomed. On their right the Skrae, now clearer than amber, mingled its waters with the sea loch. On their left was a steep bank clad with bracken, climbing up to perpendicular cliffs of basalt. These ended abruptly above the valley and the cove, and permitted a view of the Atlantic, in which, far away, the isle of the Lewis lay like a golden shield in the faint haze of the early sunset. On the other side of the sea loch, whose restless waters ever rushed in or out like a rapid river, with the change of tides, was a small village of white thatched cottages, the homes of fishermen and crofters. The neat crofts lay behind, in oblong strips, on the side of the hill. Such was the scene of a character common on the remote west coast of Sutherland.

'Alured is no maniac for fishing, luckily,' Lady Bude was saying. 'To-day he is cat-hunting.'

'I regret it,' said Merton; 'I profess myself the friend of cats.'

'He is only trying to photograph a wild cat at home in the hills; they are very scarce.'

'In fact he is Jones Harvey, the naturalist again, for the nonce, not the sportsman,' said Merton.

'It was as Jones Harvey that he—' said Lady Bude, and, blushing, stopped.

'That he grasped the skirts of happy chance,' said Merton.

'Why don't *you* grasp the skirts, Mr. Merton?' asked Lady Bude. 'Chance, or rather Lady Fortune, who wears the skirts, would, I think, be happy to have them grasped.'

'Whose skirts do you allude to?'

'The skirts, short enough in the Highlands, of Miss Macrae,' said Lady Bude; 'she is a nice girl, and a pretty girl, and a clever girl, and, after all, there are worse things than millions.'

Miss Emmeline Macrae was the daughter of the host with whom the Budes and Merton were staying at Skrae Castle, on Loch Skrae, only an easy mile and a half from the sea and the cove beside which Merton and Lady Bude were sitting.

'There is a seal crawling out on to the shore of the little island!' said Merton. 'What a brute a man must be who shoots a seal! I could watch them all day—on a day like this.'

'That is not answering my question,' said Lady Bude. 'What do you think of Miss Macrae? I *know* what you think!'

'Can a humble person like myself aspire to the daughter of the greatest living millionaire? Our host can do almost anything but bring a spate, and even *that* he could do by putting a dam with a sluice at the foot of Loch Skrae: a matter of a few thousands only. As for the lady, her heart it is another's, it never can be mine.'

'Whose it is?' asked Lady Bude.

'Is it not, or do my trained instincts deceive me, that of young Blake, the new poet? Is she not "the girl who gives to song what gold could never buy"? He is as handsome as a man has no business to be.'

'He uses belladonna for his eyes,' said Lady Bude. 'I am sure of it.'

'Well, she does not know, or does not mind, and they are pretty inseparable the last day or two.'

'That is your own fault,' said Lady Bude; 'you banter the poet so cruelly. She pities him.'

'I wonder that our host lets the fellow keep staying here,' said Merton. 'If Mr. Macrae has a foible, except that of the pedigree of the Macraes (who were here before the Macdonalds or Mackenzies, and have come back in his person), it is scientific inventions, electric lighting, and his new toy, the wireless telegraph box in the observatory. You can see the tower from here, and the pole with box on top. I don't care for that kind of thing myself, but Macrae thinks it Paradise to get messages from the Central News and the Stock Exchange up here, fifty miles from a telegraph post. Well, yesterday Blake was sneering at the whole affair.'

'What is this wireless machine? Explain it to me,' said

Lady Bude.

'How can you be so cruel?' asked Merton.

'Why cruel?'

'Oh, you know very well how your sex receives explanations. You have three ways of doing it.'

'Explain *them*!'

'Well, the first way is, if a man tries to explain what "per cent" means, or the difference of "odds on," or "odds against," that is, if they don't gamble, they cast their hands desperately abroad, and cry, "Oh, don't, I never *can* understand!" The second way is to sit and smile, and look intelligent, and think of their dressmaker, or their children, or their young man, and then to say, "Thank you, you have made it all so clear!"'

'And the third way?'

'The third way is for you to make it plain to the explainer that he does not understand what he is explaining.'

'Well, try me; how does the wireless machine work?'

'Then, to begin with a simple example in ordinary life, you know what telepathy is?'

'Of course, but tell me.'

'Suppose Jones is thinking of Smith, or rather of Smith's sister. Jones is dying, or in a row, in India. Miss Smith is in Bayswater. She sees Jones in her drawing-room. The thought of Jones has struck a receiver of some sort in the brain, say, of Miss Smith. *But* Miss Smith may not see him, somebody else may, say her aunt, or the footman. That is because the aunt or the footman has the properly tuned receiver in her or his brain, and Miss Smith has not.'

'I see, so far—but the machine?'

'That is an electric apparatus charged with a message. The message is not conducted by wires, but is merely carried along on a new sort of waves, "Hertz waves," I think, but that does not matter. They roam through space, these waves, and wherever they meet another machine of the same kind, a receiver, they communicate it.'

'Then everybody who has such a machine as Mr. Macrae's gets all Mr. Macrae's messages for nothing?' asked Lady Bude.

'They would get them,' said Merton. 'But that is where the artfulness comes in. Two Italian magicians, or electricians, Messrs. Gianesi and Giambresi, have invented an improvement suggested by a dodge of the Indians on the Amazon River. They make machines which are only in tune with each other. Their machine fires off a message which no other machine can receive or tap except that of their customer, say Mr. Macrae. The other receivers all over the world don't get it, they are not in tune. It is as if Jones could only appear as a wraith to Miss Smith, and *vice versa*.'

'How is it done?'

'Oh, don't ask me! Besides, I fancy it is a trade secret, the tuning. There's one good thing about it, you know how Highland landscape is spoiled by telegraph posts?'

'Yes, everywhere there is always a telegraph post in

the foreground.'

'Well, Mr. Macrae had them when he was here first, but he has had them all cut down, bless him, since he got the new dodge. He was explaining it all to Blake and me, and Blake only scoffed, would not understand, showed he was bored.'

'I think it delightful! What did Mr. Blake say?'

'Oh, his usual stuff. Science is an expensive and inadequate substitute for poetry and the poetic gifts of the natural man, who is still extant in Ireland. *He* can flash his thoughts, and any trifles of news he may pick up, across oceans and continents, with no machinery at all. What is done in Khartoum is known the same day in Cairo.'

'What did Mr. Macrae say?'

'He asked why the Cairo people did not make fortunes on the Stock Exchange.'

'And Mr. Blake?'

'He looked a great deal, but he said nothing. Then, as I said, he showed that he was bored when Macrae exhibited to us the machine and tried to teach us how it worked, and the philosophy of it. Blake did not understand it, nor do I, really, but of course I displayed an intelligent interest. He didn't display any. He said that the telegraph thing only brought us nearer to all that a child of nature—'

'*He* a child of nature, with his belladonna!'

'To all that a child of nature wanted to forget. The machine emitted a serpent of tape, news of Surrey *v.* Yorkshire, and something about Kaffirs, and Macrae was enormously pleased, for such are the simple joys of the millionaire, really a child of nature. Some of them keep automatic hydraulic organs and beastly machines that sing. Now Macrae is not a man of that sort, and he has only one motor up here, and only uses *that* for practical purposes to bring luggage and supplies, but the wireless thing is the apple of his eye. And Blake sneered.'

'He is usually very civil indeed, almost grovelling, to the father,' said Lady Bude. 'But I tell you for your benefit, Mr. Merton, that he has no chance with the daughter. I know it for certain. He only amuses her. Now here, you are clever.'

Merton bowed.

'Clever, or you would not have diverted me from my question with all that science. You are not ill looking.'

'Spare my blushes,' said Merton; adding, 'Lady Bude, if you must be answered, *you* are clever enough to have found me out.'

'That needed less acuteness than you suppose,' said the lady.

'I am very sorry to hear it,' said Merton. 'You know how utterly hopeless it is.'

'There I don't agree with you,' said Lady Bude.

Merton blushed. 'If you are right,' he said, 'then I have no business to be here. What am I in the eyes of a man like Mr. Macrae? An adventurer, that is what he would think me. I did think that I had done nothing, said nothing, looked nothing, but having the chance—well, I could not keep away from her. It is not honourable. I must go. . . . I love her.'

Merton turned away and gazed at the sunset without seeing it.

Lady Bude put forth her hand and laid it on his. 'Has this gone on long?' she asked.

'Rather an old story,' said Merton. 'I am a fool. That is the chief reason why I was praying for rain. She fishes, very keen on it. I would have been on the loch or the river with her. Blake does not fish, and hates getting wet.'

'You might have more of her company, if you would not torment the poet so. The green-eyed monster, jealousy, is on your back.'

Merton groaned. 'I bar the fellow, anyhow,' he said. 'But, in any case, now that I know *you* have found me out, I must be going. If only she were as poor as I am!'

'You can't go to-morrow, to-morrow is Sunday,' said Lady Bude. 'Oh, I am sorry for you. Can't we think of something? Cannot you find an opening? Do something great! Get her upset on the loch, and save her from drowning! Mr. Macrae dotes on her; he would be grateful.'

'Yes, I might take the pin out of the bottom of the boat,' said Merton. 'It is an idea! But she swims at least as well as I do. Besides—hardly sportsmanlike.'

Lady Bude tried to comfort him; it is the mission of young matrons. He must not be in such a hurry to go away. As to Mr. Blake, she could entirely reassure him. It was a beautiful evening, the lady was fair and friendly; Nature, fragrant of heather and of the sea, was hushed in a golden repose. The two talked long, and the glow of sunset was fading; the eyes of Lady Bude were a little moist, and Merton was feeling rather consoled when they rose and walked back towards

Skrae Castle. It had been an ancient seat of the Macraes, a clan in relatively modern times, say 1745, rather wild, impoverished, and dirty; but Mr. Macrae, the great Canadian millionaire, had bought the old place, with many thousands of acres 'where victual never grew.'

Though a landlord in the Highlands he was beloved, for he was the friend of crofters, as rent was no object to him, and he did not particularly care for sport. He accepted the argument, dear to the Celt, that salmon are ground game, and free to all, while the natives were allowed to use ancient flint-locked fusils on his black cocks. Mr. Macrae was a thoroughly generous man, and a tall, clean-shaved, graceful personage. His public gifts were large. He had just given 500,000*l.* to Oxford to endow chairs and students of Psychical Research, while the rest of the million was bestowed on Cambridge, to supply teaching in Elementary Logic. His way of life was comfortable, but simple, except where the comforts of science and modern improvements were concerned. There were lifts, or elevators, now in the castle of Skrae, though Blake always went by the old black corkscrew staircases, holding on by the guiding rope, after the poetical manner of our ancestors.

On a knowe which commanded the castle, in a manner that would have pained Sir Dugald Dalgetty, Mr. Macrae had erected, not a 'sconce,' but an observatory, with a telescope that 'licked the Lick thing,' as he said. Indeed it was his foible 'to see the Americans and go one better,' and he spoke without tolerance of the late boss American millionaire, the celebrated J. P. van Huytens, recently deceased.

> Duke Humphrey greater wealth computes,
> And sticks, they say, at nothing,

sings the poet. Mr. Macrae computed greater wealth than Mr.

van Huytens, though avoiding ostentation; he did not

Wear a pair of golden boots,
And silver underclothing.

The late J. P. van Huytens he regarded with moral scorn. This rival millionaire had made his wealth by the process (apparently peaceful and horticultural) of 'watering stocks,' and by the seemingly misplaced generosity of over-capitalising enterprises, and 'grabbing side shows.' The nature of these and other financial misdemeanours Merton did not understand. But he learned from Mr. Macrae that thereby J. P. van Huytens had scooped in the widow, the orphan, the clergyman, and the colonel. The two men had met in the most exclusive circles of American society; with the young van Huytenses the daughter of the millionaire had even been on friendly terms, but Mr. Macrae retired to Europe, and put a stop to all that. To do so, indeed, was one of his motives for returning to the home of his ancestors, the remote and inaccessible Castle Skrae. *The Sportsman's Guide to Scotland* says, as to Loch Skrae: 'Railway to Lairg, then walk or hire forty-five miles.' The young van Huytenses were not invited to walk or hire.

Van Huytens had been ostentatious, Mr. Macrae was the reverse. His costume was of the simplest, his favourite drink (of which he took little) was what humorists call 'the light wine of the country,' drowned in Apollinaris water. His establishment was refined, but not gaudy or luxurious, and the chief sign of wealth at Skrae was the great observatory with the laboratory, and the surmounting 'pole with box on top,' as Merton described the apparatus for the new kind of telegraphy. In the basement of the observatory was lodged the hugest balloon known to history, and a skilled expert was busied with novel experiments in aerial navigation. Happily he could swim, and his repeated descents into Loch Skrae did not daunt his soaring genius.

Above the basement of the observatory were rooms for bachelors, a smoking- room, a billiard-room, and a scientific library. The wireless telegraphy machine (looking like two boxes, one on the top of the other, to the eye of ignorance) was installed in the smoking-room, and a wire to Mr. Macrae's own rooms informed him, by ringing a bell (it also rang in the smoking-room), when the machine began to spread itself out in tape conveying the latest news. The machine communicated with another in the establishment of its vendors, Messrs. Gianesi, Giambresi & Co., in Oxford Street. Thus the millionaire, though residing nearly fifty miles from the nearest station at Lairg, was as well and promptly informed as if he dwelt in Fleet Street, and he could issue, without a moment's procrastination, his commands to sell and buy, and to do such other things as pertain to the nature of millionaires. When we add that a steam yacht of great size and comfort, doing an incredible number of knots an hour on the turbine system, lay at anchor in the sea loch, we have indicated the main peculiarities of Mr. Macrae's rural establishment. Wealth, though Merton thought so poorly of it, had supplied these potentialities of enjoyment; but, alas! disease had 'decimated' the grouse on the moors (of course to decimate now means almost to extirpate), and the crofters had increased the pleasures of stalking by making the stags excessively shy, thus adding to the arduous enjoyment of the true sportsman.

To Castle Skrae, being such as we have described, Lady Bude and Merton returned from their sentimental prowl. They found Miss Macrae, in a very short skirt of the Macrae tartan, trying to teach Mr. Blake to play ping- pong in the great hall.

We must describe the young lady, though her charms outdo

the powers of the vehicle of prose. She was tall, slim, and graceful, light of foot as a deer on the corrie. Her hair was black, save when the sun shone on it and revealed strands of golden brown; it was simply arrayed, and knotted on the whitest and shapeliest neck in Christendom. Her eyebrows were dark, her eyes large and lucid,

> The greyest of things blue,
> The bluest of things grey.

Her complexion was of a clear pallor, like the white rose beloved by her ancestors; her features were all but classic, with the charm of romance; but what made her unique was her mouth. It was faintly upturned at the corners, as in archaic Greek art; she had, in the slightest and most gracious degree, what Logan, describing her once, called 'the AEginetan grin.' This gave her an air peculiarly gay and winsome, brilliant, joyous, and alert. In brief, to use Chaucer's phrase,

> She was as wincy as a wanton colt,
> Sweet as a flower, and upright as a bolt.

She was the girl who was teaching the poet the elements of ping-pong. The poet usually missed the ball, for he was averse to and unapt for anything requiring quickness of eye and dexterity of hand. On a seat lay open a volume of the *Poetry of the Celtic Renascence*, which Blake had been reading to Miss Macrae till she used the vulgar phrase 'footle,' and invited him to be educated in ping-pong. Of these circumstances she cheerfully informed the new-comers, adding that Lord Bude had returned happy, having photographed a wild cat in its lair.

'Did he shoot it?' asked Blake.

'No. He's a sportsman!' said Miss Macrae.

'That is why I supposed he must have shot the cat,' answered Blake.

'What is Gaelic for a wild cat, Blake?' asked Merton unkindly.

Like other modern Celtic poets Mr. Blake was entirely ignorant of the melodious language of his ancestors, though it had often been stated in the literary papers that he was 'going to begin' to take lessons.

'*Sans purr*,' answered Blake; 'the Celtic wild cat has not the servile accomplishment of purring. The words, a little altered, are the motto of the Argyle and Sutherland Highlanders. This is the country of the wild cat.'

'I thought the "wild cat" was a peculiarly American financial animal,' said Merton.

Miss Macrae laughed, and, the gong sounding (by electricity, the wire being connected with the Greenwich Observatory), she ran lightly up the central staircase. Lady Bude had hurried to rejoin her lord; Merton and Blake sauntered out to their rooms in the observatory, Blake with an air of fatigue and languor.

'Learning ping-pong easily?' asked Merton.

'I have more hopes of teaching Miss Macrae the essential and intimate elements of Celtic poetry,' said Blake. 'One box of books I brought with me, another arrived to-day. I am about to begin on my Celtic drama of "Con of the Hundred Battles."'

'Have you the works of the ancient Sennachie, Macfootle?' asked Merton. He was jealous, and his usual urbanity was sorely tried by the Irish bard. In short, he was rude; stupid, too.

However, Blake had his revenge after dinner, on the roof of the observatory, where the ladies gathered round him in the faint silver light, looking over the sleeping sea. 'Far away to the west,' he said, 'lies the Celtic paradise, the Isle of Apples!'

'American apples are excellent,' said Merton, but the beauty of the scene and natural courtesy caused Miss Macrae to whisper 'Hush!'

The poet went on, 'May I speak to you the words of the emissary from the lovely land?'

'The mysterious female?' said Merton brutally. 'Dr. Hyde calls her "a mysterious female." It is in his *Literary History of Ireland*.'

'Pray let us hear the poem, Mr. Merton,' said Miss Macrae, attuned to the charm of the hour and the scene.

'She came to Bran's Court,' said Blake, 'from the Isle of Apples, and no man knew whence she came, and she chanted to them.'

'Twenty-eight quatrains, no less, a hundred and twelve lines,' said the insufferable Merton. 'Could you give us them in Gaelic?'

The bard went on, not noticing the interruption, 'I shall translate

'There is a distant isle
Around which sea horses glisten,
A fair course against the white swelling surge,
Four feet uphold it.'

'Feet of white bronze under it.'

'White bronze, what's that, eh?' asked the practical Mr.
Macrae.

'Glittering through beautiful ages!
Lovely land through the world's age,
On which the white blossoms drop.'

'Beautiful!' said Miss Macrae.

'There are twenty-six more quatrains,' said Merton.

The bard went on,

'A beautiful game, most delightful
They play—'

'Ping-pong?' murmured Merton.

'Hush!' said Lady Bude.

Miss Macrae turned to the poet.

'They play, sitting at the luxurious wine,
Men and gentle women under a bush,
Without sin, without crime.'

'They are playing still,' Blake added. 'Unbeheld, undisturbed!
I verily believe there is no Gael even now who would not in
his heart of hearts let drift by him the Elysiums of Virgil,

Dante, and Milton, to grasp at the Moy Mell, the Apple Isle, of the unknown Irish pagan! And then to play sitting at the luxurious wine,

'Men and gentle women under a bush!'

'It really cannot have been ping-pong that they played at, *sitting*. Bridge, more likely,' said Merton. 'And "good wine needs no bush!"'

The bard moved away, accompanied by his young hostess, who resented Merton's cynicism

'Tell me more of that lovely poem, Mr. Blake,' she said.

'I am jangled and out of tune,' said Blake wildly. 'The Sassenach is my torture! Let me take your hand, it is cool as the hands of the foam-footed maidens of—of—what's the name of the place?'

'Was it Clonmell?' asked Miss Macrae, letting him take her hand.

He pressed it against his burning brow.

'Though you laugh at me,' said Blake, 'sometimes you are kind! I am upset—I hardly know myself. What is yonder shape skirting the lawn? Is it the Daoine Sidh?'

'Why do you call her "the downy she"? She is no more artful than other people. She is my maid, Elspeth Mackay,' answered Miss Macrae, puzzled. They were alone, separated from the others by the breadth of the roof.

'I said the *Daoine Sidh*,' replied the poet, spelling the words. 'It means the People of Peace.'

'Quakers?'

'No, the fairies,' groaned the misunderstood bard. 'Do you know nothing of your ancestral tongue? Do you call yourself a Gael?'

'Of course I call myself a girl,' answered Miss Macrae. 'Do you want me to call myself a young lady?'

The poet sighed. 'I thought *you* understood me,' he said. 'Ah, how to escape, how to reach the undiscovered West!'

'But Columbus discovered it,' said Miss Macrae.

'The undiscovered West of the Celtic heart's desire,' explained the bard; 'the West below the waters! Thither could we twain sail in the magic boat of Bran! Ah see, the sky opens like a flower!'

Indeed, there was a sudden glow of summer lightning.

'That looks more like rain,' said Merton, who was standing with the Budes at an opposite corner of the roof.

'I say, Merton,' asked Bude, 'how can you be so uncivil to that man? He took it very well.'

'A rotter,' said Merton. 'He has just got that stuff by heart, the verse and a lot of the prose, out of a book that I brought down myself, and left in the smoking-room. I can show you the place if you like.'

'Do, Mr. Merton. But how foolish you are! *do* be civil to the man,' whispered Lady Bude, who shared his disbelief in Blake; and at that moment the tinkle of an electric bell in the smoking-room below reached the expectant ears of Mr. Macrae.

'Come down, all of you,' he said. 'The wireless telegraphy is at work.'

He waited till they were all in the smoking-room, and feverishly examined the tape.

'Escape of De Wet,' he read. 'Disasters to the Imperial Yeomanry. Strike of Cigarette Makers. Great Fire at Hackney.'

'There!' he exclaimed triumphantly. 'We might have gone to bed in London, and not known all that till we got the morning papers to-morrow. And here we are fifty miles from a railway station or a telegraph office—no, we're nearer Inchnadampf.'

'Would that I were in the Isle of Apples, Mell Moy, far, far from civilisation!' said Blake.

"There shall be no grief there or sorrow," so sings the minstrel of *The Wooing of Etain.*

"Fresh flesh of swine, banquets of new milk and ale shalt thou have with me then, fair lady," Merton read out from the book he had been speaking of to the Budes.

'Jolly place, the Celtic Paradise! Fresh flesh of swine, banquets of ale and new milk. *Quel luxe!*'

'Is that the kind of entertainment you were offering me, Mr. Blake?' asked Miss Macrae gaily. 'Mr. Blake,' she went on, 'has been inviting me to fly to the undiscovered West beneath the waters, in the magic boat of Bran.'

'Did Bran invent the submarine?' asked Mr. Macrae, and then the company saw what they had never seen before, the bard blushing. He seemed so discomposed that Miss Macrae took compassion on him.

'Never mind my father, Mr. Blake,' she said, 'he is a very good Highlander, and believes in Eachain of the Hairy Arm as much as the crofters do. Have you heard of Eachain, Mr. Blake? He is a spectre in full Highland costume, attached to our clan. When we came here first, to look round, we had only horses hired from Edinburgh, and a Lowlander—mark you, a *Lowlander*—to drive. He was in the stable one afternoon—the old stable, we have pulled it down—when suddenly the horses began to kick and rear. He looked round to the open door, and there stood a huge Highlander in our tartans, with musket, pistols, claymore, dirk, skian, and all, and soft brogues of untanned leather on his feet. The coachman, in a panic, made a blind rush at the figure, but behold, there was nobody, and a boy outside had seen no man. The horses were trembling and foaming. Now it was a Lowlander from Teviotdale that saw the man, and the crofters were delighted. They said the figure was the chief that fell at Culloden, come to welcome us back. So you must not despair of us, Mr. Blake, and you, that have "the sight," may see Eachain yourself, who knows?'

This happy turn of the conversation exactly suited Blake. He began to be very amusing about magic, and brownies, and 'the downy she,' as Miss Macrae called the People of Peace. The ladies presently declared that they were afraid to go to bed; so they went, Miss Macrae indicating her displeasure to Merton by the coldness of her demeanour.

The men, who were rather dashed by the pleasant intelligence which the telegraph had communicated, sat up smoking for a while, and then retired in a subdued state of mind.

Next morning, which was Sunday, Merton appeared rather late at breakfast, late and pallid. After a snatch of disturbed slumber, he had wakened, or seemed to waken, fretting a good deal over the rusticity of his bearing towards Blake, and over his hopeless affair of the heart. He had vexed his lady. 'If he is good enough for his hosts, he ought to be good enough for their guests,' thought Merton. 'What a brute, what a fool I am; I ought to go. I will go! I ought not to take coffee after dinner, I know I ought not, and I smoke too much,' he added, and finally he went to breathe the air on the roof.

The night was deadly soft and still, a slight mist hid the furthest verges of the sea's horizon. Behind it, the summer lightning seemed like portals that opened and shut in the heavens, revealing a glory without form, and closing again.

'I don't wonder that these Irish poets dreamed of Isles of Paradise out there:

'Lands undiscoverable in the unheard-of West,
Round which the strong stream of a sacred sea
Runs without wind for ever.'

thought Merton. 'Chicago is the realisation of their dream. Hullo, there are the lights of a big steamer, and a very low one behind it! Queer craft!'

Merton watched the lights that crossed the sea, when either the haze deepened or the fainter light on the smaller vessel vanished, and the larger ship steamed on in a southerly direction. 'Magic boat of Bran!' thought Merton. He turned and entered the staircase to go back to his room. There was a lift, of course, but, equally of course, there was nobody to manage it. Merton, who had a lighted bedroom-candle in his hand, descended the spiral staircase; at a turning he thought he saw, 'with the tail of his eye,' a plaid, draping a tall figure of a Highlander, disappear round the corner. Nobody in the castle wore the kilt except the piper, and he had not rooms in the observatory. Merton ran down as fast as he could, but he did not catch another view of the plaid and its wearer, or hear any footsteps. He went to the bottom of the staircase, opened the outer door, and looked forth. Nobody! The electric light from the open door of his own room blazed across the landing on his return. All was perfectly still, and Merton remembered that he had not heard the footsteps of the appearance. 'Was it Eachain?' he asked himself. 'Do I sleep, do I dream?'

He went back to bed and slumbered uneasily. He seemed to be awake in his room, in broad light, and to hear a slow drip, drip, on the floor. He looked up; the roof was stained with a great dark splash of a crimson hue. He got out of bed, and touched the wet spot on the floor under the blotch on the ceiling.

His fingers were reddened with blood! He woke at the horror of it: found himself in bed in the dark, pressed an electric knob, and looked at the ceiling. It was dry and white. 'I certainly have been smoking too much lately,' thought Merton, and, switching off the light, he slumbered again, so soundly that he did not hear the piper playing round the house, or the man who brought his clothes and hot water, or the gong for breakfast.

When he did wake, he was surprised at the lateness of the hour, and dressed as rapidly as possible. 'I wonder if I was dreaming when I thought that I went out on the roof, and saw mountains and marvels,' said Merton to himself. 'A queer thing, the human mind,' he reflected sagely. It occurred to him to enter the smoking-room on his way downstairs. He routed two maids who perhaps had slept too late, and were hurriedly making the room tidy. The sun was beating in at the window, and Merton noticed some tiny glittering points of white metallic light on the carpet near the new telegraphic apparatus. 'I don't believe these lazy Highland Maries have swept the room properly since the electric machine was put up,' Merton thought. He hastily seized, and took to his chamber, his book on old Irish literature, which was too clearly part of Blake's Celtic inspiration. Merton wanted no more quatrains, but he did mean to try to be civil. He then joined the party at breakfast; he admitted that he had slept ill, but, when asked by Blake, disclaimed having seen Eachain of the Hairy Arm, and did not bore or bewilder the company with his dreams.

Miss Macrae, in sabbatical raiment, was fresher than a rose and gay as a lark. Merton tried not to look at her; he failed in this endeavour.

II

Lost

The day was Sunday, and Merton, who had a holy horror of news, rejoiced to think that the telegraphic machine would probably not tinkle its bell for twenty-four hours. This was not the ideal of the millionaire. Things happen, intelligence arrives from the limits of our vast and desirable empire, even on the Day of Rest. But the electric bell was silent. Mr. Macrae, from patriotic motives, employed a Highland engineer and mechanician, so there was nothing to be got out of him in the way of work on the sabbath day. The millionaire himself did not quite understand how to work the thing. He went to the smoking-room where it dwelt and looked wistfully at it, but was afraid to try to call up his correspondents in London. As for the usual manipulator, Donald McDonald, he had started early for the distant Free Kirk. An 'Unionist' minister intended to try to preach himself in, and the majority of the congregation, being of the old Free Kirk rock, and averse to union with the United Presbyterians, intended to try to keep him out. They 'had a lad with the gift who would do the preaching fine,' and as there was no police-station within forty miles it seemed fairly long odds on the Free Kirk recalcitrants. However, there a resolute minority of crofters on the side of the minister, and every chance of an ecclesiastical battle royal. Accompanied by the stalker, two

Andrew Lang

keepers, and all the gardeners, armed with staves, the engineer had early set out for the scene of brotherly amity, and Mr. Macrae had reluctantly to admit that he was cut off from his communications.

Merton, who was with him in the smoking-room, mentally absolved the Highland housemaids. If they had not swept up the tiny glittering metallic points on the carpet before, they had done so now. Only two or three caught his eye.

Mr. Macrae, avid of news, accommodated himself in an arm-chair with newspapers of two or three days old, from which he had already sucked the heart by aid of his infernal machine. The Budes and Blake, with Miss Macrae (an Anglican), had set off to walk to the Catholic chapel, some four miles away, for crofting opinion was resolute against driving on the Lord's Day. Merton, self-denying and resolved, did not accompany his lady; he read a novel, wrote letters, and felt desolate. All was peace, all breathed of the Sabbath calm.

'Very odd there's no call from the machine,' said Mr. Macrae anxiously.

'It is Sunday,' said Merton.

'Still, they might send us something.'

'They scarcely favoured us last Sunday,' said Merton.

'No, and now I think of it, not at all on the Sunday before,' said Mr. Macrae. 'I dare say it is all right.'

'Would a thunder-storm further south derange it?' asked Merton, adding, 'There was a lot of summer lightning last night.'

'That might be it; these things have their tempers. But they are a great comfort. I can't think how we ever did without them,' said Mr. Macrae, as if these things were common in every cottage. 'Wonderful thing, science!' he added, in an original way, and Merton, who privately detested science, admitted that it was so.

'Shall we go to see the horses?' suggested Mr. Macrae, and they did go and stare, as is usual on Sunday in the country, at the hind-quarters of these noble animals. Merton strove to be as much interested as possible in Mr. Macrae's stories of his fleet American trotters. But his heart was otherwise. 'They will soon be an extinct species,' said Mr. Macrae. 'The motor has come to stay.'

Merton was not feeling very well, he was afraid of a cigarette, Mr. Macrae's conversation was not brilliant, and Merton still felt as if he were under the wrath, so well deserved, of his hostess. She did not usually go to the Catholic chapel; to be sure, in the conditions prevailing at the Free Kirk place of worship, she had no alternative if she would not abstain wholly from religious privileges. But Merton felt sure that she had really gone to comfort and console the injured feelings of Blake. Probably she would have had a little court of lordlings, Merton reflected (not that Mr. Macrae had any taste for them), but everybody knew that, what with the weather, and the crofters, and the grouse disease, the sport at Castle Skrae was remarkably bad. So the party was tiny, though a number of people were expected later, and Merton and the heiress had been on what, as he ruefully reflected, were very kind terms—rather more than kind, he had hoped, or feared, now and then. Merton saw that he had annoyed her, and thrown her, metaphorically speaking, into the arms of the Irish minstrel. All the better, perhaps, he thought, ruefully. The poet was handsome enough to be one that 'limners loved to paint, and ladies to look upon.' He generally took chaff well, and could give it, as well as take it, and there were hours when his sentiment and witchery had a chance with most women. 'But Lady Bude says there is nothing in it, and women usually know,' he reflected. Well, he must leave the girl, and save his self-respect.

When nothing more in the way of pottering could be done at the stables, when its proprietor had exhausted the pleasure of staring at the balloon in its hall, and had fed the fowls, he walked with Merton down the avenue, above the shrunken burn that whispered among its ferns and alders, to meet the returning church-goers. The Budes came first, together; they were still, they were always, honeymooning. Mr. Macrae turned back with Lady Bude; Merton walked with Bude, Blake and Miss Macrae were not yet in sight. He thought of walking on to meet them—but no, it must not be.

'Blake owes you a rare candle, Merton,' said Bude, adding, 'A great deal may be done, or said, in a long walk by a young man with his advantages. And if you had not had your knife in him last night I do not think she would have accompanied us this morning to attend the ministrations of Father McColl. He preached in Gaelic.'

'That must have been edifying,' said Merton, wincing.

'The effect, when one does not know the language, and is within six feet of an energetic Celt in the pulpit, is rather odd,' said Bude. 'But you have put your foot in it, not a doubt of that.'

This appeared only too probable. The laggards arrived late for luncheon, and after luncheon Miss Macrae allowed Blake to read his manuscript poems to her in the hall, and to discuss the prospects of the Celtic drama. Afterwards, fearing to hurt the religious sentiments of the Highland servants by playing ping-pong on Sunday in the hall, she instructed him elsewhere, and clandestinely, in that pastime till the hour of tea arrived.

Merton did not appear at the tea-table. Tired of this Castle of Indolence, loathing Blake, afraid of more talk with Lady Bude, eating his own heart, he had started alone after luncheon for a long walk round the loch. The day had darkened, and was deadly still; the water was like a mirror of leaden hue; the air heavy and sulphurous.

These atmospheric phenomena did not gladden the heart of Merton. He knew that rain was coming, but he would not be with *her* by the foaming stream, or on the black waves of the loch. Climbing to the top of the hill, he felt sure that a storm was at hand. On the east, far away, Clibrig, and Suilvean of the double peak, and the round top of Ben More, stood shadowy above the plain against the lurid light. Over the sea hung 'the ragged rims of thunder' far away, veiling in thin shadow the outermost isles, whose mountain crests looked dark as indigo. A few hot heavy drops of rain were falling as Merton began to descend. He was soaked to the skin when he reached the door of the observatory, and rushed up stairs to dress for dinner. A covered way led from the observatory to the Castle, so that he did not get drenched again on his return, which he accomplished punctually as the gong for dinner sounded.

In the drawing-room were the Budes, and Mr. Macrae was nervously pacing the length and breadth of the room.

'They must have taken refuge from the rain somewhere,' Lady Bude was saying, and 'they' were obviously Blake and the daughter of the house. Where were they? Merton's heart sank with a foolish foreboding.

'I know,' the lady went on, 'that they were only going down to the cove—where you and I were yesterday evening, Mr. Merton. It is no distance.'

'A mile and a half is a good deal in this weather, said Merton, 'and there is no cottage on this side of the sea loch. But they must have taken shelter,' he added; he must not seem anxious.

At this moment came a flash of lightning, followed by a crack like that of a cosmic whip-lash, and a long rever-berating roar of thunder.

'It is most foolish to have stayed out so late,' said Mr. Macrae. 'Any one could see that a storm was coming. I told them so, I am really annoyed.'

Every one was silent, the rain fell straight and steady, the gravel in front of the window was a series of little lakes, pale and chill in the wan twilight.

'I really think I must send a couple of men down with cloaks and umbrellas,' said the nervous father, pressing an electric knob.

The butler appeared.

'Are Donald and Sandy and Murdoch about?' asked Mr. Macrae.

'Not returned from church, sir;' said the butler.

'There was likely to be a row at the Free Kirk,' said Mr. Macrae, absently.

'You must go yourself, Benson, with Archibald and James.

Take cloaks and umbrellas, and hurry down towards the cove. Mr. Blake and Miss Macrae have probably found shelter on the way somewhere.'

The butler answered, 'Yes, sir;' but he cannot have been very well pleased with his errand. Merton wanted to offer to go, anything to be occupied; but Bude said nothing, and so Merton did not speak.

The four in the drawing-room sat chatting nervously: 'There was nothing of course to be anxious about,' they told each other. The bolt of heaven never strikes the daughters of millionaires; Miss Macrae was indifferent to a wetting, and nobody cared tremulously about Blake. Indeed the words 'confound the fellow' were in the minds of the three men.

The evening darkened rapidly, the minutes lagged by, the clock chimed the half-hour, three-quarters, nine o'clock.

Mr. Macrae was manifestly growing more and more nervous, Merton forgot to grow more and more hungry. His tongue felt dry and hard; he was afraid of he knew not what, but he bravely tried to make talk with Lady Bude.

The door opened, letting the blaze of electric light from the hall into the darkling room. They all turned eagerly towards the door. It was only one of the servants. Merton's heart felt like lead. 'Mr. Benson has returned, sir; he would be glad if he might speak to you for a moment.'

'Where is he?' asked Mr. Macrae.

'At the outer door, sir, in the porch. He is very wet.'

Mr. Macrae went out; the others found little to say to each other.

'Very awkward,' muttered Bude. 'They cannot have been climbing the cliffs, surely.'

'The bridge is far above the highest water-mark of the burn, in case they crossed the water,' said Merton.

Lady Bude was silent.

Mr. Macrae returned. 'Benson has come back,' he said, 'to say that he can find no trace of them. The other men are still searching.'

'Can they have had themselves ferried across the sea loch to the village opposite?' asked Merton.

'Emmiline had not the key of our boat,' said Mr. Macrae, 'I have made sure of that; and not a man in the village would launch a boat on Sunday.'

'We must go and help to search for them,' said Merton; he only wished to be doing something, anything.

'I shall not be a minute in changing my dress.'

Bude also volunteered, and in a few minutes, having drunk a glass of wine and eaten a crust of bread, they and Mr. Macrae were hurrying towards the cove. The storm was passing; by the time when they reached the sea-side there were rifts of clear light in the sky above them. They had walked rapidly and silently, the swollen stream roaring beneath them. It had rained torrents in the hills. There was nothing to be said, but the mind of each man was busy with the gloomiest conjectures. These had to be far- fetched, for in a country so thinly peopled, and so honest and friendly, within a couple of miles at most from home, on a Sunday evening, what conceivable harm could befall a man and a maid?

'Can we trust the man?' was in Merton's mind. 'If they have been ferried across to the village, they would have set out to return before now,' he said aloud; but there was no boat on the faint silver of the sea loch. 'The cliffs are the likeliest place for an accident, if there *was* an accident,' he considered, with a pang. The cliffs might have tempted the light-footed girl. In fancy he saw her huddled, a ghastly heap, the faint wind fluttering the folds of her dress, at the bottom of the rocks. She had been wearing a long skirt, not her wont in the Highlands; it would be dangerous to climb in that; she might have forgotten, climbed, and caught her foot, and fallen.

'Blake may have snatched at her, and been dragged down with her,' Merton thought. All the horrid fancies of keen anxiety flitted across his mind's eye. He paused, and made an effort over himself. There *must* be some other harmless explanation, an adventure to laugh at—for Blake and the girl. Poor comfort, that!

The men who had been searching were scattered about the sides of the cove, and, distinguishing the new-comers, gathered towards them.

'No,' they said, 'they had found nothing except a little book that seemed to belong to Mr. Blake.'

It had been discovered near the place where Merton and Lady Bude were sitting on the previous evening. When found it was lying open, face downwards. In the faint light Merton could see that the book was full of manuscript poems, the lines all blotted and run together by the tropical rain. He thrust it into the pocket of his ulster.

Merton took the most intelligent of the gillies aside. 'Show me where you have searched,' he said. The man pointed to the shores of the cove; they had also examined the banks of the burn, and under all the trees, clearly fearing that the lost pair might have been lightning-struck, like the nymph and swain in Pope's poem. 'You have not searched the cliffs?' asked Merton.

'No, sir,' said the man.

Merton then went to Mr. Macrae, and suggested that the boat should be sent across the sea ferry, to try if anything could be learned in the village. Mr. Macrae agreed, and himself went in the boat, which was presently unmoored, and pulled by two gillies across the loch, that ran like a river with the outgoing tide.

Merton and Bude began to search the cliffs; Merton could hear the hoarse pumping of his own heart. The cliff's base was deep in flags and bracken, then the rocks began climbing to the foot of the perpendicular basaltic crag. The sky, fortunately, was now clear in the west, and lent a wan light to the seekers. Merton had almost reached the base of the cliff, when, in the deep bracken, he stumbled over something soft. He stooped and held back the tall fronds of bracken.

It was the body of a man; the body did not stir. Merton glanced to see the face, but the face was bent round, leaning half on the earth. It was Blake. Merton's guess seemed true. They had fallen from the cliffs! But where was that other body? Merton yelled to Bude. Blake seemed dead or insensible.

Merton (he was ashamed of it presently) left the body of Blake alone; he plunged wildly in and out of the bracken, still shouting to Bude, and looking for that which he feared to find. She could not be far off. He stumbled over rocks, into rabbit holes, he dived among the soaked bracken. Below and around he hunted, feverishly panting, then he set his face to the sheer cliff, to climb; she might be lying on some higher ledge, the shadow on the rocks was dark. At this moment Bude hailed him.

'Come down!' he cried, 'she cannot be there!'

'Why not?' he gasped, arriving at the side of Bude, who was stooping, with a lantern in his hand, over the body of Blake, which faintly stirred.

'Look!' said Bude, lowering the lantern.

Then Merton saw that Blake's hands were bound down beside his body, and that the cords were fastened by pegs to the ground. His feet were fastened in the same way, and his mouth was stuffed full of wet seaweed. Bude pulled out the improvised gag, cut the ropes, turned the face upwards, and carefully dropped a little whisky from his flask into the mouth. Blake opened his eyes.

'Where are my poems?' he asked.

'Where is Miss Macrae?' shrieked Merton in agony.

'Damn the midges,' said Blake (his face was hardly recognisable from their bites). 'Oh, damn them all!' He had fainted again.

'She has been carried off,' groaned Merton. Bude and he did all that they knew for poor Blake. They rubbed his ankles and wrists, they administered more whisky, and finally got him to sit up. He scratched his hands over his face and moaned, but at last he recovered full consciousness. No sense could be extracted from him, and, as the boat was now visible on its homeward track, Bude and Merton carried him

Andrew Lang

down to the cove, anxiously waiting Mr. Macrae.

He leaped ashore.

'Have you heard anything?' asked Bude.

'They saw a boat on the loch about seven o'clock,' said Mr. Macrae, 'coming from the head of it, touching here, and then pulling west, round the cliff. They thought the crew Sabbath-breakers from the lodge at Alt Garbh. What's that,' he cried, at last seeing Blake, who lay supported against a rock, his eyes shut.

Merton rapidly explained.

'It is as I thought,' said Mr. Macrae resolutely. 'I knew it from the first. They have kidnapped her for a ransom. Let us go home.'

Merton and Bude were silent; they, too, had guessed, as soon as they discovered Blake. The girl was her father's very life, and they admired his resolution, his silence. A gate was taken from its hinges, cloaks were strewn on it, and Blake was laid on this ambulance.

Merton ventured to speak.

'May I take your boat, sir, across to the ferry, and send the fishermen from the village to search each end of the loch on their side? It is after midnight,' he added grimly. 'They will not refuse to go; it is Monday.'

'I will accompany them,' said Bude, 'with your leave, Mr. Macrae, Merton can search our side of the loch, he can borrow another boat at the village in addition to yours. You, at the Castle, can organise the measures for to-morrow.'

'Thank you both,' said Mr. Macrae. 'I should have thought of that. Thank you, Mr. Merton, for the idea. I am a little dazed. There is the key of the boat.'

Merton snatched it, and ran, followed by Bude and four gillies, to the little pier where the boat was moored. He must be doing something for her, or go mad. The six men crowded into the boat, and pulled swiftly away, Merton taking the stroke oar. Meanwhile Blake was carried by four gillies towards the Castle, the men talking low to each other in Gaelic. Mr. Macrae walked silently in front.

Such was the mournful procession that Lady Bude ran out to meet. She passed Mr. Macrae, whose face was set with an expression of deadly rage, and looked for Bude. He was not there, a gillie told her what they knew, and, with a convulsive sob, she followed Mr. Macrae into the Castle.

'Mr. Blake must be taken to his room,' said Mr. Macrae. 'Benson, bring something to eat and drink. Lady Bude, I deeply regret that this thing should have troubled your stay with me. She has been carried off, Mr. Blake has been rendered unconscious; your husband and Mr. Merton are trying nobly to find the track of the miscreants. You will excuse me, I must see to Mr. Blake.'

Mr. Macrae rose, bowed, and went out. He saw Blake carried to a bathroom in the observatory; they undressed him and put him in the hot water. Then they put him to bed, and brought him wine and food. He drank the wine eagerly.

'We were set on suddenly from behind by fellows from a boat,' he said. 'We saw them land and go up from the cove; they took us in the rear: they felled me and pegged me out. Have you my poems?'

'Mr. Merton has the poems,' said Mr. Macrae. 'What became of my daughter?'

'I don't know, I was unconscious.'

'What kind of boat was it?'

'An ordinary coble, a country boat.'

'What kind of looking men were they?'

'Rough fellows with beards. I only saw them when they first passed us at some distance. Oh, my head! Oh damn, how these bites do sting! Get me some ammonia; you'll find it in a bottle on the dressing-table.'

Mr. Macrae brought him the bottle and a handkerchief. 'That is all you know?' he asked.

But Blake was babbling some confusion of verse and prose: his wits were wandering.

Mr. Macrae turned from him, and bade one of the men watch him. He himself passed downstairs and into the hall, where Lady Bude was standing at the window, gazing to the north.

'Indeed you must not watch, Lady Bude,' said the millionaire. 'Let me persuade you to take something and go to bed. I forget myself; I do not believe that you have dined.' He himself sat down at the table, he ate and drank, and induced Lady Bude to join him. 'Now, do let me persuade you to go back and to try to sleep,' said Mr. Macrae gently. 'Your husband is well accompanied.'

'It is not for him that I am afraid,' said the lady, who was in tears.

'I must arrange for the day's work,' said the millionaire, and Lady Bude sighed and left him.

'First,' he said aloud, 'we must get the doctor from Lairg to see Blake. Over forty miles.' He rang. 'Benson,' he said to the butler, 'order the tandem for seven. The yacht to have steam up at the same hour. Breakfast at half-past six.'

The millionaire then went to his own study, where he sat lost in thought. Morning had come before the sound of voices below informed him that Bude and Merton had returned. He hurried down; their faces told him all. 'Nothing?' he asked calmly.

Nothing! They had rowed along the loch sides, touching at every cottage and landing-place. They had learned nothing. He explained his ideas for the day.

'If you will allow me to go in the yacht, I can telegraph from Lochinver in all directions to the police,' said Bude.

'We can use the wireless thing,' said Mr. Macrae. 'But if you would be so good, you could at least see the local police, and if anything occurred to you, telegraph in the ordinary way.'

'Right,' said Bude, 'I shall now take a bath.'

'You will stay with me, Mr. Merton,' said Mr. Macrae.

'It is a dreadful country for men in our position,' said Merton, for the sake of saying something. 'Police and everything so remote.'

'It gave them their chance; they have waited for it long enough, I dare say. Have you any ideas?'

'They must have a steamer somewhere.'

'That is why I have ordered the balloon, to reconnoitre the sea from,' said Mr. Macrae. 'But they have had all the night to escape in. I think they will take her to America, to some rascally southern republic, probably.'

'I have thought of the outer islands,' said Merton, 'out behind the Lewis and the Long Island.'

'We shall have them searched,' said Mr. Macrae. 'I can think of no more at present, and you are tired.'

Merton had slept ill and strangely on the night of Saturday; on Sunday night, of course, he had never lain down. Unshaven, dirty, with haggard eyes, he looked as wretched as he felt.

'I shall have a bath, and then please employ me, it does not matter on what, as long as I am at work for—you,' said Merton. He had nearly said 'for her.'

Mr. Macrae looked at him rather curiously. 'You are dying of fatigue,' he said. 'All your ideas have been excellent, but I cannot let you kill yourself. Ideas are what I want. You must stay with me to-day: I shall be communicating with London and other centres by the Giambresi machine; I shall need your advice, your suggestions. Now, do go to bed: you shall be called if you are needed.'

He wrung Merton's hand, and Merton crept up to his bedroom. He took a bath, turned in, and was wrapped in all the blessedness of sleep.

Before five o'clock the house was astir. Bude, in the yacht, steamed down the coast, touching at Lochinver, and wherever there seemed a faint hope of finding intelligence. But he learned nothing. Yachts and other vessels came and went (on Sundays, of course, more seldom), and if the heiress had been taken straight to sea, northwards or west, round the Butt of Lewis, by night, there could be no chance of news of her. Returning, Bude learned that the local search parties had found nothing but the black ashes of a burned boat in a creek on the south side of the cliffs. There the captors of Miss Macrae must have touched, burned their coble, and taken to some larger and fleeter vessel. But no such vessel had been seen by shepherd, fisher, keeper, or gillie. The grooms arrived from Lairg, in the tandem, with the doctor and a rural policeman. Bude had telegraphed to Scotland Yard from Lochinver for detectives, and to Glasgow, Oban, Tobermory, Salen, in fact to every place he thought likely, with minute particulars of Miss Macrae's appearance and dress. All this Merton learned from Bude, when, long after luncheon time, our hero awoke suddenly, refreshed in body, but with the ghastly blank of misery and doubt before the eyes of his mind.

'I wired,' said Bude, 'on the off chance that yesterday's storm might have deranged the wireless machine, and, by Jove, it is lucky I did. The wireless machine won't work, not a word of message has come through; it is jammed or something. I met Donald Macdonald, who told me.'

'Have you seen our host yet?'

'No,' said Bude, 'I was just going to him.'

They found the millionaire seated at a table, his head in his hands. On their approach he roused himself.

'Any news?' he asked Bude, who shook his head. He explained how he had himself sent various telegrams, and

Mr. Macrae thanked him.

'You did well,' he said. 'Some electric disturbance has cut us off from our London correspondent. We sent messages in the usual way, but there has been no reply. You sent to Scotland Yard for detectives, I think you said?'

'I did.'

'But, unluckily, what can London detectives do in a country like this?' said Mr. Macrae.

'I told them to send one who had the Gaelic,' said Bude.

'It was well thought of,' said Mr. Macrae, 'but this was no local job. Every man for miles round has been examined, and accounted for.'

'I hope you have slept well, Mr. Merton?' he asked.

'Excellently. Can you not put me on some work if it is only to copy telegraphic despatches? But, by the way, how is Blake?'

'The doctor is still with him,' said Mr. Macrae; 'a case of concussion of the brain, he says it is. But you go out and take the air, you must be careful of yourself.'

Bude remained with the millionaire, Merton sauntered out to look at the river: running water drew him like a magnet. By the side of the stream, on a woodland path, he met Lady Bude. She took his hand silently in her right, and patted it with her left. Merton turned his head away.

'What can I say to you?' she asked. 'Oh, this is too horrible, too cruel.'

'If I had listened to you and not irritated her I might have been with her, not Blake,' said Merton, with keen self-respect.

'I don't quite see that you would be any the better for concussion of the brain,' said Lady Bude, smiling. 'Oh, Mr. Merton, you *must* find her, I know how you have worked already. You must rescue her. Consider, this is your chance, this is your opportunity to do something great. Take courage!'

Merton answered, with a rather watery smile, 'If I had Logan with me.'

'With or without Lord Fastcastle, you *must do it*!' said Lady Bude.

They saw Mr. Macrae approaching them deep in thought and advanced to meet him.

'Mr. Macrae,' asked Lady Bude suddenly, 'have you had Donald with you long?'

'Ever since he was a lad in Canada,' answered the millionaire. 'I have every confidence in Donald's ability, and he was for half a year with Gianesi and Giambresi, learning to work their system.'

Donald's honesty, it was clear, he never dreamed of suspecting. Merton blushed, as he remembered that a doubt as to whether the engineer had been 'got at' had occurred to his own mind. For a heavy bribe (Merton had fancied) Donald might have been induced, perhaps by some Stock Exchange operator, to tamper with the wireless centre of communication. But, from Mr. Macrae's perfect confidence, he felt obliged to drop this attractive hypothesis.

They dined at the usual hour, and not long after dinner Lady Bude said good-night, while her lord, who was very tired, soon followed her example. Merton and the millionaire paid a visit to Blake, whom they found asleep, and the doctor, having taken supper and accepted an invitation to stay all night, joined the two other men in the smoking- room. In answer to inquiries about the patient, Dr. MacTavish said, 'It's jist concussion, slight concussion, and nervous shoke. No that muckle the maiter wi' him but a clour on the hairnspan, and midge bites, forbye the disagreeableness o' being clamped doon for a wheen hours in a wat tussock o' bracken.'

This diagnosis, though not perfectly intelligible to Merton, seemed to reassure Mr. Macrae.

'He's a bit concetty, the chiel,' added the worthy physician, 'and it may be a day or twa or he judges he can leave his bed. Jist nervous collapse. But, bless my soul, what's thon?'

'Thon' had brought Mr. Macrae to his feet with a bound. It was the thrill of the electric bell which preluded to communications from the wireless communicator! The instrument began to tick, and to emit its inscribed tape.

'Thank heaven,' cried the millionaire, 'now we shall have light on this mystery.' He read the message, stamped his foot with an awful execration, and then, recovering himself, handed the document to Merton. 'The message is a disgusting practical joke,' he said. 'Some one at the central agency is playing tricks with the instrument.'

'Am I to read the message aloud?' asked Merton.

It was rather a difficult question, for the doctor was a perfect stranger to all present, and the matters involved were of an intimate delicacy, affecting the most sacred domestic relations.

'Dr. MacTavish,' said Mr. Macrae, 'speaking as Highlander to Highlander, these are circumstances, are they not, under the seal of professional confidence?'

The big doctor rose to his feet.

'They are, sir, but, Mr. Macrae, I am a married man. This sad business of yours, I say it with sorrow, will be the talk of the world to-morrow, as it is of the country side to-day. If you will excuse me, I would rather know nothing, and be able to tell nothing, so I'll take my pipe outside with me.'

'Not alone, don't go alone, Dr. MacTavish,' said Merton; 'Mr. Macrae will need his telegraphic operator probably. Let me play you a hundred up at billiards.'

The doctor liked nothing better; soon the balls were rattling, while the millionaire was closeted alone with Donald Macdonald and the wireless thing.

After one game, of which he was the winner, the doctor, with much delicacy, asked leave to go to bed. Merton conducted him to his room, and, returning, was hailed by Mr. Macrae.

'Here is the pleasant result of our communications,' he said, reading aloud the message which he had first received.

'The Seven Hunters. August 9, 7.47 p.m.

'Do not be anxious about Miss Macrae. She is in perfect health, and accompanied by three chaperons accustomed to move in the first circles. The one question is How Much? Sorry to be abrupt, but the sooner the affair is satisfactorily concluded the better. A reply through your Gianesi machine will reach us, and will meet with prompt attention.'

'A practical joke,' said Merton. 'The melancholy news has reached town through Bude's telegrams, and somebody at the depot is playing tricks with the instrument.'

'I have used the instrument to communicate that opinion to the manufacturers,' said Mr. Macrae, 'but I have had no reply.'

'What does the jester mean by heading his communication "The Seven Hunters"?' asked Merton.

'The name of a real or imaginary public-house, I suppose,' said Mr. Macrae.

At this moment the electric bell gave its signal, and the tape began to exude. Mr. Macrae read the message aloud; it ran thus:

'No good wiring to Gianesi and Giambresi at headquarters. You are hitched on to us, and to nobody else. Better climb down. What are your terms?'

'This is infuriating,' said Mr. Macrae. 'It *must* be a practical joke, but how to reach the operators?'

'Let me wire to-morrow by the old-fashioned way,' said Merton; 'I hear that one need not go to Lairg to wire. One can do that from Inchnadampf, much nearer. That is quicker than steaming to Loch Inver.'

'Thank you very much, Mr. Merton; I must be here myself. You had better take the motor—trouble dazes a man—I forgot the motor when I ordered the tandem this morning.'

'Very good,' said Merton. 'At what hour shall I start?'

'We all need rest; let us say at ten o'clock.'

'All right,' replied Merton. 'Now do, pray, try to get a good night of sleep.'

Mr. Macrae smiled wanly: 'I mean to force myself to read *Emma*, by Miss Austen, till the desired effect is produced.'

Merton went to bed, marvelling at the self-command of the millionaire. He himself slept ill, absorbed in regret and darkling conjecture.

After writing out several telegrams for Merton to carry, the smitten victim of enormous opulence sought repose. But how vainly! Between him and the pages which report the prosings of Miss Bates and Mr. Woodhouse intruded visions of his daughter, a captive, perhaps crossing the Atlantic, perhaps hidden, who knew, in a shieling or a cavern in the untrodden wastes of Assynt or of Lord Reay's country. At last these appearances were merged in sleep.

III

Logan to the Rescue!

As Merton sped on the motor next day to the nearest telegraph station, with Mr. Macrae's sheaf of despatches, Dr. MacTavish found him a very dull companion. He named the lochs and hills, Quinag, Suilvean, Ben Mor, he dwelt on the merits of the trout in the lochs; he showed the melancholy improvements of the old Duke; he spoke of duchesses and of crofters, of anglers and tourists; he pointed to the ruined castle of the man who sold the great Montrose—or did not sell him. Merton was irresponsive, trying to think. What was this mystery? Why did the wireless machine bring no response from its headquarters; or how could practical jokers have intruded into the secret chambers of Messrs. Gianesi and Giambresi? These dreams or visions of his own on the night before Miss Macrae was taken—were they wholly due to tobacco and the liver?

'I thought I was awake,' said Merton to himself, 'when I was only dreaming about the crimson blot on the ceiling. Was I asleep when I saw the tartans go down the stairs? I used to walk in my sleep as a boy. It is very queer!'

'Frae the top o' Ben Mor,' the doctor was saying, 'on a fine day, they tell me, with a glass you can pick up "The

Seven Hunters."'

'Eh, what? I beg your pardon, I am so confused by this wretched affair. What did you say you can pick up?'

'Just "The Seven Hunters,"' said the doctor rather sulkily.

'And what are "The Seven Hunters"?'

'Just seven wee sma' islandies ahint the Butt of Lewis. The maps ca' them the Flanan Islands.'

Merton's heart gave a thump. The first message from the Gianesi invention was dated 'The Seven Hunters.' Here was a clue.

'Are the islands inhabited?' asked Merton.

'Just wi' wild goats, and, maybe, fishers drying their fish. And three men in a lighthouse on one of them,' said the doctor.

They now rushed up to the hotel and telegraph office of Inchnadampf. The doctor, after visiting the bar, went on in the motor to Lairg; it was to return for Merton, who had business enough on hand in sending the despatches. He was thinking over 'The Seven Hunters.' It might be, probably was, a blind, or the kidnappers, having touched there, might have departed in any direction—to Iceland, for what he knew. But the name, 'the Seven Hunters,' was not likely to have been invented by a practical joker in London. If not, the conspirators had really captured and kept to themselves Mr. Macrae's line of wireless communications. How could that have been done? Merton bitterly regretted that his general information did not include electrical science.

However, he had first to send the despatches. In one Mr. Macrae informed Gianesi and Giambresi of the condition of their instrument, and bade them send another at once with a skilled operator, and to look out for probable tamperers in their own establishment. This despatch was in a cypher which before he got the new invention, and while he used the old wires, Mr. Macrae had arranged with the electricians. The words of the despatch were, therefore, peculiar, and the Highland lass who operated, a girl of great beauty and modesty, at first declined to transmit the message.

'It's maybe no proper, for a' that I ken,' she urged, and only by invoking a local person of authority, and using the name of Mr. Macrae very freely, could Merton obtain the transmission of the despatch.

In another document Mr. Macrae ordered 'more motors' and a dozen bicycles, as the Nabob of old ordered 'more curricles.' He also telegraphed to the Home Office, the Admiralty, the Hereditary Lord High Admiral of the West Coast, to Messrs. McBrain, of the steamers, and to every one who might have any access to the control of marine police or information. He wired to the police at New York, bidding them warn all American stations, and to the leading New York newspapers, knowing the energy and inquiring, if imaginative, character of their reporters. Bude ought to have done all this on the previous day, but Bude's ideas were limited. Nothing, however, was lost, as America is not reached in forty- eight hours. The millionaire instructed Scotland Yard to warn all foreign ports, and left them *carte-blanche* as to the offer of a reward for the discovery of his missing daughter. He also put off all the guests whom he had been expecting at Castle Skrae.

Merton was amazed at the energy and intelligence of a paternal mind smitten by sudden grief. Mr. Macrae had even telegraphed to every London newspaper, and to the leading Scottish and provincial journals, 'No Interviewers need Apply.' Several hours were spent, as may be imagined, in getting off these despatches from a Highland rural office, and Merton tried to reward the fair operator. But she declined to accept a present for doing her duty, and expressed lively sympathy for the poor young lady who was lost. In a few days a diamond-studded watch and chain arrived for Miss MacTurk.

Merton himself wired to Logan, imploring him, in the name of friendship, to abandon all engagements, and come to Inchnadampf. Where kidnapping was concerned he knew that Logan must be interested, and might be useful; but, of course, he could not invite him to Castle Skrae. Meanwhile he secured rooms for Logan at the excellent inn. Lady Fastcastle, he knew, was in England, brooding over her first-born, the Master of Fastcastle.

Before these duties were performed the motor returned from Lairg, bearing the two London detectives, one disguised as a gillie (he was the detective who had the Gaelic), the other as a clergyman of the Church of England. To Merton he whispered that he was to be an early friend of Mr. Macrae, come to comfort him on the first news of his disaster. As to the other, the gillie, Mr. Macrae was known to have been in want of an assistant to the stalker, and Duncan Mackay (of Scotland Yard) had accepted the situation. Merton approved of these arrangements; they were such as he would himself have suggested.

'But I don't see what we can do, sir,' said the clerical detective (the Rev. Mr. Williams), 'except perhaps find out if it was a put up thing from within.'

Merton gave him a succinct sketch of the events, and he

could see that Mr. Williams already suspected Donald Macdonald, the engineer. Merton, Mr. Williams, and the driver now got into the motor, and were followed by the gillie-detective and a man to drive in a dog-cart hired from the inn. Merton ordered all answers to telegrams to be sent by boys on bicycles.

It was late ere he returned to Castle Skrae. There nothing of importance had occurred, except the arrival of more messages from the wireless machine. They insisted that Miss Macrae was in perfect health, but implored the millionaire to settle instantly, lest anxiety for a father's grief should undermine her constitution.

Mr. Williams had a long interview with Mr. Macrae. It was arranged that he should read family prayers in the morning and evening. He left *The Church Quarterly Review* and numbers of *The Expositor*, *The Guardian*, and *The Pilot* in the hall with his great coat, and on the whole his entry was very well staged. Duncan Mackay occupied a room at the keeper's, who had only eight children.

Mr. Williams asked if he might see Mr. Blake; he could impart religious consolation. Merton carried this message, in answer to which Blake, who was in bed very sulky and sleepy, merely replied, 'Kick out the hell-hound.'

Merton was obliged to soften this rude message, saying that unfortunately Mr. Blake was of the older faith, though he had expressed no wish for the ministrations of Father McColl.

On hearing this Mr. Williams merely sighed, as the Budes were present. He had been informed as to their tenets, and had even expressed a desire to labour for their enlighten-ment, by way of giving local colour. He had, he said, some stirring Protestant tracts among his clerical properties. Mr. Macrae, however, had gently curbed this zeal, so on hearing of Blake's religious beliefs the sigh of Mr. Williams was delicately subdued.

Dinner-time arrived. Blake did not appear; the butler said that he supported existence solely on dried toast and milk and soda-water. He was one of the people who keep a private clinical thermometer, and he sent the bulletin that his temperature was 103. He hoped to come downstairs to-morrow. Mr. Williams gave the party some news of the outer world. He had brought the *Scotsman*, and Mr. Macrae had the gloomy satisfaction of reading a wildly inaccurate report of his misfortune. Correct news had not reached the press, but deep sympathy was expressed. The melancholy party soon broke up, Mr. Williams conducting family prayers with much unction, after the Budes had withdrawn.

In a private interview with the millionaire Merton told him how he had discovered the real meaning of 'The Seven Hunters,' whence the first telegram of the kidnappers was dated. Neither man thought the circumstance very important.

'They would hardly have ventured to name the islands if they had any idea of staying there,' the millionaire said, 'besides any heartless jester could find the name on a map.'

This was obvious, but as Lady Bude was much to be pitied, alone, in the circumstances, Mr. Macrae determined to send her and Bude on the yacht, the *Flora Macdonald*, to cruise round the Butt of Lewis and examine the islets. Both Bude and his wife were devoted to yachting, and the isles might yield something in the way of natural history.

Next day (Wednesday) the Budes steamed away, and there came many answers to the telegrams of Mr. Macrae, and one from Logan to Merton. Logan was hard by, cruising with his cousin, Admiral Chirnside, at the naval manoeuvres on the northeast coast. He would come to Inchnadampf at once. Mr. Macrae heard from Gianesi and Giambresi. Gianesi himself was coming with a fresh machine. Mr. Macrae wished it had been Giambresi, whom he knew; Gianesi he had never met. Condolences, of course, poured in from all quarters, even the most exalted. The Emperor of Germany was most sympathetic. But there was no news of importance. Several yachting parties had been suspected and examined; three young ladies at Oban, Applecross, and Tobermory, had established their identity and proved that they were not Miss Macrae.

All day the wireless machine was silent. Mr. Williams was shown all the rooms in the castle, and met Blake, who appeared at luncheon. Blake was most civil. He asked for a private interview with Mr. Macrae, who inquired whether his school friend, Mr. Williams, might share it? Blake was pleased to give them both all the information he had, though his head, he admitted, still rang with the cowardly blow that had stunned him. He was told of the discovery of the burned boat, and was asked whether it had approached from east or west, from the side of the Atlantic, or from the head of the sea loch.

'From Kinlocharty,' he said, 'from the head of the loch, the landward side.' This agreed with the evidence of the villagers on the other side of the sea loch.

Would he recognise the crew? He had only seen them at a certain distance, when they landed, but in spite of the blow on his head he remembered the black beard of one man, and the red beard of another. To be sure they might shave off their beards, yet these two he thought he could identify. Speaking to Miss Macrae as the men passed them, he had called one Donald Dubh, or 'black,' and the other Donald Ban, or 'fair.' They carried heavy shepherds' crooks in their hands. Their dress was Lowland, but they wore unusually broad bonnets of the old sort, drooping over the eyes. Blake knew no more, except his anguish from the midges.

He expressed his hope to be well enough to go away on Friday; he would retire to the inn at Scourie, and try to persevere with his literary work. Mr. Macrae would not hear of this; as, if the miscreants were captured, Blake alone could have a chance of identifying them. To this Blake replied that, as long as Mr. Macrae thought that he might be useful, he was at his service.

To Merton, Blake displayed himself in a new light. He said that he remembered little of what occurred after he was found at the foot of the cliff. Probably he was snappish and selfish; he was suffering very much. His head, indeed, was still bound up, and his face showed how he had suffered. Merton shook hands with him, and said that he hoped Blake would forget his own behaviour, for which he was sincerely sorry.

'Oh, the chaff?' said Blake. 'Never mind, I dare say I played the fool. I have been thinking, when my brain would give me leave, as I lay in bed. Merton, you are a trifle my senior, and you know the world much better. I have lived in a writing and painting set, where we talked nonsense till it went to our heads, and we half believed it. And, to tell you the truth, the presence of women always sets me off. I am a humbug; I do *not* know Gaelic, but I mean to work away at my drama for all that. This kind of shock against the realities of life sobers a fellow.'

Blake spoke simply, in an unaffected, manly way.

'*Semel in saninivimus omnes*!' said Merton.

'*Nec lusisse pudet*!' said Blake, 'and the rest of it. I know there's a parallel in the *Greek Anthology*, somewhere. I'll go and get my copy.'

He went into the observatory (they had been sitting on a garden seat outside), and Merton thought to himself:

'He is not such a bad fellow. Not many of your young poets know anything but French.'

Blake seemed to have some difficulty in finding his Anthology. At last he came out with rather a 'carried' look, as the Scots say, rather excited.

'Here it is,' he said, and handed Merton the little volume, of a Tauchnitz edition, open at the right page. Merton read the epigram. 'Very neat and good,' he said.

'Now, Merton,' said Blake, 'it is not usual, is it, for ministers of the Anglican sect to play the spy?'

'What in the world do you mean?' asked Merton. 'Oh, I guess, the Rev. Mr. Williams! Were you not told that his cure of souls is in Scotland Yard? I ought to have told you, I thought our host would have done so. What was the holy man doing?'

'I was not told,' said Blake, 'I suppose Mr. Macrae was too busy. So I was rather surprised, when I went into my room for my book, to find the clergyman examining my things and taking books out of one of my book boxes.'

'Good heavens!' exclaimed Merton. 'What did you do?'

'I locked the door of the room, and handed Mr. Williams the key of my despatch box. "I have a few private trifles there," I said, "the key may save you trouble." Then I sat down and wrote a note to Mr. Macrae, and rang the bell and asked the servant to carry the note to his master. Mr. Macrae came, and I explained the situation and asked him to be kind enough to order the motor, if he could spare it, or anything to carry me to the nearest inn.'

'I shall order it, Mr. Blake,' said Mr. Macrae, 'but it will be to remove this person, whom I especially forbade to molest any of my guests. I don't know how I forgot to tell you who he is, a detective; the others were told.'

'He confounded himself in excuses; it was horribly awkward.'

'Horribly!' said Merton.

'He rated the man for visiting his guests' rooms without his knowledge. I dare say the parson has turned over all *your* things.'

Merton blenched. He had some of the correspondence of the Disentanglers with him, rather private matter, naturally.

'He had not the key of my despatch box,' said Merton.

'He could open it with a quill, I believe,' said Blake. 'They do—in novels.'

Merton felt very uneasy. 'What was the end of it?' he asked.

'Oh, I said that if the man was within his duty the accident was only one of those which so singular a misfortune brings with it. I would stay while Mr. Macrae wanted me. I handed over my keys, and insisted that all my luggage and drawers and things should be examined. But Mr. Macrae would not listen to me, and forbade the fellow to enter any of—the bedrooms.'

'Begad, I'll go and look at my own despatch box,' said Merton.

'I shall sit in the shade,' said Blake.

Merton did examine his box, but could not see that any of the papers had been disarranged. Still, as the receptacle was full of family secrets he did not feel precisely comfortable. Going out on the lawn he met Mr. Macrae, who took him into a retired place and told him what had occurred.

'I had given the man the strictest orders not to invade the rooms of any of my guests,' he said; 'it is too odious.'

The Rev. Mr. Williams being indisposed, dined alone in his room that night; so did Blake, who was still far from well.

The only other incident was that Donald Macdonald and the new gillie, Duncan Mackay, were reported to be 'lying around in a frightfully dissolute state.' Donald was a sober man, but Mackay, he explained next morning, proved to be his long lost cousin, hence the revel. Mackay, separately, stated that he had made Donald intoxicated for the purpose of eliciting any guilty secret which he might possess. But whisky had elicited nothing.

On the whole the London detectives had not been entirely a success. Mr. Macrae therefore arranged to send both of them back to Lairg, where they would strike the line, and return to the metropolis.

Merton had casually talked of Logan (Lord Fastcastle) to Mr. Macrae on the previous evening, and mentioned that he was now likely to be at Inchnadampf. Mr. Macrae knew something of Logan, and before he sped the parting detectives, asked Merton whether he thought that he might send a note to Inchnadampf inviting his friend to come and bear him company? Merton gravely said that in such a crisis as theirs he thought that Logan would be extremely helpful, and that he was a friend of the Budes. Perhaps he himself had better go and pick up Logan and inform him fully as to the mysterious events? As Mr. Gianesi was also expected from London on that day (Thursday) to examine the wireless machine, which had been silent, Mr. Macrae sent off several vehicles, as well as the motor that carried the detectives. Merton drove the tandem himself.

Merton found Logan, with his Spanish bull-dog, Bouncer, loafing outside the hotel door at Inchnadampf. He greeted Merton in a state of suppressed glee; the whole adventure was much to the taste of the scion of Rostalrig. Merton handed him Mr. Macrae's letter of invitation.

'Come, won't I come, rather!' said Logan.

'Of course we must wait to rest the horses,' said Merton. 'The motor has gone on to Lairg, carrying two detectives who have made a pretty foozle of it, and it will bring back an electrician.'

'What for?' asked Logan.

'I must tell you the whole story,' said Merton. 'Let us walk a little way—too many gillies and people loafing about here.'

They walked up the road and sat down by little Loch Awe, the lochan on the way to Alt-na-gealgach. Merton told all the tale, beginning with his curious experiences on the night before the disappearance of Miss Macrae, and ending with the dismissal of the detectives. He also confided to Logan the importance of the matter to himself, and entreated him to be serious.

Logan listened very attentively.

When Merton had ended, Logan said, 'Old boy, you were the making of me: you may trust me. Serious it is. A great deal of capital must have been put into this business.'

'A sprat to catch a whale,' said Merton. 'You mean about nobbling the electric machine? How could *that* be done?'

'That—and other things. I don't know *how* the machine was nobbled, but it could not be done cheap. Would you mind telling me your dreams again?'

Merton repeated the story.

Logan was silent.

'Do you see your way?' asked Merton.

'I must have time to think it out,' said Logan. 'It is rather mixed. When was Bude to return from his cruise to "The Seven Hunters"?'

'Perhaps to-night,' said Merton. 'We cannot be sure. She is a very swift yacht, the *Flora Macdonald*.'

'I'll think it all over, Bude may give us a tip.'

No more would Logan say, beyond asking questions, which Merton could not answer, about the transatlantic past of the vanished heiress.

They loitered back towards the hotel and lunched. The room was almost empty, all the guests of the place were out fishing. Presently the motor returned from Lairg, bringing Mr. Gianesi and a large box of his electrical appliances. Merton rapidly told him all that he did not already know through Mr. Macrae's telegrams. He was a reserved man, rather young, and beyond thanking Merton, said little, but pushed on towards Castle Skrae in the motor. 'Some other motors,' he said, 'had arrived, and were being detained at Lairg.' They came later.

Merton and Logan followed in the tandem, Logan driving; they had handed to Gianesi a sheaf of telegrams for the millionaire. As to the objects of interest on the now familiar road, Merton enlightened Logan, who seemed as absent-minded as Merton had been, when instructed by Dr. MacTavish. As they approached the Castle, Merton observed, from a height, the *Flora Macdonald* steaming into the sea loch.

'Let us drive straight down to the cove and meet them,' he said.

They arrived at the cove just as the boat from the yacht touched the shore. The Budes were astonished and delighted to see their old friend, Logan, and his dog, Bouncer, a tawny black muzzled, bow-legged hero, was admired by Lady Bude.

Merton rapidly explained. 'Now, what tidings?' he asked.

The party walked aside on the shore, and Bude swiftly narrated what he had discovered.

'They *have* been there,' he said. 'We drew six of the islets blank, including the islet of the lighthouse. The men there had seen a large yacht, two ladies and a gentleman from it had visited them. They knew no more. Desert places, the other isles are, full of birds. On the seventh isle we found some Highland fishermen from the Lewis in a great state of excitement. They had only landed an hour before to pick up some fish they had left to dry on the rocks. They had no English, but one of our crew had the Gaelic, and interpreted in Scots. Regular Gaels, they did not want to speak, but I offered money, gold, let them see it. Then they took us to a cave. Do you know Mackinnon's cave in Mull, opposite Iona?'

'Yes, drive on!' said Merton, much interested.

'Well, inside it was pitched an empty corrugated iron house, quite new, and another, on the further side, outside the cave.'

'I picked up this in the interior of the cave,' said Lady Bude.

'This' was a golden hair-pin of peculiar make.

'That's the kind of hair-pin she wears,' said Lady Bude.

'By Jove!' said Merton and Logan in one voice.

'But that was all,' said Bude. 'There was no other trace, except that plainly people had been coming and going, and living there. They had left some empty bottles, and two intact champagne bottles. We tasted it, it was excellent! The Lewis men, who had not heard of the affair, could tell nothing more, except, what is absurd, that they had lately seen a dragon flying far off over the sea. A *dragon volant*, did you ever hear such nonsense? The interpreter pronounced it "draigon." He had not too much English himself.'

'The Highlanders are so delightfully superstitious,' said Lady Bude.

Logan opened his lips to speak, but said nothing.

'I don't think we should keep Mr. Macrae waiting,' said Lady Bude.

'If Bude will take the reins,' said Merton, 'you and he can be at the Castle in no time. We shall walk.'

'Excuse me a moment,' said Logan. 'A word with you, Bude.'

He took Bude aside, uttered a few rapid sentences, and then helped Lady Bude into the tandem. Bude followed, and drove away.

'Is your secret to be kept from me?' asked Merton.

'Well, old boy, you never told *me* the mystery of the Emu's feathers! Secret for secret, out with it; how did the feathers help you, if they *did* help you, to find out my uncle, the Marquis? *Gifgaff*, as we say in Berwickshire. Out with your feathers! and I'll produce my *dragon volant*, tail and all.'

Merton was horrified. The secret of the Emu's feathers involved the father of Lady Fastcastle, of his old friend's wife, in a very distasteful way. Logan, since his marriage, had never shown any curiosity in the matter. His was a joyous nature; no one was less of a self-tormentor.

'Well, old fellow,' said Merton, 'keep your dragon, and I'll keep my Emu.'

'I won't keep him long, I assure you,' said Logan. 'Only for a day or two, I dare say; then you'll know; sooner perhaps.

But, for excellent reasons, I asked Bude and Lady Bude to say nothing about the hallucination of these second-sighted Highland fishers. I have a plan. I think we shall run in the kidnappers; keep your pecker up. You shall be in it!'

With this promise, and with Logan's jovial confidence (he kept breaking into laughter as he went) Merton had to be satisfied, though in no humour for laughing.

'I'm working up to my *denouement*.' Logan said. 'Tremendously dramatic! You shall be on all through; I am keeping the fat for you, Merton. It is no bad thing for a young man to render the highest possible services to a generous millionaire, especially in the circumstances.'

'You're rather patronising,' said Merton, a little hurt.

'No, no,' said Logan. 'I have played second fiddle to you often, do let me take command this time—or, at all events, wait till you see my plot unfolded. Then you can take your part, or leave it alone, or modify to taste. Nothing can be fairer.'

Merton admitted that these proposals were loyal, and worthy of their old and tried friendship.

'*Un dragon volant*, flying over the empty sea!' said Logan. 'The Highlanders beat the world for fantastic visions, and the Islanders beat the Highlanders. But, look here, am I too inquisitive? The night when we first thought of the Disentanglers you said there was—somebody. But I understood that she and you were of one mind, and that only parents and poverty were in the way. And now, from what you told me this morning at Inchnadampf, it seems that there is no understanding between you and *this* lady, Miss Macrae.'

'There is none,' said Merton. 'I tried to keep my feelings to myself—I'm ashamed to say that I doubt if I succeeded.'

'Any chance?' asked Logan, putting his arm in Merton's in the old schoolboy way.

'I would rather not speak about it,' said Merton. 'I had meant to go myself on the Monday. Then came the affair of Sunday night,' and he sighed.

'Then the somebody before was another somebody?'

'Yes,' said Merton, turning rather red.

'Men have died and the worms have eaten them, but not for love,' muttered Logan.

IV

The Adventure of Eachain of the Hairy Arm

On arriving at the Castle Logan and Merton found poor Mr. Macrae comparatively cheerful. Bude and Lady Bude had told what they had gleaned, and the millionaire, recognising his daughter's hair-pin, had all but broken down. Lady Bude herself had wept as he thanked her for this first trace, this endearing relic, of the missing girl, and he warmly welcomed Merton, who had detected the probable meaning of the enigmatic 'Seven Hunters.'

'It is to *you*,' he said, 'Mr. Merton, that I owe the intelligence of my daughter's life and probable comfort.'

Lady Bude caught Merton's eye; one of hers was slightly veiled by her long lashes.

The telegrams of the day had only brought the usual stories of the fruitless examination of yachts, and of hopes unfulfilled and clues that led to nothing. The outermost islets were being searched, and a steamer had been sent to St. Kilda. At home Mr. Gianesi had explained to Mr. Macrae that he and his partner were forced, reluctantly, by the nature of the case, to suspect treason within their own establishment in London, a thing hitherto unprecedented. They had therefore installed a new machine in a carefully locked chamber at their place, and Mr. Gianesi was ready at once to set up a corresponding recipient engine at Castle Skrae. Mr. Macrae wished first to remove the machine in the smoking-room, but Blake ventured to suggest that it had better be left where it was.

'The conspirators,' he said, 'have made one blunder already, by mentioning "The Seven Hunters," unless, indeed, that was intentional; they *may* have meant to lighten our anxiety, without leaving any useful clue. They may make another mistake: in any case it is as well to be in touch with them.'

At this moment the smoking-room machine began to tick and emitted a message. It ran, 'Glad you visited the Hunters. You see we do ourselves very well. Hope you drank our health, we left some bottles of champagne on purpose. No nasty feeling, only a matter of business. Do hurry up and come to terms.'

'Impudent dogs!' said Mr. Macrae. 'But I think you are right, Mr. Blake; we had better leave these communications open.'

Mr. Gianesi agreed that Blake had spoken words of wisdom. Merton felt surprised at his practical common sense. It was necessary to get another pole to erect on the roof of the observatory, with another box at top for the new machine, but a flagstaff from the Castle leads was found to serve the purpose, and the rest of the day was passed in arranging the installation, the new machine being placed in Mr. Merton's own study. Before dinner was over, Mr. Gianesi, who worked like a horse, was able to announce that all was complete, and that a brief message, 'Yours received, all right,' had passed through from his firm in London.

Soon after dinner Blake retired to his room; his head was still suffering, and he could not bear smoke. Gianesi and Mr. Macrae were in the Castle, Mr. Macrae feverishly reading the newspaper speculations on the melancholy affair: leading articles on Science and Crime, the potentialities of both, the perils of wealth, and such other thoughts as occurred to active minds in Fleet Street. Gianesi's room was in the observatory, but he remained with Mr. Macrae in case he might be needed. Merton and Logan were alone in the smoking-room, where Bude left them early.

'Now, Merton,' said Logan, 'you are going to come on in the next scene. Have you a revolver?'

'Heaven forbid!' said Merton.

'Well, I have! Now this is what you are to do. We shall both turn in about twelve, and make a good deal of clatter and talk as we do so. You will come with me into my room. I'll hand you the revolver, loaded, silently, while we talk fishing shop with the door open. Then you will go rather noisily to your room, bang the door, take off your shoes, and slip out again—absolutely noiselessly—back into the smoking-room. You see that window in the embrasure here, next the door, looking out towards the loch? The curtain is drawn already, you will go on the window-seat and sit tight! Don't fall asleep! I shall give you my portable electric lamp for reading in the train. You may find it useful. Only don't fall asleep. When the row begins I shall come on.'

'I see,' said Merton. 'But look here! Suppose you slip out of your own room, locking the door quietly, and into mine, where you can snore, you know—I snore myself—in case anybody takes a fancy to see whether I am asleep? Leave your dog in your own room, *he* snores, all Spanish bull- dogs do.'

'Yes, that will serve,' said Logan. 'Merton, your mind is not wholly inactive.'

They had some whisky and soda-water, and carried out the manoeuvres on which they had decided.

Merton, unshod, silently re-entered the smoking-room, his shoes in his hand; Logan as tactfully occupied Merton's room, and then they waited. Presently, the smoking-room door being slightly ajar, Merton heard Logan snoring very naturally; the Spanish bull-dog was yet more sonorous. Gianesi came in, walked upstairs to his bedroom, and shut his door; in half an hour he also was snoring; it was a nasal trio.

Merton 'drove the night along,' like Dr. Johnson, by repeating Latin and other verses. He dared not turn on the light of his portable electric lamp and read; he was afraid to smoke; he heard the owls towhitting and towhooing from the woods, and the clock on the Castle tower striking the quarters and the hours.

One o'clock passed, two o'clock passed, a quarter after two, then the bell of the wireless machine rang, the machine began to tick; Merton sat tight, listening. All the curtains of the windows were drawn, the room was almost perfectly dark; the snorings had sometimes lulled, sometimes revived. Merton lay behind the curtains on the window-seat, facing the door. He knew, almost without the help of his ears, that the door was slowly, slowly opening. Something entered, something paused, something stole silently towards the wireless machine, and paused again. Then a glow suffused the further end of the room, a disc of electric light, clearly from a portable lamp. A draped form, in deep shadow, was exposed to Merton's view. He stole forward on tiptoe with noiseless feet; he leaped on the back of the figure, threw his left arm round its neck, caught its right wrist in a grip of steel, and yelled:

'Mr. Eachain of the Hairy Arm, if I am not mistaken!'

At the same moment there came a click, the electric light was switched on, Logan bounced on to the figure, tore away a revolver from the right hand of which Merton held the wrist, and the two fell on the floor above a struggling Highland warrior in the tartans of the Macraes. The figure was thrown on its face.

'Got you now, Mr. Blake!' said Logan, turning the head to the light. 'D—n!' he added; 'it is Gianesi! I thought we had the Irish minstrel.'

The figure only snarled, and swore in Italian.

'First thing, anyhow, to tie him up,' said Logan, producing a serviceable cord.

Both Logan and Merton were muscular men, and presently had the intruder tightly swathed in inextricable knots and gagged in a homely but sufficient fashion.

'Now, Merton,' said Logan, 'this is a bitter disappointment! From your dream, or vision, of Eachain of the Hairy Arm, it was clear to me that somebody, the poet for choice, had heard the yarn of the Highland ghost, and was masquerading in the kilt for the purpose of tampering with the electric dodge and communicating with the kidnappers. Apparently I owe the bard an apology. You'll sit on this fellow's chest while I go and bring Mr. Macrae.'

'A message has come in on the machine,' said Merton.

'Well, he can read it; it is not our affair.'

Logan went off; Merton poured out a glass of Apollinaris water, added a little whisky, and lit a cigarette. The figure on the floor wriggled; Merton put the revolver which the man had dropped and Logan's pistol into a drawer of the writing-table, which he locked.

'I do detest all that cheap revolver business,' said Merton.

The row had awakened Logan's dog, which was howling dolefully in the neighbouring room.

'Queer situation, eh?' said Merton to the prostrate figure.

Hurrying footsteps climbed the stairs; Mr. Macrae (with a shot-gun) and Logan entered.

Mr. Macrae all but embraced Merton. 'Had I a son, I could have wished him to be like you,' he said; 'but my poor boy—' his voice broke. Merton had not known before that the millionaire had lost a son. He did understand, however, that the judicious Logan had given *him* the whole credit of the exploit, for reasons too obvious to Merton.

'Don't thank *me*,' he was saying, when Logan interrupted:

'Don't you think, Mr. Macrae, you had better examine the message that has just come in?'

Mr. Macrae read, 'Glad they found the hair-pin, it will console the old boy. Do not quite see how to communicate, if Gianesi, who, you say, has arrived, removes the machine.'

'Look here,' cried Merton, 'excuse my offering advice, but we ought, I think, to send for Donald Macdonald *at once*. We must flash back a message to those brutes, so they may think they are still in communication with the traitor in our camp.

That beast on the floor could work it, of course, but he would only warn *them*; we can't check him. We must use Donald, and keep them thinking that they are sending news to the traitor.'

'But, by Jove,' said Logan, 'they have heard from *him*, whoever he is, since Bude came back, for they know about the finding of the hair-pin. You,' he said to the wretched captive, 'have you been at this machine?'

The man, being gagged, only gasped.

'There's this, too,' said Merton, 'the senders of the last message clearly think that Gianesi is against them. If Gianesi removes the machine, they say—'

Merton did not finish his sentence, he rushed out of the room. Presently he hurried back. 'Mr. Macrae,' he said, 'Blake's door is locked. I can't waken him, and, if he were in his room, the noise we have made must have wakened him already. Logan, ungag that creature!'

Logan removed the gag.

'Who are *you*?' he asked.

The captive was silent.

'Mr. Macrae,' said Merton, 'may I run and bring Donald and the other servants here? Donald must work the machine at once, and we must break in Blake's door, and, if he is off, we must rouse the country after him.'

Mr. Macrae seemed almost dazed, the rapid sequence of unusual circumstances being remote from his experience. In spite of the blaze of electric light, the morning was beginning to steal into the room; the refreshments on the table looked oddly dissipated, there was a heavy stale smell of tobacco, and of whisky from a bottle that had been upset in the struggle. Mr. Macrae opened a window and inhaled the fresh air from the Atlantic.

This revived him. 'I'll ring the alarm bell,' he said, and, putting a small key to an unnoticed keyhole in a panel, he opened a tiny door, thrust in his hand, and pressed a knob. Instantly from the Castle tower came the thunderous knell of the alarm. 'I had it put in in case of fire or burglars,' explained the millionaire, adding automatically, 'every modern improvement.'

In a few minutes the servants and gillies had gathered, hastily clad; they were met by Logan, who briefly bade some bring hammers, and the caber, or pine-tree trunk that is tossed in Highland sports. It would make a good battering-ram. Donald Macdonald he sent at once to Mr. Macrae. He met Bude and Lady Bude, and rapidly explained that there was no danger of fire. The Countess went back to her rooms, Bude returned with Logan into the observatory. Here they found Donald telegraphing to the conspirators, by the wireless engine, a message dictated by Merton:

'Don't be alarmed about communications. I have got them to leave our machine in its place on the chance that you might say something that would give you away. Gianesi suspects nothing. Wire as usual, at about half-past two in the morning, when you mean it for me.'

'That ought to be good enough,' said Logan approvingly, while the hammers and the caber, under Mr. Macrae's directions, were thundering on the door of Blake's room. The door, which was very strong, gave way at last with a crash; in they burst. The room was empty, a rope fastened to the ironwork of the bedstead showed the poet's means of escape, for a long rope-ladder swung from the window. On the table lay a letter directed to

Thomas Merton, Esq.,
care of Ronald Macrae, Esq.,
Castle Skrae.

Mr. Macrae took the letter, bidding Benson, the butler, search the room, and conveyed the epistle to Merton, who opened it. It ran thus:—

'DEAR MERTON,—As a man of the world, and slightly my senior, you must have expected to meet me in the smoking-room to-night, or at least Lord Fastcastle probably entertained that hope. I saw that things were getting a little too warm, and made other arrangements. It is a little hard on the poor fellow whom you have probably mauled, if you have not shot each other. As he has probably informed you, he is not Mr. Gianesi, but a dismissed *employe*, whom we enlisted, and whom I found it desirable to leave behind me. These discomforts will occur; I myself did not look for so severe an assault as I suffered down at the cove on Sunday evening. The others carried out their parts only too conscientiously in my case. You will not easily find an opportunity of renewing our acquaintance, as I slit and cut the tyres of all the motors, except that on which I am now retiring from hospitable Castle Skrae, having also slit largely the tyres of the bicycles. Mr. Macrae's new wireless machine has been rendered useless by my unfortunate associate, and, as I have rather spiked all the wheeled conveyances (I could not manage to scuttle the yacht), you will be put to some inconvenience to re-establish communications. By that time my trail will be lost. I enclose a banknote for 10*l*., which pray, if you would oblige me, distribute among the servants at the Castle. Please thank Mr. Macrae for all his hospitality. Among my books you may find something to interest you. You may keep my manuscript poems.

Very faithfully yours,
GERALD BLAKE.'

'P. S.—The genuine Gianesi will probably arrive at Lairg to-morrow. My unfortunate associate (whom I cannot sufficiently pity), relieved him of his ingenious machine *en route*, and left him, heavily drugged, in a train bound for Fort William. Or perhaps Gianesi may come by sea to Loch Inver. G.B.'

When Merton had read this elegant epistle aloud, Benson entered, bearing electrical apparatus which had been found in the book boxes abandoned by Blake. What he had done was obvious enough. He had merely smuggled in, in his book boxes, a machine which corresponded with that of the kidnappers, and had substituted its mechanism for that supplied to Mr. Macrae by Gianesi and Giambresi. This he must have arranged on the Saturday night, when Merton saw the kilted appearance of Eachain of the Hairy Arm. A few metallic atoms from the coherer on the floor of the smoking-room had caught Merton's eye before breakfast on Sunday morning. Now it was Friday morning! And still no means of detecting and capturing the kidnappers had been discovered.

Out of the captive nothing could be extracted. The room had been cleared, save for Mr. Macrae, Logan, and Bude, and the man had been interrogated. He refused to answer any questions, and demanded to be taken before a magistrate. Now, where was there a magistrate?

Logan lighted the smoking-room fire, thrust the poker into it, and began tying hard knots in a length of cord, all this silently. His brows were knit, his lips were set, in his eye shone the wild light of the blood of Restalrig. Bude and Mr. Macrae looked on aghast.

'What *are* you about?' asked Merton.

'There are methods of extracting information from reluctant witnesses,' snarled Logan.

'Oh, bosh!' said Merton. 'Mr. Macrae cannot permit you to revive your ancestral proceedings.'

Logan threw down his knotted cord. 'I beg your pardon, Mr. Macrae,' he said, 'but if I had that dog in my house of Kirkburn—' he then went out.

'Lord Fastcastle is a little moved,' said Merton. 'He comes of a wild stock, but I never saw him like this.'

Mr. Macrae allowed that the circumstances were unusual.

A horrible thought occurred to Merton. 'Mr. Macrae,' he exclaimed, 'may I speak to you privately? Bude, I dare say, will be kind enough to remain with that person.'

Mr. Macrae followed Merton into the billiard-room.

'My dear sir,' said the pallid Merton, 'Logan and I have made a terrible blunder! We never doubted that, if we caught any one, our captive would be Blake. I do not deny that this man is his accomplice, but we have literally no proof. He may persist, if taken before a magistrate, that he is Gianesi. He may say that, being in your employment as an electrician, he naturally entered the smoking-room when the electric bell rang. He can easily account for his possession of a revolver, in a place where a mysterious crime has just been committed.

As to the Highland costume, he may urge that, like many Southrons, he had bought it to wear on a Highland tour, and was trying it on. How can you keep him? You have no longer the right of Pit and Gallows. Before what magistrate can you take him, and where? The sheriff-substitute may be at Golspie, or Tongue, or Dingwall, or I don't know where. What can we do? What have we against the man? "Loitering with intent"? And here Logan and I have knocked him down, and tied him up, and Logan wanted to torture him.'

'Dear Mr. Merton,' replied Mr. Macrae, with paternal tenderness, 'you are overwrought. You have not slept all night. I must insist that you go to bed, and do not rise till you are called. The man is certainly guilty of conspiracy, that will be proved when the real Gianesi comes to hand. If not, I do not doubt that I can secure his silence. You forget the power of money. Make yourself easy, go to sleep; meanwhile I must re-establish communications. Good-night, golden slumbers!'

He wrung Merton's hand, and left him admiring the calm resolution of one whose conversation, 'in the mad pride of intellectuality,' he had recently despised. The millionaire, Merton felt, was worthy to be his daughter's father.

'The power of money!' mused Mr. Macrae; 'what is it in circumstances like mine? Surrounded by all the resources of science, I am baffled by a clever rogue and in a civilised country the aid of the law and the police is as remote and inaccessible as in the Great Sahara! But to business!'

He sent for Benson, bade him, with some gillies, carry the prisoner into the dungeon of the old castle, loose his bonds, place food before him, and leave him in charge of the stalker. He informed Bude that breakfast would be ready at eight, and then retired to his study, where he matured his plans.

The yacht he would send to Lochinver to await the real Gianesi there, and to send telegrams descriptive of Blake in all directions. Giambresi must be telegraphed to again, and entreated to come in person, with yet another electric machine, for that brought by the false Gianesi had been, by the same envoy, rendered useless. A mounted man must be despatched to Lairg to collect vehicles and transport there, and to meet the real Gianesi if he came that way. Thus Mr. Macrae, with cool patience and forethought, endeavoured to recover his position, happy in the reflection that treachery had at last been eliminated. He did not forget to write telegrams to remote sheriff-substitutes and procurators fiscal.

As to the kidnappers, he determined to amuse them with protracted negotiations on the subject of his daughter's ransom. These would be despatched, of course, by the wireless engine which was in tune and touch with their own. During the parleyings the wretches might make some blunder, and Mr. Macrae could perhaps think out some plan for their detection and capture, without risk to his daughter. If not, he must pay ransom.

Having written out his orders and telegrams, Mr. Macrae went downstairs to visit the stables. He gave his commands to his servants, and, as he returned, he met Logan, who had been on the watch for him.

'I am myself again, Mr. Macrae,' said Logan, smiling. 'After all, we are living in the twentieth century, not the sixteenth, worse luck! And now can you give me your attention for a few minutes?'

'Willingly,' said Mr. Macrae, and they walked together to a point in the garden where they were secure from being overheard.

'I must ask you to lend me a horse to ride to Lairg and the railway at once,' said Logan.

'Must you leave us? You cannot, I fear, catch the 12.50 train south.'

'I shall take a special train if I cannot catch the one I want,' said Logan, adding, 'I have a scheme for baffling these miscreants and rescuing Miss Macrae, while disappointing them of the monstrous ransom which they are certain to claim. If you can trust me, you will enter into protracted negotiations with them on the matter through the wireless machine.'

'That I had already determined to do,' said the millionaire. 'But may I inquire what is your scheme?'

'Would it be asking too much to request you to let me keep it concealed, even from you? Everything depends on the most absolute secrecy. It must not appear that you are concerned—must not be suspected. My plan has been suggested to me by trifling indications which no one else has remarked. It is a plan which, I confess, appears wild, but what is *not* wild in this unhappy affair? Science, as a rule beneficent, has given birth to potentialities of crime which exceed the dreams of oriental romance. But science, like the spear of Achilles, can cure the wounds which herself inflicts.'

Logan spoke calmly, but eloquently, as every reader must observe. He was no longer the fierce Border baron of an hour agone, but the polished modern gentleman. The millionaire marked the change.

'Any further mystery cannot but be distasteful, Lord Fastcastle,' said Mr. Macrae.

'The truth is,' said Logan, 'that if my plan takes shape important persons and interests will be involved. I myself will be involved, and, for reasons both public and private, it seems to me to the last degree essential that you should in no way appear; that you should be able, honestly, to profess entire ignorance. If I fail, I give you my word of honour that your position will be in no respect modified by my action. If I succeed—'

'Then you will, indeed, be my preserver,' said the millionaire.

'Not I, but my friend, Mr. Merton,' said Logan, 'who, by the way, ought to accompany me. In Mr. Merton's genius for success in adventures entailing a mystery more dark, and personal dangers far greater, than those involved by my scheme (which is really quite safe), I have confidence based on large experience. To Merton alone I owe it that I am a married, a happy, and, speaking to any one but yourself, I might say an affluent man. This adventure must be achieved, if at all, *auspice Merton*.'

'I also have much confidence in him, and I sincerely love him,' said Mr. Macrae, to the delight of Logan. He then paced silently up and down in deep thought. 'You say that your scheme involves you in no personal danger?' he asked.

'In none, or only in such as men encounter daily in several professions. Merton and I like it.'

'And you will not suffer in character if you fail?'

'Certainly not in character; no gentleman of my coat ever entered on enterprise so free from moral blame,' said Logan, 'since my ancestor and namesake, Sir Robert, fell at the side of the good Lord James of Douglas, above the Heart of Bruce.'

He thrilled and changed colour as he spoke.

'Yet it would not do for *me* to be known to be connected with the enterprise?' asked Mr. Macrae.

'Indeed it would not! Your notorious opulence would arouse ideas in the public mind, ideas false, indeed, but fatally compromising.'

'I may not even subsidise the affair—put a million to Mr. Merton's account?'

'In no sort! Afterwards, *after* he succeeds, then I don't say, if Merton will consent; but that is highly improbable. I know my friend.'

Mr. Macrae sighed deeply and remained pensive. 'Well,' he answered at last, 'I accept your very gallant and generous proposal.'

'I am overjoyed!' said Logan. He had never been in such a big thing before.

'I shall order my two best horses to be saddled after breakfast,' said Mr. Macrae. 'You will bait at Inchnadampf.'

'Here is my address; this will always find me,' said Logan, writing rapidly on a leaf of his note-book.

'You will wire all news of your negotiations with the pirates to me, by the new wireless machine, when Giambresi brings it, and his firm in town will telegraph it on to me, at the address I gave you, *in cypher*. To save time, we must use a book cypher, we can settle it in the house in ten minutes,' said Logan, now entirely in his element.

They chose *The Bonnie Brier Bush*, by Mr. Ian Maclaren—a work too popular to excite suspicion; and arranged the method of secret correspondence with great rapidity. Logan then rushed up to Merton's room, hastily communicated the scheme to him, and overcame his objections, nay, awoke in him, by his report of Mr. Macrae's words, the hopes of a lover. They came down to breakfast, and arranged that their baggage should be sent after them as soon as communications were restored.

Merton contrived to have a brief interview with Lady Bude. Her joyous spirit shone in her eyes.

'I do not know what Lord Fastcastle's plan is,' she said, 'but I wish you good fortune. You have won the *father's* heart, and now I am about to be false to my sex'—she whispered—'the daughter's is all but your own! I can help you a little,' she added, and, after warmly clasping both her hands in his, Merton hurried to the front of the house, where the horses stood, and sprang into the saddle. No motors, no bicycles, no scientific vehicles to-day; the clean wind piped to him from the mountains; a good steed was between his thighs! Logan mounted, after entrusting Bouncer to Lady Bude, and they galloped eastwards.

V

The Adventure of the Flora Macdonald

'This is the point indicated, latitude so and so, longitude so and so,' said Mr Macrae. 'But I do not see a sail or a funnel on the western horizon. Nothing since we left the Fleet behind us, far to the East. Yet it is the hour. It is strange!'

Mr. Macrae was addressing Bude. They stood together on the deck of the *Flora Macdonald*, the vast yacht of the millionaire. She was lying to on a sea as glassy and radiant, under a blazing August sun, as the Atlantic can show in her mildest moods. On the quarter-deck of the yacht were piled great iron boxes containing the millions in gold with which the millionaire had at last consented to ransom his daughter. He had been negotiating with her captors through the wireless machine, and, as Logan could not promise any certain release, Mr. Macrae had finally surrendered, while informing Logan of the circumstances and details of his rendezvous with the kidnappers. The amassing of the gold had shaken the exchanges of two worlds. Banks trembled, rates were enormous, but the precious metal had been accumulated. The pirates would not take Mr. Macrae's cheque; bank notes they laughed at, the millions must be paid in gold. Now at last the gold was on the spot of ocean indicated by the kidnappers, but there was no sign of sail or ship, no promise of their coming. Men with telescopes in the rigging of the *Flora* were on the outlook in vain. They could pick up one of the floating giants of our fleet, far off to the East, but North, West and South were empty wastes of water.

'Three o'clock has come and gone. I hope there has been no accident,' said Mr. Macrae nervously. 'But where are those thieves?' He absently pressed his repeater, it tingled out the half-hour.

'It *is* odd,' said Bude. 'Hullo, look there, what's *that*?'

That was a slim spar, which suddenly shot from the plain of ocean, at a distance of a hundred yards. On its apex a small black hood twisted itself this way and that like a living thing; so tranquil was the hour that the spar with its dull hood was distinctly reflected in the mirror- like waters of the ocean.

'By gad, it is the periscope of a submarine!' said Bude.

There could not be a doubt of it. The invention of Napier of Merchistoun and of M. Jules Verne, now at last an actual engine of human warfare, had been employed by the kidnappers of the daughter of the millionaire!

A light flashed on the mind, steady and serviceable, but not brilliantly ingenious, of Mr. Macrae. 'This,' he exclaimed rather superfluously, 'accounts for the fiendish skill with which these miscreants took cover when pursued by the Marine Police. *This* explains the subtle art with which they dodged observation. Doubtless they had always, somewhere, a well-found normal yacht containing their supplies. Do you not agree with me, my lord?'

'In my opinion,' said Bude, 'you have satisfactorily explained what has so long puzzled us. But look! The periscope, having reconnoitred us, is sinking again!'

It was true. The slim spar gracefully descended to the abyss. Again ocean smiled with innumerable laughters (as the Athenian sings), smiled, empty, azure, effulgent! The *Flora Macdonald* was once more alone on a wide, wide sea!

Two slight jars were now just felt by the owner, skipper, and crew of the *Flora Macdonald*. 'What's that?' asked Mr. Macrae sharply. 'A reef?'

'In my opinion,' said the captain, 'the beggars in the submarine have torpedoed us. Attached torpedoes to our keel, sir,' he explained, respectfully touching his cap and shifting the quid in his cheek. He was a bluff tar of the good old school.

'Merciful heavens!' exclaimed Mr. Macrae, his face paling. 'What can this new outrage mean? Here on our deck is the gold; if they explode their torpedoes the bullion sinks to join the exhaustless treasures of the main!'

'A bit of bluff and blackmail on their part I fancy,' said Bude, lighting a cigarette.

'No doubt! No doubt!' said Mr. Macrae, rather unsteadily. 'They would never be such fools as to blow up the millions. Still, an accident might have awful results.'

'Look there, sir, if you please,' said the captain of the *Flora Macdonald*, 'there's that spar of theirs up again.'

It was so. The spar, the periscope, shot up on the larboard side of the yacht. After it had reconnoitred, the mirror of ocean was stirred into dazzling circling waves, and the deck of a submarine slowly emerged. The deck was long and flat, and of a much larger area than submarines in general have. It would seem to indicate the presence below the water of a body or hull of noble proportions. A voice hailed the yacht from the submarine, though no speaker was visible.

'You have no consort?' the voice yelled.

'For ten years I have been a widower,' replied Mr. Macrae, his voice trembling with emotion.

'Most sorry to have unintentionally awakened unavailing regrets,' came the voice. 'But I mean, honour bright, you have no attendant armed vessel?'

'None, I promised you so,' said Mr. Macrae; 'I am a man of my word. Come on deck if you doubt me and look for yourself.'

'Not me, and get shot by a rifleman,' said the voice.

'It is very distressing to be distrusted in this manner,' replied Mr. Macrae. 'Captain McClosky,' he said to the skipper, 'pray request all hands to oblige me by going below.'

The captain issued this order, which the yacht's crew rather reluctantly obeyed. Their interest and curiosity were strongly excited by a scene without precedent in the experience of the oldest mariner.

When they had disappeared Mr. Macrae again addressed the invisible owner of the voice. 'All my crew are below. Nobody is on deck but Captain McClosky, the Earl of Bude, and myself. We are entirely unarmed. You can see for yourself.' {406}

The owner of the voice replied: 'You have no torpedoes?'

'We have only the armament agreed upon by you to protect this immense mass of bullion from the attacks of the unscrupulous,' said Mr. Macrae. 'I take heaven to witness that I am honourably observing every article of our agreement, as *per* yours of August 21.'

'All right,' answered the voice. 'I dare say you are honest. But I may as well tell you *this*, that while passing under your yacht we attached two slabs of gun-cotton to her keel. The knob connected with them is under my hand. We placed them where they are, not necessarily for publication— explosion, I mean—but merely as a guarantee of good faith. You understand?'

'Perfectly,' said Mr. Macrae, 'though I regard your proceeding as a fresh and unmerited insult.'

'Merely a precaution usual in business,' said the voice. 'And now,' it went on, 'for the main transaction. You will lower your gold into boats, row it across, and land it here on my deck. When it is all there, *and* has been inspected by me, you will send one boat rowed by *two men only*, into which Miss Macrae shall be placed and sent back to you. When that has been done we shall part, I hope, on friendly terms and with mutual respect.'

'Captain McClosky,' said Mr. Macrae, 'will you kindly pipe all hands on board to discharge cargo?' The captain obeyed.

Mr. Macrae turned to Bude. 'This is a moment,' he said, 'which tries a father's heart! Presently I must see Emmeline, hear her voice, clasp her to my breast.' Bude mutely wrung the hand of the millionaire, and turned away to conceal his emotion. Seldom, perhaps never, has a father purchased back an only and beloved child at such a cost as Mr. Macrae was now paying without a murmur.

The boats of the *Flora Macdonald* were lowered and manned, the winches slowly swung each huge box of the precious metal aboard the boats. Mr. Macrae entrusted the keys of the gold-chests to his officers.

'Remember,' cried the voice from the submarine, 'we must have the gold on board, inspected, and weighed, before we return Miss Macrae.'

'Mean to the last,' whispered the millionaire to the earl; but aloud he only said, 'Very well; I regret, for your own sake, your suspicious character, but, in the circumstances, I have no choice.'

To Bude he added: 'This is terrible! When he has secured the bullion he may submerge his submarine and go off without returning my daughter.'

This was so manifestly true that Bude could only shake his head and mutter something about 'honour among thieves.'

The crew got the gold on board the boats, and, after several journeys, had the boxes piled on the deck of the submarine.

When they had placed the boxes on board they again retired, and one of the men of the submarine, who seemed to be in command, and wore a mask, coolly weighed the glittering metal on the deck, returning each package, after weighing and inspection, to its coffer. The process was long and tedious; at length it was completed.

Then at last the form of Miss Macrae, in an elegant and tasteful yachting costume, appeared on the deck of the submarine. The boat's crew of the *Flora Macdonald* (to whom she was endeared) lifted their oars and cheered. The masked pirate in command handed her into a boat of the

Flora's with stately courtesy, placing in her hand a bouquet of the rarest orchids. He then placed his hand on his heart, and bowed with a grace remarkable in one of his trade. This man was no common desperado.

The crew pulled off, and at that moment, to the horror of all who were on the *Flora's* deck, two slight jars again thrilled through her from stem to stern.

Mr. Macrae and Bude gazed on each other with ashen faces. What had occurred? But still the boat's crew pulled gallantly towards the *Flora*, and, in a few moments, Miss Macrae stepped on deck, and was in her father's arms. It was a scene over which art cannot linger. Self- restraint was thrown to the winds; the father and child acted as if no eyes were regarding them. Miss Macrae sobbed convulsively, her sire was shaken by long-pent emotion. Bude had averted his gaze, he looked towards the submarine, on the deck of which the crew were busy, beginning to lower the bullion into the interior.

To Bude's extreme and speechless amazement, another periscope arose from ocean at about fifty yards from the further side of the submarine! Bude spoke no word; the father and daughter were absorbed in each other; the crew had no eyes but for them.

Presently, unmarked by the busy seamen of the hostile submarine, the platform and look-out hood of *another* submarine appeared. The new boat seemed to be pointing directly for the middle of the hostile submarine and at right angles to it.

'*Hands up!*' pealed a voice from the second submarine.

It was the voice of Merton!

At the well-known sound Miss Macrae tore herself from her father's embrace and hurried below. She deemed that a fond illusion of the senses had beguiled her.

Mr. Macrae looked wildly towards the two submarines.

The masked captain of the hostile vessel, leaping up, shook his fist at the *Flora Macdonald* and yelled, 'Damn your foolish treachery, you money- grubbing hunks! You *have* a consort.'

'I assure you that nobody is more surprised than myself,' cried Mr. Macrae.

'One minute more and you, your ship, and your crew will be sent to your own place!' yelled the masked captain.

He vanished below, doubtless to explode the mines under the *Flora*.

Bude crossed himself; Mr. Macrae, folding his arms, stood calm and defiant on his deck. One sailor (the cook) leaped overboard in terror, the others hastily drew themselves up in a double line, to die like Britons.

A minute passed, a minute charged with terror. Mr. Macrae took out his watch to mark the time. Another minute passed, and no explosion.

The captain of the pirate vessel reappeared on her deck. He cast his hands desperately abroad; his curses, happily, were unheard by Miss Macrae, who was below.

'Hands up!' again rang out the voice of Merton, adding, 'if you begin to submerge your craft, if she stirs an inch, I send you skyward at least as a preliminary measure. My diver has detached your mines from the keel of the *Flora Macdonald* and has cut the wires leading to them; my bow-tube is pointing directly for you, if I press the switch the torpedo must go home, and then heaven have mercy on your souls!'

A crow of laughter arose from the yachtsmen of the *Flora Macdonald*, who freely launched terms of maritime contempt at the crew of the pirate submarine, with comments on the probable future of the souls to which Merton had alluded.

On his desk the masked captain stood silent. 'We have women on board!' he answered Merton at last.

'You may lower them in a collapsible boat, if you have one,' answered Merton. 'But, on the faintest suspicion of treachery—the faintest surmise, mark you, I switch on my torpedo.'

'What are your terms?' asked the pirate captain.

'The return of the bullion, that is all,' replied the voice of Merton. 'I give you two minutes to decide.'

Before a minute and a half had passed the masked captain had capitulated. 'I climb down,' he said.

'The boats of the *Flora* will come for it,' said Merton; 'your men will help load it in the boats. Look sharp, and be civil, or I blow you out of the water!'

The pirates had no choice; rapidly, if sullenly, they effected the transfer.

When all was done, when the coffers had been hoisted aboard the *Flora Macdonald*, Merton, for the first time, hailed the yacht.

'Will you kindly send a boat round here for me, Mr. Macrae, if you do not object to my joining you on the return voyage?'

Mr. Macrae shouted a welcome, the yacht's crew cheered as only Britons can. Mr. Macrae's piper struck up the march of the clan, '*A' the wild McCraws are coming*!'

'If any of you scoundrels shoot,' cried Merton to his enemies, 'up you will all go. You shall stay here, after we depart, in front of that torpedo, just as long as the skipper of my vessel pleases.'

Meanwhile the boat of the *Flora* approached the friendly submarine; Merton stepped aboard, and soon was on the deck of the *Flora Macdonald.*

Mr. Macrae welcomed him with all the joy of a father reunited to his daughter, of a capitalist restored to his millions.

Bude shook Merton's hand warmly, exclaiming, 'Well played, old boy!'

Merton's eyes eagerly searched the deck for one beloved form. Mr. Macrae drew him aside. 'Emmeline is below,' he whispered; 'you will find her in the saloon.' Merton looked steadfastly at the millionaire, who smiled with unmistakable meaning. The lover hurried down the companion, while the *Flora*, which had rapidly got up steam, sped eastward.

Merton entered the saloon, his heart beating as hard as when he had sought his beloved among the bracken beneath the cliffs at Castle Skrae. She rose at his entrance; their eyes met, Merton's dim with a supreme doubt, Emmeline's frank and clear. A blush rose divinely over the white rose of her face, her lips curved in the resistless AEginetan smile, and, without a word spoken, the twain were in each other's arms.

* * * * * *

Half an hour later Mr. Macrae, heralding his arrival with a sonorous hem! entered the saloon. Smiling, he embraced his daughter, who hid her head on his ample shoulder, while with his right hand the father grasped that of Merton.

'My daughter is restored to me—and my son,' said the millionaire softly.

There was silence. Mr. Macrae was the first to recover his self-possession. 'Sit down, dear,' he said, gently disengaging Emmeline, 'and tell me all about it. Who were the wretches? I can forgive them now.'

Miss Macrae's eyes were bent on the carpet; she seemed reluctant to speak. At last, in timid and faltering accents, she whispered, 'It was the Van Huytens boy.'

'Rudolph Van Huytens! I might have guessed it,' cried the millionaire. 'His motive is too plain! His wealth did not equal mine by several millions. The ransom which he demanded, and but for Tom here' (he indicated Merton) 'would now possess, exactly reversed our relative positions. Carrying on his father's ambition, he would, but for Tom, have held the world's record for opulence. The villain!'

'You do not flatter *me*, father,' said Miss Macrae, 'and you are unjust to Mr. Van Huytens. He had another, *he* said a stronger, motive. Me!' she murmured, blushing like a red rose, and adding, 'he really was rather nice. The submarine was comfy; the yacht delightful. His sisters and his aunt were very kind. But—' and the beautiful girl looked up archly and shyly at Merton.

'In fact if it had not been for Tom,' Mr. Macrae was exclaiming, when Emmeline laid her lily hand on his lips, and again hid her burning blushes on his shoulder.

'So Rudolph had no chance?' asked Mr. Macrae gaily.

'I used rather to like him, long ago—before—' murmured Emmeline.

A thrill of happy pride passed through Merton. He also, he remembered of old, had thought that he loved. But now he privately registered an oath that he would never make any confessions as to the buried past (a course which the chronicler earnestly recommends to young readers).

'Now tell us all about your adventures, Emmie,' said Mr. Macrae, sitting down and taking his daughter's hand in his own.

The narrative may have been anticipated. After Blake was felled, Miss Macrae, screaming and struggling, had been carried to the boat. The crew had rapidly pulled round the cliff, the submarine had risen, to the captive's horrified amazement, from the deep, she had been taken on board, and, yet more to her surprise, had been welcomed by the Misses Van Huytens and their aunt. The brother had always behaved with respect, till, finding that his suit was hopeless, he had avoided her presence as much as possible, and—

'Had gone for the dollars,' said Macrae.

They had wandered from rocky desert isle to desert isle, in the archipelago of the Hebrides, meeting at night with a swift attendant yacht. Usually they had slept on shore under canvas; the corrugated iron houses had been left behind at 'The Seven Hunters,' with the champagne, to alleviate the anxiety of Mr. Macrae. Ample supplies of costume and other necessaries for Miss Macrae had always been at hand.

'They really did me very well,' she said, smiling, 'but I was miserable about *you*,' and she embraced her father.

'Only about *me*?' asked Mr. Macrae.

'I did not know, I was not sure,' said Emmeline, crying a little, and laughing rather hysterically.

'You go and lie down, my dear,' said Mr. Macrae. 'Your maid is in your cabin,' and thither he conducted the overwrought girl, Merton anxiously following her with his eyes.

'We are neglecting Lord Bude,' said Mr. Macrae. 'Come on deck, Tom, and tell us how you managed that delightful surprise.'

'Oh, pardon me, sir,' said Merton, 'I am under oath, I am solemnly bound to Logan and others never to reveal the circumstances. It was necessary to keep you uninformed, that you might honourably make your arrangement to meet Mr. Van Huytens without being aware that you had a submarine consort. Logan takes any dishonour on himself, and he wished to offer Mr. Van Huytens—as that is his name— every satisfaction, but I dissuaded him. His connection with the affair cannot be kept too secret. Though Logan put me forward, you really owe all to *him*.'

'But without *you*, I should never have had his aid,' said Mr. Macrae: 'Where *is* Lord Fastcastle?' he asked.

'In the friendly submarine,' said Merton.

'Oh, I think I can guess!' said Mr. Macrae, smiling. 'I shall ask no more questions. Let us join Lord Bude.'

If the reader is curious as to how the rescue was managed, it is enough to say that Logan was the cousin and intimate friend of Admiral Chirnside, that the Admiral was commanding a fleet engaged in naval manoeuvres around the North coast, that he had a flotilla of submarines, and that the point of ocean where the pirates met the *Flora Macdonald* was not far west of the Orkneys.

On deck Bude asked Merton how Logan (for he knew that Logan was the guiding spirit) had guessed the secret of the submarine.

'Do you remember,' said Merton, 'that when you came back from "The Seven Hunters," you reported that the fishermen had a silly story of seeing a dragon flying above the empty sea?'

'I remember, *un dragon volant*,' said Bude.

'And Logan asked you not to tell Mr. Macrae?'

'Yes, but I don't understand.'

'A dragon is the Scotch word for a kite—not the bird—a boy's kite. You did not know; *I* did not know, but Mr. Macrae would have known, being a Scot, and Logan wanted to keep his plan dark, and the kite had let him into the secret of the submarine.'

'I still don't see how.'

'Why the submarine must have been flying a kite, with a pendent wire, to catch messages from Blake and the wireless machine at Castle Skrae. How else could a kite—"a dragon," the sailor said—have been flying above the empty sea?'

'Logan is rather sharp,' said Bude.

'But, Mr. Macrae,' asked Merton, 'how about the false Gianesi?'

'Oh, when Gianesi came of course we settled *his* business. We had him tight, as a conspirator. He had been met, when expelled for misdeeds from Gianesi's and Giambresi's, by a beautiful young man, to whom he sold himself. He believed the beautiful young man to be the devil, but, of course, it was our friend Blake. *He*, in turn, must have been purchased by Van Huytens while he was lecturing in America as a poet-Fenian. In fact, he really had a singular genius for electric engineering; he had done very well at some German university. But he was a fellow of no principle! We are well quit of a rogue. I turned his unlucky victim, the false Gianesi, loose, with money enough for life to keep him honest if he chooses. His pension stops if ever a word of the method of rescue comes out. The same with my crew. They shall all be rich men, for their station, *till* the tale is whispered and reaches my ears. In that case—all pensions stop. I think we can trust the crew of the friendly submarine to keep their own counsel.'

'Certainly!' said Merton. 'Wealth has its uses after all,' he thought in his heart.

* * * * * *

Merton and Logan gave a farewell dinner in autumn to the Disentanglers—to such of them as were still unmarried. In her napkin each lady of the Society found a cheque on Coutts for 25,000*l.* signed with the magic name Ronald Macrae.

The millionaire had insisted on being allowed to perform this act of munificence, the salvage for the recovered millions, he said.

Miss Martin, after dinner, carried Mr. Macrae's health in a toast. In a humorous speech she announced her own approaching nuptials, and intimated that she had the permission of the other ladies present to make the same general confession for all of them.

'Like every novel of my own,' said Miss Martin, smiling, 'this enterprise of the Disentanglers has a HAPPY ENDING.'

Footnotes:

{232} Part III. No. I, 1896. Baptist Mission Press. Calcutta, 1897.

{242} See also Monsieur Henri Junod, in *Les Ba-Ronga*. Attinger, Neuchatel, 1898. Unlike Mr. Skertchley, M. Junod has not himself seen the creature.

{406} Periscope not necessary with conning tower out of water. Man could see out of port.

ABOUT THE AUTHOR

 **Andrew Lang** Born in Selkirk, Scotland (March 31, 1844 – July 20, 1912) was a prolific Scots man of letters. He was a poet, novelist, and literary critic, and contributor to anthropology. He now is best known as the collector of folk and fairy tales.

The Andrew Lang lectures at St Andrews University are named for him.

Lang is now chiefly known for his publications on folklore, mythology, and religion. The earliest of his publications is Custom and Myth (1884). In Myth, Ritual and Religion (1887) he explained the "irrational" elements of mythology as survivals from more primitive forms. Lang's Making of Religion was heavily influenced by the 18th century idea of the "noble savage": in it, he maintained the existence of high spiritual ideas among so-called "savage" races, drawing parallels with the contemporary interest in occult phenomena in England. His Blue Fairy Book (1889) was a beautifully produced and illustrated edition of fairy tales that has become a classic. This was followed by many other collections of fairy tales, collectively known as Andrew Lang's Fairy Books. Lang examined the origins of totemism in Social Origins (1903).

Choose from Thousands of 1stWorldLibrary Classics By

A. M. Barnard
Ada Leverson
Adolphus William Ward
Aesop
Agatha Christie
Alexander Aaronsohn
Alexander Kielland
Alexandre Dumas
Alfred Gatty
Alfred Ollivant
Alice Duer Miller
Alice Turner Curtis
Alice Dunbar
Allen Chapman
Alleyne Ireland
Ambrose Bierce
Amelia E. Barr
Amory H. Bradford
Andrew Lang
Andrew McFarland Davis
Andy Adams
Angela Brazil
Anna Alice Chapin
Anna Sewell
Annie Besant
Annie Hamilton Donnell
Annie Payson Call
Annie Roe Carr
Annonaymous
Anton Chekhov
Archibald Lee Fletcher
Arnold Bennett
Arthur C. Benson
Arthur Conan Doyle
Arthur M. Winfield
Arthur Ransome
Arthur Schnitzler
Arthur Train
Atticus
B.H. Baden-Powell
B. M. Bower
B. C. Chatterjee
Baroness Emmuska Orczy
Baroness Orczy
Basil King
Bayard Taylor
Ben Macomber
Bertha Muzzy Bower
Bjornstjerne Bjornson

Booth Tarkington
Boyd Cable
Bram Stoker
C. Collodi
C. E. Orr
C. M. Ingleby
Carolyn Wells
Catherine Parr Traill
Charles A. Eastman
Charles Amory Beach
Charles Dickens
Charles Dudley Warner
Charles Farrar Browne
Charles Ives
Charles Kingsley
Charles Klein
Charles Hanson Towne
Charles Lathrop Pack
Charles Romyn Dake
Charles Whibley
Charles Willing Beale
Charlotte M. Braeme
Charlotte M. Yonge
Charlotte Perkins Stetson
Clair W. Hayes
Clarence Day Jr.
Clarence E. Mulford
Clemence Housman
Confucius
Coningsby Dawson
Cornelis DeWitt Wilcox
Cyril Burleigh
D. H. Lawrence
Daniel Defoe
David Garnett
Dinah Craik
Don Carlos Janes
Donald Keyhoe
Dorothy Kilner
Dougan Clark
Douglas Fairbanks
E. Nesbit
E. P. Roe
E. Phillips Oppenheim
E. S. Brooks
Earl Barnes
Edgar Rice Burroughs
Edith Van Dyne
Edith Wharton

Edward Everett Hale
Edward J. O'Biren
Edward S. Ellis
Edwin L. Arnold
Eleanor Atkins
Eleanor Hallowell Abbott
Eliot Gregory
Elizabeth Gaskell
Elizabeth McCracken
Elizabeth Von Arnim
Ellem Key
Emerson Hough
Emilie F. Carlen
Emily Bronte
Emily Dickinson
Enid Bagnold
Enilor Macartney Lane
Erasmus W. Jones
Ernie Howard Pie
Ethel May Dell
Ethel Turner
Ethel Watts Mumford
Eugene Sue
Eugenie Foa
Eugene Wood
Eustace Hale Ball
Evelyn Everett-green
Everard Cotes
F. H. Cheley
F. J. Cross
F. Marion Crawford
Fannie E. Newberry
Federick Austin Ogg
Ferdinand Ossendowski
Fergus Hume
Florence A. Kilpatrick
Fremont B. Deering
Francis Bacon
Francis Darwin
Frances Hodgson Burnett
Frances Parkinson Keyes
Frank Gee Patchin
Frank Harris
Frank Jewett Mather
Frank L. Packard
Frank V. Webster
Frederic Stewart Isham
Frederick Trevor Hill
Frederick Winslow Taylor

Friedrich Kerst
Friedrich Nietzsche
Fyodor Dostoyevsky
G.A. Henty
G.K. Chesterton
Gabrielle E. Jackson
Garrett P. Serviss
Gaston Leroux
George A. Warren
George Ade
Geroge Bernard Shaw
George Cary Eggleston
George Durston
George Ebers
George Eliot
George Gissing
George MacDonald
George Meredith
George Orwell
George Sylvester Viereck
George Tucker
George W. Cable
George Wharton James
Gertrude Atherton
Gordon Casserly
Grace E. King
Grace Gallatin
Grace Greenwood
Grant Allen
Guillermo A. Sherwell
Gulielma Zollinger
Gustav Flaubert
H. A. Cody
H. B. Irving
H.C. Bailey
H. G. Wells
H. H. Munro
H. Irving Hancock
H. R. Naylor
H. Rider Haggard
H. W. C. Davis
Haldeman Julius
Hall Caine
Hamilton Wright Mabie
Hans Christian Andersen
Harold Avery
Harold McGrath
Harriet Beecher Stowe
Harry Castlemon
Harry Coghill
Harry Houidini

Hayden Carruth
Helent Hunt Jackson
Helen Nicolay
Hendrik Conscience
Hendy David Thoreau
Henri Barbusse
Henrik Ibsen
Henry Adams
Henry Ford
Henry Frost
Henry James
Henry Jones Ford
Henry Seton Merriman
Henry W Longfellow
Herbert A. Giles
Herbert Carter
Herbert N. Casson
Herman Hesse
Hildegard G. Frey
Homer
Honore De Balzac
Horace B. Day
Horace Walpole
Horatio Alger Jr.
Howard Pyle
Howard R. Garis
Hugh Lofting
Hugh Walpole
Humphry Ward
Ian Maclaren
Inez Haynes Gillmore
Irving Bacheller
Isabel Cecilia Williams
Isabel Hornibrook
Israel Abrahams
Ivan Turgenev
J.G.Austin
J. Henri Fabre
J. M. Barrie
J. M. Walsh
J. Macdonald Oxley
J. R. Miller
J. S. Fletcher
J. S. Knowles
J. Storer Clouston
J. W. Duffield
Jack London
Jacob Abbott
James Allen
James Andrews
James Baldwin

James Branch Cabell
James DeMille
James Joyce
James Lane Allen
James Lane Allen
James Oliver Curwood
James Oppenheim
James Otis
James R. Driscoll
Jane Abbott
Jane Austen
Jane L. Stewart
Janet Aldridge
Jens Peter Jacobsen
Jerome K. Jerome
Jessie Graham Flower
John Buchan
John Burroughs
John Cournos
John F. Kennedy
John Gay
John Glasworthy
John Habberton
John Joy Bell
John Kendrick Bangs
John Milton
John Philip Sousa
John Taintor Foote
Jonas Lauritz Idemil Lie
Jonathan Swift
Joseph A. Altsheler
Joseph Carey
Joseph Conrad
Joseph E. Badger Jr
Joseph Hergesheimer
Joseph Jacobs
Jules Vernes
Julian Hawthrone
Julie A Lippmann
Justin Huntly McCarthy
Kakuzo Okakura
Karle Wilson Baker
Kate Chopin
Kenneth Grahame
Kenneth McGaffey
Kate Langley Bosher
Kate Langley Bosher
Katherine Cecil Thurston
Katherine Stokes
L. A. Abbot
L. T. Meade

L. Frank Baum
Latta Griswold
Laura Dent Crane
Laura Lee Hope
Laurence Housman
Lawrence Beasley
Leo Tolstoy
Leonid Andreyev
Lewis Carroll
Lewis Sperry Chafer
Lilian Bell
Lloyd Osbourne
Louis Hughes
Louis Joseph Vance
Louis Tracy
Louisa May Alcott
Lucy Fitch Perkins
Lucy Maud Montgomery
Luther Benson
Lydia Miller Middleton
Lyndon Orr
M. Corvus
M. H. Adams
Margaret E. Sangster
Margret Howth
Margaret Vandercook
Margaret W. Hungerford
Margret Penrose
Maria Edgeworth
Maria Thompson Daviess
Mariano Azuela
Marion Polk Angellotti
Mark Overton
Mark Twain
Mary Austin
Mary Catherine Crowley
Mary Cole
Mary Hastings Bradley
Mary Roberts Rinehart
Mary Rowlandson
M. Wollstonecraft Shelley
Maud Lindsay
Max Beerbohm
Myra Kelly
Nathaniel Hawthrone
Nicolo Machiavelli
O. F. Walton
Oscar Wilde

Owen Johnson
P.G. Wodehouse
Paul and Mabel Thorne
Paul G. Tomlinson
Paul Severing
Percy Brebner
Percy Keese Fitzhugh
Peter B. Kyne
Plato
Quincy Allen
R. Derby Holmes
R. L. Stevenson
R. S. Ball
Rabindranath Tagore
Rahul Alvares
Ralph Bonehill
Ralph Henry Barbour
Ralph Victor
Ralph Waldo Emmerson
Rene Descartes
Ray Cummings
Rex Beach
Rex E. Beach
Richard Harding Davis
Richard Jefferies
Richard Le Gallienne
Robert Barr
Robert Frost
Robert Gordon Anderson
Robert L. Drake
Robert Lansing
Robert Lynd
Robert Michael Ballantyne
Robert W. Chambers
Rosa Nouchette Carey
Rudyard Kipling
Saint Augustine
Samuel B. Allison
Samuel Hopkins Adams
Sarah Bernhardt
Sarah C. Hallowell
Selma Lagerlof
Sherwood Anderson
Sigmund Freud
Standish O'Grady
Stanley Weyman
Stella Benson
Stella M. Francis

Stephen Crane
Stewart Edward White
Stijn Streuvels
Swami Abhedananda
Swami Parmananda
T. S. Ackland
T. S. Arthur
The Princess Der Ling
Thomas A. Janvier
Thomas A Kempis
Thomas Anderton
Thomas Bailey Aldrich
Thomas Bulfinch
Thomas De Quincey
Thomas Dixon
Thomas H. Huxley
Thomas Hardy
Thomas More
Thornton W. Burgess
U. S. Grant
Upton Sinclair
Valentine Williams
Various Authors
Vaughan Kester
Victor Appleton
Victor G. Durham
Victoria Cross
Virginia Woolf
Wadsworth Camp
Walter Camp
Walter Scott
Washington Irving
Wilbur Lawton
Wilkie Collins
Willa Cather
Willard F. Baker
William Dean Howells
William le Queux
W. Makepeace Thackeray
William W. Walter
William Shakespeare
Winston Churchill
Yei Theodora Ozaki
Yogi Ramacharaka
Young E. Allison
Zane Grey

www.ingramcontent.com/pod-product-compliance
Lightning Source LLC
Chambersburg PA
CBHW030759260626
47169CB00001B/113